EYE TO EYE

EYE TO EYE

The Quest for the New Paradigm

THIRD EDITION

KEN WILBER

Afterword by Frances Vaughan

SHAMBHALA
Boston & London
1996

Sнамвнаla Publications, Inc.
Horticultural Hall
300 Massachusetts Avenue
Boston, Massachusetts 02115

"Eye to Eye," "The Problem of Proof," "Physics, Mysticism, and the
New Holographic Paradigm," "Reflections on the New Age Paradigm,"
and "The Pre/Trans Fallacy" first appeared in *ReVision*.
"A Mandalic Map of Consciousness," "Development, Meditation,
and the Unconscious," and "Structure, Stage, and Self" first appeared,
in a different form, in the *Journal of Transpersonal Psychology*. Copyright © by the
Journal of Transpersonal Psychology.
Reprinted by permission.
"The Ultimate State of Consciousness" first appeared in the
Journal of Altered States of Consciousness. Copyright © by
the *Journal of Altered States of Consciousness*.
Reprinted by permission.

9 8 7 6 5 4 3 2 1

Printed in the United States of America
⊗This edition is printed on acid-free paper that meets the
American National Standards Institute Z39.48 Standard.
Distributed in the United States by Random House
and in Canada by Random House of Canada Ltd.
Distributed in the United Kingdom by Element Books, Ltd.

Library of Congress Cataloging-in-Publication Data
Wilber, Ken.
Eye to eye: the quest for the new paradigm / by Ken Wilber.—
Revised ed.
p. cm.
Includes bibliographical references and index.
ISBN 1-57062-249-3 (alk. paper)
1. Knowledge, Theory of. 2. Religion. 3. Consciousness.
I. Title.
BD161.W46 1996   96-7679
121—dc20   CIP

To
FRANCES AND ROGER,
JUDY AND WHIT,
BOB, BILL, AND KEN

Contents

Preface to the Third Edition

THE VAST MAJORITY of the great philosophers of the West have maintained that there does indeed exist some sort of Absolute, from the Good to God to Geist. That has never seriously been doubted by the vast majority. The burning question, rather, has always been this: What is the relation of the absolute One to the world of the relative Many?

And this crucial question has, like many of the most profound questions in Western philosophy, generated a series of utterly intractable difficulties, paradoxes, absurdities. Like the mind/body problem and the question of free will versus determinism, the absolute/relative issue has been a bloody thorn in the side of the Western tradition, a thorn that has utterly refused to either go away or have the good sense to be solved.

And, more intriguingly, all of these central issues—mind/body, mind/brain, free will/fate, absolute/relative, noumenon/phenomena —are, we will see, precisely the same problem.

And they all have precisely the same answer.

Aristotle gave the classic statement of a God that has nothing substantial to do with the relative world. Aristotle's God is a God of pure Perfection, and for such a God to dirty its hands with the

ix

relative world—to be involved with relative and finite creatures—would surely indicate a lack of fullness, a lack of completeness, and thus a lack of self-contained perfection. Since God requires nothing, there is certainly no reason for God to produce or create a relative world. In fact, if God actually created the relative world, that would indicate that God lacked something in its own being, which obviously is not possible (you don't get to be God by lacking something!). Thus, God is "in" the relative world only as final cause: the Good toward which all relative creatures strive but never, never reach.

Aspects of Plato's writing could certainly be interpreted to support Aristotle's notion of an untouchable, uninvolved, totally self-contained God. This world, after all, could be seen as nothing but the fleeting and shadowy reflection of the real world, a world utterly transcendent to the relative world of sense and confused opinion.

But that is only half of Plato, so to speak. The other (and less noted) half confirms in the strongest way that the entire relative world is a production, an emanation, a mark of the Plenitude of the Good. Thus, in the *Timaeus*—arguably the most influential book of Western cosmology—an Absolute that cannot create a world is described as decidedly inferior to an Absolute that can. Contrary to Aristotle's conclusion—that God must be totally self-contained to be perfect—the conclusion of the *Timaeus* is that a God that cannot create is no God at all. (It is even implied that a God who cannot create is envious of a God who can!) Thus, through the Absolute's *creative outflowing,* the entire manifest realm issues forth, so that all things are essentially the Plenitude of the Good. Therefore this very earth Plato describes as a "visible, sensible God."

And thus would begin this version of the West's most intractable dualism: the Absolute versus the relative, and what exactly is their relation?

The great difficulty with Aristotle's position is that it simply leaves the dualism as it finds it. Aristotle's God creates nothing; all things are driven by their desire to reach up to that God, but none of them make it. And however "clean" this might be logically, it leaves the Kosmos with a divisive wedge driven violently into its heart. God over there, us over here, and the two meet only in perpetually unrequited love.

And yet the other side of the attempted solution—God is present in the world as Plenitude—also had its own grave difficulties, at least as it was usually preached. Namely, if we intellectually picture the Absolute as substantially creating the relative world, then how do we account for the existence of evil? If God has his, her, or its hand in this world, then doesn't God get blamed for Auschwitz? If so, what kind of grotesque monster is that God?

This dualism between the Absolute and the relative—and their relation, if any—would split the entire tradition of Western philosophy and theology into two warring and utterly irreconcilable camps: those who saw God strongly (or even totally) in this world versus those who saw God strongly (or even totally) out of this world: this-worldly versus otherworldly, the Descenders versus the Ascenders, the immanentists versus the transcendentalists, empiricists versus rationalists, one flavor or another.

The Aristotelian tradition simply stood back from the commotion of the relative world, and refused to have its God dirty its fingers. God is a self-contained and unitary perfection, and thus that God has no need to create the world or anything else. How could anything so utterly Perfect do anything further without falling away from Perfection? To create implies that something is lacking now, and God lacks nothing; hence God does not create. Where the world came from, and why, is thus left literally hanging, though buried deep in the relative world's heart is the burning desire to reach the state of utter God-perfection, which would actually mean, for this autistic God, to simply be done with all its neighbors and disappear into its own self-contained absoluteness, basking in the wonders of its unending specialness.

But the alternative intellectual position—that the Perfect One nonetheless got itself involved with imperfect creatures—is scarcely more attractive. If the Perfect One steps down into imperfect evil, something has gone terribly wrong somewhere, and the blame for that can only rest with the One itself.

Christian theologians would, for the most part, maintain that God's Will creates the world, and since freedom is a good component of that world, God allows, but does not create, evil. The Gnostics headed in the other direction: this world is so obviously evil (as in the famous Gnostic line, "What kind of God is this?") that they maintained the entire world was created, not by the real Absolute, but by a Demiurge, an evil or at least inferior spirit. This tricky attempt to keep God out of the world! Because if we let God into the world, something has gone horribly, wretchedly wrong.

Approaching the dualism in this intellectual fashion does nothing to ameliorate it. If, as the Gnostics maintain, this world is phenomenal, illusory, evil, the product of the Demiurge and not of the real Godhead, then the Demiurge itself comes perilously close to absolute status, and indeed some Gnostics would simply claim that the Demiurge itself creates but is not created, and that is in fact a definition of the Absolute. So now we have two absolutes: an absolute Good, and an absolute Evil, and we have reintroduced exactly the dualism we set out to overcome.

This intractable dualism, I maintain, is the central dualism in the Western tradition, and it would appear and reappear in numerous disguises: it would show up as the dualism between noumenon and phenomena, between mind and body, between free will and determinism, morals and nature, transcendent and immanent, ascending and descending. That these are essentially the same dualism is a theme I carefully pursued in *Sex, Ecology, Spirituality* (and its popular version, *A Brief History of Everything*), and the interested reader might consult those sources for a much more detailed look.

But what I would like to emphasize here is simply that, buried in the Western tradition—and in the Eastern—is a *radical and compelling solution to these massive dualisms,* a literal solution to the West's most intractable philosophical problems, from the absolute/relative to the mind/body dilemma. But this solution—appropriately known as "nondualism"—has an unbelievably awkward characteristic: namely, its utterly compelling answer cannot be captured in words, a type of metaphysical catch-22 that absolutely guarantees to solve all your problems as long as you don't ask it to.

And that is where *Eye to Eye* comes in.

The premise of *Eye to Eye* is that there is a great spectrum of human consciousness; and this means that men and women have available to them a spectrum of different modes of knowing, each of which discloses a different type of world (a different worldspace, with different objects, different subjects, different modes of space-time, different motivations, and so on).

Put in its simplest form, there is the eye of flesh, the eye of mind, and the eye of contemplation. An exclusive or predominant reliance on one of these modes produces, for example, empiricism, rationalism, and mysticism.

The claim of *Eye to Eye* is that each of these modes of knowing has its own specific and quite valid set of referents: *sensibilia, intelligibilia,* and *transcendelia.* Thus, all three of these modes of knowing can be validated with similar degrees of confidence; and thus all three modes are perfectly valid types of knowledge. Accordingly, any attempt at a comprehensive and graceful understanding of the Kosmos will most definitely include all three types of knowing; and anything less comprehensive than that is gravely, *gravely* suspect on its own merits.

Once we allow that the Kosmos is an altogether big and wondrous thing, and once we allow that at least these three types of knowing are necessary to get a decent taste of this miracle of existence, then we very well might find that some of our most recalcitrant philosophical problems are not so recalcitrant after all. And that includes, yes, the most aggravating dualism of all—the absolute and the relative—and its dozen or so bastard offspring, from the mind/body problem to fate and free will.

In order to see the moons of Jupiter, you need a telescope. In order to understand *Hamlet,* you need to learn to read. In order to vote on the truth of the Pythagorean theorem, you must learn geometry. In other words, all valid forms of knowledge have, as one of their significant components, an *injunction*—if you want to *know* this, you must *do* this. (This, for example, is the actual meaning of Kuhn's term "paradigm" or "exemplar"—a type of practice or injunction that discloses a particular domain.)

As you will see outlined in the following pages, the injunctive strand of all valid knowledge leads to an *apprehension* or an *illumination,* a direct disclosing of the data or referents in the worldspace brought forth by the injunction, and this illumination is then *checked* (confirmed or refuted) by all those who have adequately performed the injunction and thus disclosed the data.

In short, all valid forms of knowledge have an *injunction,* an *illu-*

mination, and a *confirmation;* and this is true whether we are looking at the moons of Jupiter, the Pythagorean theorem, or . . . the nature of the Absolute.

And where the moons of Jupiter can be disclosed by the eye of flesh (by the senses of their extensions—sensibilia), and the Pythagorean theorem can be disclosed by the eye of mind and its inward apprehensions (intelligibilia), the nature of the Absolute can only be disclosed by the *eye of contemplation* and its directly disclosed referents—its transcendelia, its spiritual data, the hard facts of the spiritual worldspace.

But in order to gain access to any of these valid modes of knowing, I must be *adequate* to the injunction—I must successfully complete the injunctive strand. This is true in the physical sciences, the mental sciences, and the spiritual sciences. If we want to *know* this, we must *do* this. And where the exemplar in physical sciences might be a telescope, and in the human sciences might be linguistic interpretation, in the spiritual sciences the exemplar, the injunction, the paradigm, the practice is: meditation or contemplation. It too has its injunctions, its illuminations, and its confirmations, all of which are perfectly repeatable, verifiable or falsifiable—and all of which therefore constitute a perfectly valid mode of knowledge acquisition.

But in all cases, we must engage the injunction. We must take up the exemplary practice, and this is certainly true for the spiritual sciences as well. If we do not take up the injunctive practice, then we will not have a genuine paradigm, and therefore we will never see the data of the spiritual worldspace. We will in effect be no different from the Churchmen who refused to follow Galileo's injunction and look through the telescope itself.

And that is where the catch-22 comes in.

As I will argue in the following pages, *we cannot solve the absolute/ relative problem using the eye of flesh or the eye of mind.* This deepest of problems and mysteries directly yields its resolution only to the eye of contemplation. And, as both Kant and Nagarjuna forcefully demonstrated, if you try to state this solution in intellectual or rational terms, you will generate nothing but antimonies, paradox, contradiction.

In other words, we cannot solve the absolute/relative problem empirically, using the eye of flesh and its sensibilia; nor can we solve it rationally, using the eye of mind and its intelligibilia. The solution, rather, involves the direct apprehension of transcendelia, which are disclosed only by the eye of contemplation and are most definitely verifiable or falsifiable in that domain, using what are in fact quite *public* procedures—public, that is, to all who have completed the injunction and disclosed the illumination.

And likewise again with fate and free will, the one and the many, mind and brain, noumenon and phenomena. *Eye to Eye* argues that only with the higher stages of the spectrum of consciousness development—part and parcel of the meditative or contemplative unfolding—does the solution to these dilemmas become obvious. But that is not an empirical discovery nor a rational proposition; it is a contemplative discovery and apprehension.

And thus, to the question, what is the relation of mind and body—or mind and brain—typical Western answers include the *identity thesis* (they are two different aspects of the same thing), *dualism* (they are two different things), *interactionism* (they are different but mutually causal), *parallel* (two different things that never speak to each other), *epiphenomenal* (one is the byproduct of the other). And yet, despite what their adherents all claim, not one of those positions has been able to carry the day, simply because they are all, all of them, deeply flawed in one way or another.

And the reason, a more integral philosophy would maintain, is that the mind/body problem cannot be satisfactorily solved with the eye of flesh or the eye of mind, since those are exactly the two modes that need to be integrated, something neither of them could accomplish on their own.

Thus, the only *acceptable response* to the question "What is the relation of the mind and body?" is to *carefully explain the actual injunctions*—the contemplative practices or paradigms or exemplars—and invite the questioners to take up the practice and see for themselves. If you want to *know* this, you must *do* this. Although both the empiricist and the rationalist will not find this answer satisfactory—they wish only to engage their own paradigms and exemplars—nonetheless this is the only acceptable answer and course of action.

Both the rationalist and the empiricist press us: they want us to state our contemplative conclusions and let them check these conclusions *against their own world views.* That is, they want our words without our injunctions. They want to try to follow our words without the pain of having to follow our exemplars. And so we must remind them: Words without injunctions are meaningless. That is, words without injunctions have no means of verification whatsoever. Our conclusions can indeed be carefully justified and verified or rejected, but only if the injunctions are engaged.

And so when the empiricist and the rationalist demand our conclusions without the injunctions, they have guaranteed a *meaningless* answer—and they blame us for the meaninglessness! Our data cannot be generated by their particular paradigms and exemplars, and so they scratch their heads. They will *not* do this, and therefore they will *not* know this. They circle in the orbit of their self-imposed blindness, and they call this blindness reality.

In the East, Zen would handle the problem of the One and the Many in the following way. The question might be, as a famous Zen *koan* has it, "If all things return to the One, to what does the One return?" This is, of course, that intractable dilemma: what is the relation of the absolute and the relative, the One and the Many?

But Zen, of course, will reject every intellectual response. A clever student might respond, "To the Many!," which is a perfectly good intellectual answer, yet it will earn only a severe blow from the Master. Any intellectual response will be radically rejected, no matter what its content!

Rather, the student must take up an *injunction,* a paradigm, an exemplar, a practice, which in this case is *zazen,* sitting meditation. And—to make a very long and complex story brutally short—after an average of five or six years of this exemplary training, the student may begin to have a series of profound illuminations. And you will simply have to trust me that no one would go through this extended hell in order to be rewarded only with an epileptic fit, a schizophrenic hallucination, or a socially induced illusion.

No, this is Ph.D. training in the realm of transcendelia. And once this injunctive training begins to bear fruit, a series of illuminations—commonly called *kensho* or *satori*—begin to flash forth into direct and immediate awareness, and this data is then checked (confirmed or refuted) by the community of those who have completed the injunctive and the illuminative strands. At this point, the answer to the question "To what does the One return?" will become extremely clear and straightforward—and I will give that answer in a moment.

But the point is, the *answer* to the question, What is the relation of the One and the Many, the absolute and the relative, free will and fate, consciousness and form, mind and body?—the technically correct and precise answer is: satori. The technically correct answer is: take up the injunction, perform the experiment, gather the data, the illuminations, and check them with a community of the similarly adequate.

We can't *state* what the answer is other than that, because if we did, we would have merely words without injunctions, and they would indeed be utterly meaningless. It's very like baking a pie: you follow the recipe (the injunctions), you bake the pie, and then you actually taste it. In answer to the question "What does the pie taste like?" we can only give the person the recipe, and let them make it and taste it themselves. We *cannot* theoretically or verbally or philosophically or rationally describe the answer in any other satisfactory fashion: if you want to *know* this, you must *do* this.

And thus: take up the injunction or paradigm of meditation; practice and polish that cognitive tool until awareness learns to discern the incredibly subtle phenomena of transcendelia; check your observations with others who have done so, much as mathematicians will check their proofs with others who have completed the injunctions; and thus confirm or reject your results. And in the verification of that transcendelia, the relation of the One and the Many will become perfectly clear—at least as clear as rocks are to the eye of flesh and geometry is to the eye of mind—and thus will that most intractable of dualisms quite literally come unglued.

The answer to the relation of the Absolute and the relative is therefore most definitely *not*: the Absolute created the world. It most definitely is *not*: the world is illusory and the Absolute alone is real. It is *not*: we perceive only the phenomenal reflection of a noumenal reality. It is *not*: fate and free will are two aspects of one and the same process. It is *not*: all things and events are different aspects of a single interwoven web-of-life. It is *not*: the body alone is real and the mind is a reflection of that only reality. It is *not*: mind and body are two different aspects of the total organism. It is *not*: mind emerges from hierarchical brain structure. In fact, it is not even: noumenon and phenomena are not-two and nondual.

Those are all merely *intellectual symbols* that purport to give the answer, but the real answer does not lie in sensibilia or intelligibilia, it lies in transcendelia, and that domain only discloses itself after the meditative exemplar is engaged, whereupon every single one of those intellectual answers is seen to be utterly inadequate and totally off the mark; each generates nothing but more insolvable and insuperable difficulties and absurd dilemmas and outrageous contradictions. The answer is not more talk; the answer is satori, by whatever name we wish to use to convey valid contemplative awareness.

And, much more to the point, even if this answer could be stated in words—and in fact, the answer most definitely can be stated in words, because Zen Masters talk about it all the time!—nonetheless, it would make no sense whatsoever to anybody who had not also performed the injunction, just as mathematical symbols can be seen by anybody but understood only by those who have completed the training.

But open the eye of contemplation, and the answer is as obvious, as perfect, as unmistakable as the play of sunlight on a crystal clear pond, early on a cool spring morning.

You see, that was the answer.

In subsequent books, particularly *Sex, Ecology, Spirituality,* I have elaborated on themes first presented in *Eye to Eye.* But looking back on the almost fifteen years since I wrote this book, subsequent theory and research have convinced me more than ever of the basic fruitfulness and soundness of the book's approach. I have engaged in a certain fine-tuning and refinement of some of the central issues, but they basically remain exactly as presented here, I trust in a clear and concise fashion.

The first two chapters—"Eye to Eye" and "The Problem of Proof"—set forth the general notion of the three eyes of knowing, and prepare the ground for all that follows. Chapter 3, "A Mandalic Map of Consciousness," is perhaps noteworthy in that it was something of a historical first: critics agreed that it was the first presentation of a genuinely "full-spectrum" model of human growth and development, a model that plausibly integrated both Eastern and Western approaches to psychology and spirituality (an approach that was fleshed out in *The Atman Project* and *Transformations of Consciousness*). This model is further explored in chapter 4, "Development, Meditation, and the Unconscious," and in chapter 9, "Structure, Stage, and Self."

Chapters 5 and 6 take a critical look at various "new age" paradigms. The whole new age movement—as exemplified, for example, in any issue of *New Age Journal*—is unfortunately shot through with regressive and antirational prejudices, and thus any true and genuine "integral paradigm" must include a sharply critical stance to those approaches that claim to be trans-rational but are in fact pre-rational, antiprogressive, antiliberal, and all too often retrograde. These two chapters explore ways in which a truly transcendental and mystical orientation can be rescued from the new Dark Age.

Chapter 7, "The Pre/Trans Fallacy," has received perhaps more attention than any of the other essays in this volume. It has been reprinted in numerous languages around the world, and has become something of a standard reference in the field—both for those who agree with it and those who don't. The essence of the pre/trans fallacy is simple and straightforward: since pre-rational and trans-rational are both non-rational, then they appear similar or even identical to the untutored eye. And if they are confused—if prepersonal is confused with transpersonal, if preverbal is confused with transverbal, if subconscious is confused with superconscious—then one of two things happen: the trans states are reduced to pre states (and thus explained away), or the pre states are elevated to trans glory (thus elevating nonsense to God). These twin disasters—reductionism and elevationism—are the topics of this essay.

Chapter 8, "Legitimacy, Authenticity, and Authority in the New Religions," takes a careful look at various new religious movements, both those deemed generally benign or even beneficial (Zen, Vedanta, Taoism), and those deemed disastrous (Jonestown, the Moonies, cults in general). This chapter suggests a set of criteria that have, in the cases tested so far, spotted those movements that are potentially dangerous.

The last chapter, chapter 10, is called "The Ultimate State of Consciousness," and it is about exactly that. What is the ultimate state? Does that even make any sense? I believe it does, and this chapter attempts to explain why. It is really a statement of the "Always Already" schools of truth, such as Dzogchen, Zen, and Vedanta. It contains a set of "pointing out instructions" for the location of Spirit in the midst of one's ordinary and present state of consciousness. As such, it is an altogether appropriate way to end this volume.

And as for the answer to the great Western dualism? The final answer to the mind/body problem? To the One and the Many? God and creation? Was God at Auschwitz? Are we fated or free willed? It's all the same question, you see, so here is another perfectly complete answer:

> This slowly drifting cloud is pitiful!
> What dreamwalkers we all are!
> Awakened, the one great truth:
> Black rain on the temple roof.

In the following pages I will attempt to explain exactly why that is so.

Boulder, Colo.
February 1996

Preface to the Second Edition

THIS IS A BOOK about an overall or "comprehensive" knowledge quest—not with a view toward any sort of *finality* in
knowledge, but with a view toward some sort of *balance* in the
quest itself. It is about empirical science, philosophy, psychology, and
transcendental religion; about sensory knowledge, symbolic knowledge, and spiritual knowledge; and about how they might all fit
together. It discusses what a "comprehensive" paradigm might
eventually look like, and—just as important or perhaps more important—it attempts to expose and unravel some of the major obstacles to the emergence of such a paradigm.

Each chapter is meant to be something of a self-contained unit;
indeed, most were originally written and circulated as independent
presentations. Nonetheless, each chapter builds upon its predecessor
to drive home the point of the book as a whole: A new and comprehensive paradigm is *possible;* this is what aspects of it might look
like; and here are some of the greatest obstacles now preventing its
emergence.

In looking over this book for its new release, I remain more convinced than ever of the truth and cogency of its central points. In
fact, the existing orthodox *and* new age paradigms have both severely narrowed and distorted the full range of human knowing

and being. Both approaches have fallen considerably short of offering a new and comprehensive paradigm, because both have consistently failed to take a *full-spectrum* view of the human condition in its secular as well as divine possibilities. The orthodox tend to deny the higher reaches of the human spirit, while the new-agers, equally blind but in the other eye, ignore or underestimate the lower and primitive roots of the human animal. Both are terribly half-sighted.

This is a book about what a new and comprehensive paradigm might look like if a full-spectrum approach is taken, an approach that attempts to restore vision to the many eyes of the human spirit.

Boulder, Colo.
December 1989

EYE TO EYE

1

Eye to Eye

WE HEAR A LOT TODAY about "paradigms," and especially about "new and higher" paradigms—"supertheories" that would include, beyond the physical sciences, the higher knowledge claims of philosophy-psychology *and* of transcendental-mystical religion—a type of truly unified world view. The vision itself is fascinating: finally, an overall paradigm or theory that would unite science, philosophy-psychology, and religion-mysticism; finally, a truly "unified field theory"; finally, a comprehensive overview. Some very skilled, very sober, very gifted scholars, from all sorts of different fields, are today talking exactly that. Extraordinary.

The precise implications and meanings of all this will become, I believe, more obvious as we proceed; for the moment, let us simply call any such paradigm, however tentative or fledgling (and assuming it is even possible), an "integral paradigm," meaning an *overall* knowledge quest that would include not only the "hard ware" of physical sciences but also the "soft ware" of philosophy and psychology and the "transcendental ware" of mystical-spiritual religion. If this type of new, higher, and comprehensive paradigm is indeed starting to emerge—and I think it is—then it is probably true that the single greatest issue it must face—an issue it has *not* yet adequately treated—is its relation to *empirical science*. For, the argument goes, if any sort of "new and higher" paradigm is not an empirical science, then it has no valid epistemology—no valid means of acquiring knowledge—and thus anything it says or proclaims, no matter how otherwise comforting, must therefore be invalid, nonsensical, and meaningless. There is no use trying to figure out the range or scope or methods of knowledge of the "new and higher" paradigm, which wishes to include philosophy and mysticism, until you can demonstrate that you *have* actual knowledge of any sort to begin with. Make no mistake about it:

> We do not deny *a priori* that the mystic is able to discover truths by his own special methods. We wait to hear what are the propositions which embody his discoveries, in order to see whether they are verified or confuted by our empirical observations. But the mystic, so far from producing propositions which are empirically verified, is unable to produce any intelligible propositions at all.[3]

The statement is from A. J. Ayer, the noted philosopher, and he concludes that the fact that the mystic "cannot reveal what he 'knows' or even himself devise an empirical test to validate his 'knowledge' shows that his state of mystical intuition is not a genuinely cognitive state."[3]

Would a new integral paradigm be an empirical science? If not, could it claim genuine cognition and knowledge? Or, for that matter—and this is really the whole point of our discussion—can any sort of higher philosophical or spiritual truths be adequately "validated"? There has been an immense amount written on these subjects, but I personally find that most of it just slides off the main issues, like greasy hands chasing soap. In this chapter and the next, then, I would like to examine briefly the nature of empirical science, the meaning of philosophical knowledge, and the essence of transcendental or spiritual knowledge, as well as the relationships between them—and that might help us more easily envision the nature of a new and truly comprehensive paradigm, if such, indeed, exists.

THREE EYES OF THE SOUL

St. Bonaventure, the great *Doctor Seraphicus* of the Church and a favorite philosopher of Western mystics, taught that men and women have at least three modes of attaining knowledge—"three eyes," as he put it (following Hugh of St. Victor, another famous mystic): the *eye of flesh,* by which we perceive the external world of space, time, and objects; the *eye of reason,* by which we attain a knowledge of philosophy, logic, and the mind itself; and the *eye of contemplation,* by which we rise to a knowledge of transcendent realities.

Further, said St. Bonaventure, all knowledge is a type of *illumination.* There is exterior and inferior illumination *(lumen exterius* and *lumen inferius),* which lights the eye of flesh and gives us knowledge of sense objects. There is *lumen interius,* which lights the eye of reason and gives us knowledge of philosophical truths. And there is *lumen superius,* the light of transcendent Being which illumines the eye of contemplation and reveals salutary truth, "truth which is unto liberation."

In the external world, said St. Bonaventure, we find a *vestigium* or "vestige of God"—and the eye of flesh perceives this vestige (which appears as separate objects in space and time). In ourselves, in our psyches—especially in the "threefold activity of the soul" (memory, reason, and will)—we find an *imago* of God, revealed by the mental eye. And ultimately, through the eye of contemplation, lighted by the *lumen superius,* we find the whole transcendent realm itself, beyond sense and reason—the Divine Ultimate itself.

All of this fits precisely with Hugh of St. Victor (first of the great Victorine mystics), who distinguished between *cogitatio, meditatio,* and *contemplatio. Cogitatio,* or simple empirical cognition, is a seeking for the facts of the material world using the eye of flesh. *Meditatio* is a seeking for the truths within the psyche itself (the *imago* of God) using the mind's eye. *Contemplatio* is the knowledge whereby the psyche or soul is united instantly with Godhead in transcendent insight (revealed by the eye of contemplation).

Now that particular wording—eye of flesh, mind, and contemplation—is Christian; but similar ideas can be found in every major school of traditional psychology, philosophy, and religion. The "three eyes" of a human being correspond, in fact, to the three major realms of being described by the perennial philosophy, which are the gross (flesh and material), the subtle (mental and animic), and the causal (transcendent and contemplative). These realms have been described extensively elsewhere, and I wish here only to point to their unanimity among traditional psychologists and philosophers.[107,110,137]

To extend St. Bonaventure's insights, we moderns might say that the eye of flesh—the *cogitatio,* the *lumen inferius/exterius*—participates in a select world of shared sensory experience, which it partially creates and partially discloses. This is the "gross realm," the realm of space, time, and matter (the subconscient). It is the realm *shared* by all those possessing a similar eye of flesh. Thus humans can even share this realm, to some degree, with other higher animals (especially mammals), because the eyes of flesh are quite similar. If a human holds a piece of meat in front of a dog, the dog will respond—a rock or plant will not. (The meat does not exist for the organism lacking the necessary mode of knowledge and perception, the necessary eye of flesh.) In the gross realm, an object is never *A* and not-*A;* it is either *A* or not-*A*. A rock is never a tree, a tree is never a mountain, one rock is not another rock, and so on. This is basic sensorimotor intelligence—object constancy—the eye of flesh. It is the *empirical eye,* the eye of sensory experience. (It should be said, at the start, that I am using the term "empirical" as it is employed in philosophy: capable of detection by the five human senses or their extensions. When empiricists like Locke concluded that all knowledge is experiential, they meant that all knowledge in the mind is first in the five senses. When Buddhists say that "meditation is experiential," they do *not* mean the same thing as Locke; they are rather using the term "experience" to mean "directly conscious, not mediated by forms or symbols." We will return to this topic in the next chapter; in the meantime, I will use "empirical" as the empiricists use it: "sensory experience.")

The eye of reason, or more generally, the eye of mind—the *meditatio,* the *lumen interius*—participates in a world of ideas, images, logic, and concepts. This is the subtle realm (or more precisely, the lower portion of the subtle, but the only one I will discuss here). Because so much of modern thought is based solely on the empirical eye, the eye of flesh, it is important to remember that the mental eye *cannot* be reduced to the fleshy eye. The mental field includes but transcends the sensory field. While not excluding it, the mind's eye rises far above the eye of flesh: in imagination, it can *picture* sensory objects not immediately present, and thus transcend the flesh's imprisonment in the simply present world; in logic, it can internally operate upon sensorimotor objects, and so transcend actual motor sequences; in will, it can delay the flesh's instinctual and impulsive discharges and thus transcend the merely animal and subhuman aspects of the organism.

Although the eye of mind relies upon the eye of flesh for much of its information, not all mental knowledge comes strictly from fleshy knowledge, nor does it deal solely with the objects of the flesh. Our knowledge is *not* entirely empirical and fleshy. "According to the sensationalists [that is, empiricists]," says Schuon, "all knowledge originates in sensorial experience [the eye of flesh]. They go so far as to maintain that human knowledge can have no access to any suprasensory knowledge and are unaware of the fact that the suprasensible can be the object of a genuine perception and hence of a concrete experience [notice that Schuon correctly refuses to equate empirical and experiential, since there are supraempirical or suprasensory experiences]. Thus, it is upon an intellectual infirmity that these thinkers build their systems, without their appearing to be in the least impressed by the fact that countless men as intelligent as themselves have thought otherwise than they do."[106]

The point is precisely as Schumacher said: "In short, we 'see' not simply with our eyes but with a great part of our mental equipment as well [the eye of mind]. . . . With the light of the intellect [the *lumen interius*] we can see things which are invisible to our bodily senses. . . . The truth of ideas cannot be seen by the senses."[105] For example, mathematics is a nonempirical knowledge or a supraempirical knowledge. It is discovered, illuminated, and implemented by the eye of reason, not by the eye of flesh.

Even introductory philosophy texts are quite certain on that point: "Whether these [mathematical] expressions are to be understood as referring to anything physical is not his concern but that of the physicist. For the mathematician, statements are viewed as statements of logical relationships; he is not interested in their empirical or factual meaning [if they have any]."[96] Thus, no one has ever seen, with the eye of flesh, the square root of a negative one. That is a transempirical entity, and can only be seen by the mind's eye. Most of mathematics, as Whitehead says, is transempirical and even *a priori* (in the Pythagorean sense).

Likewise with logic. The truth of a logical deduction is based on internal consistency—it is not based upon its relation to sensory objects. Thus, a valid logical syllogism might say, "All unicorns are mortal. Tarnac is a unicorn. Therefore Tarnac is mortal." Logically that is valid; empirically it is meaningless (not sound), for the simple reason that no one has ever seen a unicorn in the first place. Logic is transempirical. Thus many philosophers, such as Whitehead, have held that the abstract (or mental) sphere is necessary and *a priori* for the manifestation of the natural/sensory realm, and this is approximately what the Eastern traditions mean when they say that the gross arises from the subtle (which arises from the causal).

In mathematics, in logic—and more: in imagination, in conceptual understanding, in psychologic insight, in creativity—we *see* things with the mind's eye which are not fully present to the eye of flesh. Thus we say that the mental field includes but greatly transcends the fleshy field.

The eye of contemplation is to the eye of reason as the eye of reason is to the eye of flesh. Just as reason transcends flesh, so contemplation transcends reason. Just as reason cannot be reduced to, nor derived solely from, fleshy knowledge, so contemplation cannot be reduced to nor derived from reason. Where the eye of reason is transempirical, the eye of contemplation is transrational, translogical, and transmental. "Gnosis [the eye of contemplation, the *lumen superius*] transcends the mental realm and *a fortiori* the realm of the sentiments [the sensory realm]. This transcendence results from the 'supernaturally natural' function of [gnosis], namely the contemplation of the Immutable, of the Self which is Reality, Consciousness, and Bliss. The quest of philosophers, therefore, has nothing in common with that of contemplatives, since its basic principle of exhaustive verbal adequacy is opposed to any liberating finality, to any transcending of the sphere of words."[106]

We will be returning to these three different fields of knowledge throughout this chapter. In the meantime, let us simply assume that all men and women possess an eye of flesh, an eye of reason, and an eye of contemplation; that each eye has its own objects of knowledge (sensory, mental, and transcendental); that a higher eye cannot be reduced to nor explained solely in terms of a lower eye; that each eye is valid and useful in its own field, but commits a fallacy when it attempts, by itself, to fully grasp higher or lower realms.

Within that context, I will try to demonstrate that while an integral or truly comprehensive paradigm will draw freely on the eye of flesh and the eye of mind, it must also draw significantly on the eye of contemplation. This means that a new and integral paradigm—if such is ever to exist—would be in the extremely favorable position of being able to use and integrate all three eyes—gross, subtle, and causal. I will also argue that, by and large, empiric-analytic science belongs to the eye of flesh, phenomenological philosophy and psychology to the eye of mind, and religion/meditation to the eye of contemplation. Thus a new and integral paradigm would ideally and ultimately be a synthesis and integration of empiricism, rationalism, and transcendentalism (whether this overall endeavor can or should be called a "higher science" will be dealt with in the next chapter; in this chapter, "science" will refer to classical empiric-analytic science).

But there is one major difficulty and one major hazard which is first to be overcome, and that is the tendency toward *category error,* which is the attempt of one eye to usurp the roles of the other two. I will point out some of the major category errors committed by religion, by philosophy, and by science, and then—as one example—I will discuss the historical category errors that led to the rise of modern scientism. I do not mean to pick on science in this regard—religion and philosophy have been just as guilty, as we will see. However, historically speaking, the most recent and most pervasive category error has concerned the role of empirical science, and it is important to try to understand that error as carefully as we can, not only because, of all the category errors, it has probably had the most impact, but also because in many subtle ways it is still with us.

Following those assumptions, we can begin with an examination of the rise and meaning of empirical science.

THE RISE OF SCIENCE

It is not generally realized that science—by which I mean, for the moment, what Kepler, Galileo, and Newton did—was *not* a rationalistic system, but an empirical one. As we have seen, these two are not at all the same: rationalism lays stress on the eye of reason; empiricism, the eye of flesh. Science, in fact, began as an *anti*rationalism, as a direct revolt against the rational systems of the scholastic age. As Whitehead put it: "Galileo keeps harping on how things happen, whereas his [rationally minded] adversaries had a complete theory as to why things happen. Unfortunately the two theories did not bring out the same results. Galileo insists upon 'irreducible and stubborn facts,' and Simplicius, his opponent, brings forward *reasons.*"[130]

Notice that the clash between Galileo, with his "irreducible and stubborn facts," and Simplicius, with his "satisfactory reasons," is precisely a clash between the eye of flesh and the eye of reason— between empiricism and rationalism. Whitehead is very insistent on that point: "It is a great mistake to conceive this historical revolt [of science] as an appeal to reason. On the contrary, it was through and through an anti-intellectualist movement. It was a return to the contemplation of brute fact [the eye of flesh; empiricism]; and it was based on a recoil from the inflexible rationality of medieval thought."[130] Again and again Whitehead drives home that crucial point: "We cannot too carefully realize that science started with the organization of ordinary [sense] experiences. It was in this way that it coalesced so readily with the antirationalistic bias of the historical revolt."[130] Science was, as Bertrand Russell remarked, nothing more than consistent *common sense,* which actually means: based on the most commonsense organ we all possess: the eye of flesh.

It is very easy to see why science began as a revolt against rationalism. Recall that logic, in and by itself, so transcends the subhuman eye of flesh that at times it seems almost disembodied, totally unrelated to the world of fleshy objects. This in itself does not constitute a flaw in logic, as so many romantics seem to think, but rather constitutes its very strength: to reason about an activity means not to have to actually perform that activity with the flesh. The very power of logic lies in its transcendence of sensory objects (as Piaget has demonstrated, formal operational thinking or rational logic operates *upon,* and thus transcends, concrete and sensorimotor experience).

But logic—or in general, the entire eye of mind—can be severely misused. The only final test of "correct reasoning" is whether the train of logical thought is itself internally consistent, and whether it has violated any canons of logic in the process. If it meets these criteria, then it is, in its own realm, quite valid. It starts with an initial premise, and through subtle processes of abstract (or formal operational) reasoning, draws out all of the implications and deductions enfolded in that premise.

The premise itself—the initial starting proposition—can originate in any of the three realms: fleshy, mental, or contemplative. If the initial starting point originates in the realm of the eye of flesh, and is itself valid, we speak of "indubitable facts" (Russell) or Galileo's "irreducible and stubborn facts" or simply empiric-analytic facts. If the initial starting point originates in the realm of the eye of mind, we speak of "indubitable principles of reference" (Russell) or "intuitively self-evident truths" (Descartes) or of "direct phenomenological apprehensions" (Husserl), which can be either philosophical or psychological. If the proposition is influenced by the higher eye of contemplation, we speak broadly of revelation or mandalic reasoning (as we will explain). At any rate, let us note the three starting points for reasoning: irreducible facts (flesh), self-evident or axiomatic truths (mind), and revelatory insights (spirit).

Now we mentioned that logic can be put to a grave misuse, and it is this: In the *selection of the initial premises* for reasoning, all sorts of errors and even frauds can be committed. Outstanding among these is the "category error," which occurs when one of the three realms is made to wholly substitute for another realm—or, we might say, when things (flesh) are confused with thoughts (mind) are confused with transcendental insights (contemplation). For once that occurs, then facts try to replace principles and principles try to replace God.

For example, a true rationalist is one who claims all valid knowledge comes only from the eye of reason and dismisses the eye of flesh (not to mention contemplation) as being wholly unreliable. Descartes was such a philosopher. "We should never allow ourselves to be persuaded excepting by the evidence of our Reason," he said, and by that he explicitly meant evidence "of our Reason and not of our senses." For Descartes, reason—and reason alone—could discover ultimately self-evident truths, an apprehension Descartes called intuition (rational intuition, not spiritual intuition):

> By *intuition* I understand not the fluctuating testimony of the senses, but the conception which an unclouded and attentive mind gives us so readily and distinctly that we are wholly freed from doubt about that which we understand. Or, what comes to the same thing, *intuition* springs from the light of reason alone. . . .[96]

"Intuition springs from the light of reason alone. . . ." And rational-intuition alone could discover self-evident truths. Once we have arrived at self-evident truths, then, according to Descartes, we may deduce from those truths a whole series of secondary truths. And, he says, "These two methods [the initial rational truth and deduction] are the most certain routes to knowledge, and the mind should admit no others. All the rest should be rejected as suspect of error and dangerous."[96]

There is the statement of a pure rationalist, one who believes only in the eye of reason, and discards the eye of flesh and the eye of contemplation. But what a severe limitation! For now the eye of reason is forced to try to disclose empirical truths as well as contemplative truths, a task it simply is not equipped to do, and a task that therefore leads inexorably to category errors. It is quite obvious that the eye of reason cannot adequately disclose the realm of contemplation; and it soon became obvious that the eye of reason could not itself, by itself, disclose the truths lying in the realm of the objective and sensory world. As we will soon see, it was the role of modern science to show precisely why reasoning alone could not disclose empirical facts. The truth in the domain of the eye of flesh can be checked only with the eye of flesh.

The only point I wish to emphasize here is that when one eye tries to usurp the role of any of the other eyes, a category error occurs. And it can occur in any direction: the eye of contemplation is as ill-equipped to disclose the facts of the eye of flesh as the eye of flesh is incapable of grasping the truths of the eye of contemplation. Sensation, reason, and contemplation disclose their own truths in their own realms, and anytime one eye tries to see for another eye, blurred vision results.

Now that type of category error has been *the* great problem for almost every major religion: the great sages of Hinduism, Buddhism, Christianity, Islam, and so on all opened, to one degree or another, the eye of contemplation—the third eye. But that does not mean, at all, that they then automatically became experts in the realms of the first and second eyes. Enlightenment, for instance, does not carry the information that water is composed of two hydrogen and one oxygen atoms. If it did, then that fact would appear in at least one religious text, whereas in fact it is in none.

Unfortunately, the Revelation—given by the eye of contemplation—is then taken as the supreme arbiter of truth for the eye of flesh and the eye of reason. The *Book of Genesis,* for instance, is a Revelation of the evolution of the manifest realm from the Unmanifest, which occurs in seven major stages (seven days). It is a translation of a *supramental* insight into the poetic images of the mind's eye. Alas, those whose own eye of contemplation remains closed, take the Revelation as both an *empirical fact* and a *rational truth.* And that is a category error. And science discovered that error—with a vengeance.

Thus, for example, in A.D. 535, the Christian monk Cosmas wrote a book called *Christian Topography.* Based entirely upon a literal reading of the Bible, Cosmas demonstrated once and for all that the earth had neither North nor South Pole, but was a flat parallelogram whose length is double its width. Dogmatic theology abounds with that type of howling error—and that is true of both Eastern and Western religions. The Hindus and Buddhists, for instance, believed that the earth, because it must be supported, was sitting on an elephant which, because it must also be supported, was sitting on a turtle (and to the question, "Upon what, then, rests the turtle," the answer was given, "Let us now change the subject").

The point is that Buddhism and Christianity and other genuine religions contained, at their summit, ultimate insights into ultimate reality, but these transverbal insights were invariably all mixed up with rational truths and empirical facts. Humanity had not, as it were, yet learned to differentiate and separate the eyes of flesh, reason, and contemplation. And because Revelation was confused with logic and with empirical fact, and all three were presented as *one truth,* then two things happened: the philosophers came in and de-

stroyed the rational side of religion, and science came in and destroyed the empirical side. I will argue that that was as it should be.
However, theology—which in the West had a somewhat weak eye
of contemplation anyway—was so heavily dependent upon its rationalism and its empirical "facts" (the sun circles the earth as the Bible
says), that when these two eyes were taken away by philosophy and
science, Western spirituality all but went blind. It did not fall back
on its eye of contemplation—but merely fell apart and spent its time
in futile argument with the philosophers and scientists. From that
point on, spirituality in the West was dismantled, and only philosophy and science seriously remained.

Within a century, however, philosophy as a rational system—a
system based on the eye of mind—was in its own turn decimated,
and decimated by the new scientific empiricism. At that point,
human knowledge was *reduced* to only the eye of flesh. Gone was
the contemplative eye; gone the mental eye—and human beings had
enough collective low self-esteem to restrict their means of valid
knowledge to the eye of flesh—the eye we share with animals.
Knowing became, in source and referent, essentially subhuman.

THE NEW SCIENCE

Understand that this dismal restriction of human knowledge was
not the fault of science. Empiric-analytic science is simply the organized body of verifiable knowledge *grounded* by the eye of flesh. To
say we should not have that knowledge nor rely on it is to say we
shouldn't have flesh. Something else—almost sinister—occurred,
which converted science into scientism, and that is what will concern us.

But first the rise of science itself. By historical account, we are
now reaching the year A.D. 1600. Prior to that time human knowledge was dominated by the Church—by a dogma which confused
and combined the eyes of contemplation, of reason, and of sense. If
the Bible said the earth was created in six days, so be it; if the dogma
said an object ten times heavier than another object falls to earth ten
times faster, so be it. In this confused state, nobody bothered to
carefully exercise the eye of flesh and *simply look at the natural world.*
In fact, did a heavier object fall faster than a light object, as the
Church said? Why not test it out?

If civilized men and women have been on the face of the earth for, say, ten thousand years, then it took ten thousand years for someone to think of that simple idea and actually carry it through. But then, around the year 1600, one Galileo Galilei stood on the Pisa Tower and dropped two objects—one heavy, one light—and they hit the ground at the same time. The world has never, but never, been the same.

The scientific method was invented independently and simultaneously by Galileo and Kepler about A.D. 1600. It would not be too far wrong to say that they simply used the eye of flesh to *look* at the realm of flesh, for that is essentially what happened. "Prior to the time of Kepler and Galileo," says L. L. Whyte, "the only developed systems of thought had been religious [the eye of contemplation] or philosphic [the eye of reason] organizations of subjective experience, while such objective observations of nature as had been collected had remained relatively unorganized. Medieval rationalism was subjective; there was as yet no rational philosophy of nature [no empiric-analytic thought] of comparable complexity or precision."[131]

But what Kepler and Galileo did was actually much more brilliant than just using the eye of flesh carefully and precisely. Many before them had looked carefully and steadily at nature (e.g., Aristotle), but none before them had invented the scientific method. Please mark that point well, because everybody seems to miss that fact: If the term "scientific method" has any historical meaning whatsoever, then it can be said to have been invented and practiced by Kepler and Galileo.

For Kepler and Galileo used the eye of flesh not just to look at nature, but to look at nature in a particular way, and that particular way constituted a new discovery: the scientific method, modern science, real empirical science. It is popular today to say that science just means "knowledge," or that it is basically "good observation," but that is not true. As Whyte points out: "For two thousand years man had been observing, comparing, and seeking to classify his observations, but as yet there was no system of thought concerning nature which provided any method which might be systematically used for facilitating the process of discovery. . . ."[131] Science was not just good observation, which had been around for thousands of years; it was a peculiar type of observation.

Before I describe the heart of that particular type of observation, let me set forth a few of its auxiliary characteristics. First of all, the new scientific method was empirical-experimental. Suppose we have a question: "Does an object twice as heavy as another fall twice as fast?" A medieval rationalist might proceed as follows: "We know in all respects that as a natural object increases in one physical quantity it increases in all others proportionately. For instance, a wooden rod twice as long as another weighs twice as much. Weight is a physical quantity, and so is speed. Therefore any object twice as heavy as another must fall twice as fast." Galileo, on the other hand, simply went out and tried it.

Notice that the logic of the rationalist was valid. Starting from initial premises, it deduced correctly a set of conclusions. Problem is, the initial premises were wrong. Deduction is a sound mode of knowledge, provided one's initial premises are sound. Some initial premises are indeed self-evident and true; as the history of philosophy has shown, however, some are self-evident and false. What Galileo and Kepler needed was a way to decide, as regards the sensory realm, whether an initial proposition was true or false. *Not a rational way*—because there is none—but a sensory way, an empirical way. And that way, in short, was the empirical experiment: Devise a situation such that all variables are held constant except one. Run the experiment several times, each time changing that one variable, then look at the results.

For Galileo it meant gathering several objects—all the *same* size, dropped from the *same* height, at the *same* time. But consisting of *different* weights. If the objects fall at different speeds, then the weight of the objects is the likely reason. If they fall at the same speed (actually, acceleration), then the weight is unimportant. As it turns out, they fell at the same speed; therefore, the proposition that "heavier objects fall faster" is disproved. All objects (in a vacuum) fall at the same rate of acceleration—and there is an initial premise you may *now* use in deductive logic.

This scientific proof is empirical and inductive; it is not rational and deductive (although, obviously, science uses logic and deduction, only it makes them subservient to empirical induction). Induction—systematically proposed by Francis Bacon—is the formation of general laws on the basis of numerous specific instances (the opposite of deduction). For instance, after Galileo tried his experiment on metallic objects, he might try it on wooden ones, then clay ones, then paper ones, and so on and see if he got the same results. That is induction: the suggested proposition is tested in all sorts of new circumstances; if it is *not disproved* in those circumstances, it is to that extent confirmed. The proposition itself is generally called a *hypothesis.* A hypothesis not yet disproved (without extenuating circumstances) is generally called a *theory.* And a theory that looks like it may in fact never be disproved (supplemented, perhaps, but not fundamentally invalidated in its own realm) is generally called a *law.* Galileo discovered two laws of earthly motion; Kepler discovered three laws of planetary motion; and the genius Newton put these laws *together* to join the forces of heaven with those of earth: he showed that an apple falls to earth (Galileo) for the same reason that the planets circle the sun (Kepler)—namely, gravity.

The point is that the classic scientific method was empirical and inductive, not rational and deductive. What Bacon and Kepler and Galileo did was simply promise to yoke the eye of reason to the eye of flesh when the proposition in question concerns the domain of flesh. Odd as it sounds today, that was a stroke of genius: let the eye of flesh itself check facts in the domain of flesh, and thus avoid the category errors of confusing flesh with reason and contemplation. I am going to suggest that not only was that a great benefit to science, but also a potentially great benefit to religion, because it acts to strip religion of its nonessential and pseudoscientific dross, which has contaminated every major religion bar none.

But there is one other point in regard to Galileo and Kepler, and the most important point at that, the very heart of the matter. We saw that others before them had carefully used the eye of flesh; and others before them had, in a crude sense, used a type of induction, trying to validate their theories in several circumstances. But Galileo and Kepler hit upon the real and essential secret of empirical-inductive proof: in a scientific experiment, one desires to see if a particular event occurs; if it does, something changed. In the physical world, change necessarily involves some sort of displacement in space-time; displacement can be *measured.* Conversely, if an event cannot be measured, it cannot be the object of an empiric-scientific experiment; and, as far as *that* science is concerned, it does not exist.

Thus, it is only a slight exaggeration to say that empiric-analytic science is measurement. Measurement, and virtually measurement alone, gives the data of scientific experiments. Galileo measured. Kepler measured. Newton measured. *There* was the real genius of Kepler and Galileo. The reason modern science was not discovered before Kepler and Galileo was that nobody really measured before Kepler and Galileo. "We have here reached a moment of great significance," says L. L. Whyte. "About 1600 Kepler and Galileo simultaneously and independently formulatd the principle that the laws of nature are to be discovered by measurement, and applied this principle in their own work. Where Aristotle had classified, Kepler and Galileo sought to measure."[131] Whyte is at pains to emphasize: "The process of measurement was the one objectively reliable approach to the structure of nature and the numbers so obtained were the key to the order of nature. After 1600 mankind was thus in possession of a systematic method of research into those aspects of nature which were accessible to measurement. The centuries since 1600 may well be regarded as the age of quantity. Never before had such a technique been available. . . ."[131]

Whitehead is just as certain: Aristotle, he said, tended to mislead the physicists because "in effect, these doctrines said to the physicist *classify* when they should have said *measure*." For, says Whitehead, "if only the schoolmen had measured instead of classifying, how much they might have learnt!"[130] Whitehead summarizes the essence of the new empiric-analytic method: "Search for *measurable* elements among your phenomena, and then search for relations between these measures of physical quantities." That, he says, is a "rule of science."[130]

I am not going to make a drawn-out argument for this, but take it as obvious that "the scientific gauge is quantity: space, size, and strength of forces can all be reckoned numerically. . . . A number is a number, and number is the language of science."[110] Psychology is considered an empirical science only if it offers *measurable* patterns, which is why behaviorism is an empirical science and psychoanalysis is not. (Notice I did not say that behaviorism is therefore valid and psychoanalysis is not; they are two sets of data gathered through two different eyes, both of which are valid, one of which is empirical, and one of which is mental-phenomenological.) Even psychoanalysis realized this right off. As the pioneering analyst Melanie Klein put it:

> It has to be kept in mind that the evidence which the analyst can present differs essentially from that which is required in physical sciences, because the whole nature of psychoanalysis is different. In my view, endeavors to provide comparable exact data result in a pseudoscientific approach, because the workings of the unconscious mind, and the response of the psychoanalyst to them, cannot be submitted to measurement. . . .[73]

In summary, we have this: The ingenius and enduring contribution of Galileo and Kepler was the demonstration that, as regards the physical or sensorimotor world, the eye of reason can and must be linked to and grounded in the eye of flesh by inductive experimentation, whose very heart is repeatable measurement (number). Let the eye of flesh speak for the eye of flesh—and empirical science was invented for just that purpose.

KANT AND THE BEYOND

The epitome of fleshy truth is empirical fact; the epitome of mental truth is philosophic and psychologic insight; and the epitome of contemplative truth is spiritual wisdom. We saw that prior to the modern era men and women had not sufficiently differentiated the eyes of flesh, reason, and contemplation, and thus tended to confuse them. Religion *tried* to be scientific, philosophy tried to be religious, science tried to be philosophic—and all were, to just that extent, wrong. They were guilty of category errors.

Thus, Galileo and Kepler, in delineating the true nature of empiric-scientific truth, actually did religion and philosophy a great service. They actually separated out the eye of flesh from its confusion with the eyes of mind and contemplation. Science, by performing its duty faithfully and honestly, could liberate both philosophy and religion from trying to be pseudoscience. The monk Cosmas would not have to spend his time trying to figure out the shape of the earth; the science of geology could do that and free Cosmas for the pursuit of contemplation. By showing us precisely what truth is in the realm of the eye of flesh, it would eventually, by subtraction, help us rediscover the mind's eye and the contemplative eye.

Now what Galileo and Kepler did for the eye of flesh, vis-à-vis religion, Kant did for the eye of reason. That is to say, as Galileo and Kepler helped to strip religion of its nonessential "scientific" dross, Kant helped strip it of its nonessential rationalizing. And that was to have extraordinary, if almost wholly misunderstood, repercussions.

Prior to Kant, the philosophers were not only trying to *deduce* scientific facts—which we saw was impossible—they were also trying to *deduce* contemplative or spiritual truths, which is just as impossible but twice as dangerous. Both secular and religious philosophers were making all sorts of rational statements which they claimed were about ultimate realities and ultimate truths. Thus, Thomas Aquinas had put forth rational "proofs" for the existence of God; so had Descartes—and Aristotle and Anselm and others. Their common mistake lay in trying to prove with the eye of reason that which can only be seen with the eye of contemplation. And somebody, sooner or later, was bound to find it out.

This was Kant's brilliance. He himself did indeed believe in God, in a Transcendent Ultimate, in noumenon. And he correctly believed that it was transempirical, transsensory. But he demonstrated that anytime we attempt to *reason* about this transempirical reality, we find that *we can create arguments for either of two completely contradictory views with equal plausibility*—and that plainly shows that such reasoning is futile (or, at any rate, does not carry near the weight it had so generously given itself under the title of "metaphysics"). But here were all these philosophers and theologians cranking out rational statements about God (or Buddha or Tao) and about ultimate reality as if they were speaking directly and actually of the Real itself, whereas in fact, as Kant demonstrated, they were speaking nonsense. Pure reason is simply incapable of grasping transcendent realities, and when it tries, it finds that its contradictory can be put with equal plausibility. (This insight was by no means confined to the West. Almost fifteen hundred years before Kant, the Buddhist genius Nagarjuna—founder of Madhyamika Buddhism—arrived at virtually the same conclusion, a conclusion echoed and amplified in succeeding generations by every major school of Eastern philosophy and psychology: Reason cannot grasp the essence of absolute reality, and when it tries, it generates only dualistic incompatibilities.)

One of the reasons for this—if I may speak poetically—is that, as disclosed by contemplation, the Ultimate is a "coincidence of opposites" (Nicholas de Cusa) or as Hinduism and Buddhism put it, *advaita* or *advaya,* which means "nondual" or "not-two," a fact that *cannot* be pictured in logic. You cannot, for instance, picture a thing being itself *and* not being itself *at the same time.* You *cannot* see it raining and not raining at the same time in the same spot. You cannot picture nor reason accurately about nonduality, about ultimate reality. If you attempt to translate nondual Reality into dualistic reason, then you will create two opposites where there are in fact none, and therefore each of these opposites can be rationally argued with absolutely equal plausibility—and that, to return to Kant, shows why reason only generates paradox when it tries to grasp God or the Absolute. To indulge in metaphysical speculation (solely with the eye of pure reason) is thus to indulge in nonsense. To say "Reality is absolute subject" is not false, it is nonsensical, it is meaningless, it is neither true nor false but empty, because its opposite can be put with equal force: "Reality is absolute object." In the East, the same nonsense would exist ("Reality is Atman" versus "Reality is Anatman") until totally dismantled by Nagarjuna in precisely the same way followed by Kant.

What Kant demonstrated was that—as Wittgenstein would later put it—most metaphysical problems are not false, they are nonsensical. Not that the answer is bad, but that the question is silly. . . . It is supported by a category error: The eye of pure reason is trying to see into Heaven. Now I don't mean to imply that Kant was enlightened (i.e., that his eye of contemplation was fully opened). Clearly, he was not. An excellent way to grasp Kant's position is by studying the aforementioned Buddhist genius, Nagarjuna, because Nagarjuna applies the same critical philosophy to reason, but he does so not just to show the limitations of reason but to push further and help open the eye of contemplation *(prajna),* which knows the Ultimate directly, nonconceptually, and immediately. Kant doesn't really know about *prajna* or contemplation, but since he *does* know that God is beyond sense and reason, he thinks God is therefore forever hidden to direct awareness. Soon Schopenhauer would point out just that shortcoming in Kant.

But the only point I want to stress is that Kant correctly demonstrated that the eye of pure reason *cannot,* by its very nature, see into the realm of spirit. Philosophy, that is, cannot reach God—at most it can posit God morally (practically). This demonstration actually stripped religion of the burden to rationalize God, just as Galileo and Kepler relieved religion of the necessity to putter around with molecules. As McPherson put it:

> Perhaps positivistic philosophy has done a service to religion. By showing, in their own way, the absurdity of what theologians try to utter, positivists have helped to suggest that religion belongs to the sphere of the unutterable. . . . Positivists may be the enemies of theology, but the friends of religion.[85]

Thus, both scientific fact and rational philosophy—besides being correct and excellent uses of their own respective eyes of flesh and reason—were potentially quite beneficial to religion in that they could help to strip spirituality of its nonessentials, and clarify its own role in human knowledge and illumination. For what we learn, if we put Galileo and Kepler and Kant and Christ together, is that sensorimotor intelligence is not philosophic insight is not spiritual wisdom—neither can be reduced to the others, neither can be dispensed with.

But within mere decades of Kant, the eye of flesh, blinded by Newton's light, thought that it, and it alone, was worthy of knowledge. For empirical science, spurred on by the likes of Auguste Comte, became scientism. It did not just speak for the eye of flesh, but for the eye of mind and for the eye of contemplation as well. In so doing, it fell prey to precisely the same category errors that it discovered in dogmatic theology, and for which it made religion dearly pay. The scienticians tried to force *empirical* science, with its eye of flesh, to work for all three eyes. And that is a category error. And for that the world, not science, has paid dearly.

THE NEW SCIENTISM

Empiric-analytic science is one aspect of the knowledge to be gained in the realm of the eye of flesh (not all sensory knowledge is scientific: aesthetic impact, for instance). Of course, empiric-analytic science does indeed use the eye of reason, and I believe it even uses the eye of contemplation for creative insight, but all are made subservient to, or grounded in, the eye of flesh and its data. And from being thus one aspect of the lowest eye, it came in the hands of the scienticians to claim all aspects of all three. What happened?

There are many ways to state the fallacy of scientism. It went from saying, "That which cannot be seen by the eye of flesh cannot be empirically verified" to "That which cannot be seen by the eye of flesh does not exist." It went from saying, "There is an excellent method for gaining knowledge in the realm of the five senses" to "Thus the knowledge gained by mind and contemplation is invalid." As Smith put it: "With science there can be no quarrel. Scientism is another matter. Whereas science is positive, contenting itself with reporting what it discovers, scientism is negative. It goes beyond the actual findings of science to deny that other approaches to knowledge are valid and other truths true."[110] Or, more to the point: "The triumphs of modern science went to man's head in something of the way rum does, causing him to grow loose in his logic. He came to think that what science discovers somehow casts doubt on things it does not discover; that the success it realizes in its own domain throws into question the reality of domains its devices cannot touch."[110]

Recall that the extraordinary significance of Kepler and Galileo lay in the discovery of a method to settle once and for all the truth-value of a sensory-empirical proposition. "Does a heavy object fall faster than a light one" is *not* to be thought about with the *lumen interius* of reason, it is *not* to be contemplated with the *lumen superius* in *contemplatio*—it is to be *tested* with the eye of flesh. Prior to that time there simply was no accepted method of settling such disputes, there was no method whereby one could demonstrate empirically that an opponent's ideas were wrong. But now, with Galileo and Kepler, there was a means to decide such empirical disputes—propositions could be shown to be true or false, and shown in such a way that all reasonable men and women would acknowledge agreement.

And with that, the impact of science began to floor theologians and philosophers (God is not a verifiable proposition, but the ground of all propositions, and thus God cannot pass the scientific quiz). *The* test had arrived, and philosophers, religionists, theologians, mystics, and poets were flunking it by the thousands. In fact, they should have refused to take the test—they should have realized that transcendent values are not empiric facts revealed to the eye of flesh but contemplative and nonverbal insights revealed by the *lumen superius* in the cave of the Heart. As it was, they simply began a long series of undignified retreats, trying to think of ways to prove that God was an object, like a rock, or a proposition, like $F = ma$. The work of Galileo and Kepler culminated in Newton's great *Principia,* which in many ways represents (to this day) the pinnacle of the empiric-scientific method. The *Principia* is full of "stubborn and irreducible facts," and such logical laws as conform to those facts. It was an overwhelming achievement for the eye of flesh.

Newton's impact on philosophy was naturally immense. The philosophers, quite simply, wanted in on a good thing. Given the disastrous years of unchecked rationalism and unused contemplation, the philosophers simply swung over their allegiance to the eye of flesh and its greatest proponent, Newton. Even Kant, for all his brilliance, fell prey to this Newtonian religion. It is well known that Kant wanted to be a physicist if he weren't a philosopher, and his critical philosophy, aside from its importance in delineating the sphere of pure reason, is otherwise wrecked with its physicalism. As Gilson so precisely points out: "Kant was not shifting from mathematics to philosophy, but from mathematics to physics. As Kant himself immediately concluded: 'The true method of metaphysics is fundamentally the same as that which Newton has introduced into natural science, and which has there yielded such fruitful results. . . .' " In a sentence, Gilson concludes that Kant's *"Critique of Pure Reason* is a masterly description of what the structure of the human mind should be, in order to account for the existence of a Newtonian conception of Nature."[53]

In other words, what began to occur is that all three eyes of knowledge were reduced to the lowest: they were all modeled on and collapsed to the Newtonian eye of flesh. On the one hand, the philosophers were envious of Newtonian success: Adam could name the stars, Pythagoras could count them, but Newton could tell you how much they weighed to the nearest pound. On the other hand, the more science advanced and the more individuals trained the eye of flesh, the less relevant the mental and contemplative eyes seemed. Science viewed the world largely as quantitative and objective, and that left little room for contemplative or even properly mental interventions. As Whyte put it, the empiric-scientific view of nature, since it was quantitative and objective, "drew attention away from the organizing aspects of personality which are known subjectively [that is, via the *lumen interius* or mental eye], and this encouraged the decline of confidence in the powers of the subjective mind. . . . Instead of the subject being dominant to the object, the object now dominated the subject, though in the new picture of objective nature there was no element corresponding to the constructive mental processes of the subject."[131] In plain language, the eye of mind was closed out, as the eye of contemplation before it. Scientism was not only relieving humanity from God, it was relieving it from the responsibility of thinking.

Thus, in effect, the sole criterion of truth came to be the empiric criterion—that is to say, a sensorimotor test by the eye of flesh (or its extensions) usually based on measurement. The empirical verification principle came to apply not only to the eye of flesh, which was valid, but to the eye of mind and the eye of contemplation as well, which was, as William James himself put it, pure bosh. In the words of Thomas McPherson, "Because the scientist's observation statements are empirically verifiable, the test for sense becomes 'amenability to verification by sense experience,' and whatever is not so verifiable accordingly is non-sense."[85] Understand at once that *this does not mean verifiable by direct experience in general; it means verifiable by sense experience.* That is, empirically verifiable. The scientific philosophers disallow the direct experiences of the mystic/meditator, because these are not capable of detection by the five senses, however otherwise direct the mystic claims them to be. (This is a point we will return to.)

In the meantime, we simply note that nonfleshy came to mean unreal, and on that the new crop of scientific philosophers perched. "Anyone who in practise or theory disregarded them was denounced with unsparing vigor,"[130] says Whitehead. And yet here is the real point: "This position on the part of the scientists was pure bluff, if one may credit them with [actually] believing their own statements."[130] Science was becoming scientism, known also as positivism, known also as scientific materialism, and *that* was a bluff of the part playing the whole. "Thereby," Whitehead concludes, "modern philosophy has been ruined."[130]

It has been ruined because it has been reduced, just as spirituality before it. Bad enough the eye of contemplation was closed, but so was the eye of proper philosophical speculation, synthesis, and criticism. Whitehead is perfectly explicit on that point. So is J. J. Van der Leeuw: "Mutual contempt of philosophy and science is as harmful as it is unfounded, but we must ever be on our guard against asking of one a question belonging to the domain of the other [category error]. A scientific answer to a philosophical question will necessarily be unsatisfactory and beside the point, just as a philosophical solution to a scientific question would be empty of meaning and scientifically valueless. We honour both best by understanding their respective spheres of knowledge and by coordinating them to their greatest benefit, never by confusing their respective tasks."[121]

But that coordination is what the eye of flesh refused to do. Instead it came to say, what it can't see does not exist; whereas what it should have said was, what it can't see it can't see. Kant did *not* say God doesn't exist—he said that sense and scientific reason cannot grasp the Absolute. As Wittgenstein would put it, "Whereof one cannot speak, thereof one must be silent," which the scienticians perverted into, "That of which one cannot speak, is not there."

For example: Recall that one of Kant's contributions was the clear demonstration that anytime you try to reason about the Absolute, you can always reason in two contradictory but equally plausible directions. This is not, as later positivists thought, a sufficient proof that Godhead doesn't exist, but a demonstration that It transcends reason.

Whenever higher dimensions are represented on lower ones, they necessarily lose something in the translation. As a simple example, whenever a three-dimensional sphere is reduced on a two-dimensional surface, it becomes a circle. The sphere, as it were, is cut in half so as to fit on the paper. And notice that the sphere can be cut in two totally different directions—say, from east to west and from west to east—*and it still appears as the same circle.* We would say, then, that whenever a circle tries to think about a sphere, it can

manufacture two totally contradictory statements with equal plausibility, because—to the circle—*both* are indeed correct. It is the same
with reason and spirit.

The positivists think that this means the sphere doesn't exist—
and all it means is that spheres can't be grasped by circles.

Kant firmly believed in the Transcendent, although he knew it
couldn't be grasped by sense or scientific reason. But his half-follow-
ers—Comte, Mach, and down to today, Ayer, Flew, Quine, and
all—had not even that good sense. Upset by the role of proper speculative philosophy, and totally blind to the eye of contemplation, the
scienticians gave all knowledge over the lowly eye of flesh, and *no*
knowledge other than that was henceforth deemed respectable.

There was the new empirical scientism—it simply said, as it says
today, that only the eye of flesh and its number quantities are real.
All else, the mind's eye, the eye of contemplation, God, Buddha,
Brahman, and Tao—all of that is meaningless because none of that
appears as an object "out there." Because scientism could not get a
ruler on God, it proclaimed Spirit nonsensical and meaningless.
Christ was therefore deluded, Buddha was schizophrenic, Krishna
was hallucinating, Lao Tzu was psychotic.

And so there, just there, was the perverted legacy of Galileo and
Kepler. From them to Newton, from Newton to Kant, from Kant
to Comte and Mach and Ayer and down to Willard Quine. "The
best way to characterize Quine's world view is to say that . . . there
is fundamentally only one kind of entity in the world, and that is
the kind studied by natural scientists—physical objects; and second,
that there is only one kind of knowledge in the world, and it is the
kind that natural scientists have."[110]

And Willard Quine? "Willard Quine is the most influential
American philosopher of the last twenty years."[110]

THE NATURE OF SCIENTISM

"However you disguise it," says Whitehead, "this is the practical
outcome of the characteristic scientific philosophy which closed the
seventeenth century." Viewed through the scientific eye, he says,
"Nature is a dull affair, soundless, scentless, colourless; merely the
hurrying of material, endlessly, meaninglessly."[130] That's all there is,
and all there is worth knowing.

But worse:

> We must note its astounding efficiency as a system of concepts for
> the organization of scientific research. In this respect, it is fully
> worthy of the genius of the century which produced it. It has held
> its own as the guiding principle of scientific studies ever since. It
> is still reigning. Every university in the world organizes itself in
> accordance with it. No alternative system of organizing the pursuit
> of scientific truth has been suggested. It is not only reigning, but it
> is without a rival. And yet—it is quite unbelievable.[130]

There is Whitehead's famous judgment of the scientific world
view. Others have been even less charitable: "The issue is not the
conscious structure of science, but the unconscious strata of the scientific ego, in the scientific character-structure. Whitehead called
the modern scientific point of view 'quite unbelievable.' Psychoanalysis adds the crucial point: it is insane."[26] As the psychiatrist Karl
Stern put it: "Such a view is crazy. And I do not at all mean crazy
in the sense of slangy invective but rather in the technical meaning
of psychotic. Indeed such a view has much in common with certain
aspects of schizophrenic thinking."[105]

Scientists aren't totally mad, but only because they don't totally
believe the empiric-scientific world view. Or, if they do believe it,
they genuinely *value* science; or they are appropriately *proud* of it;
or they find science *meaningful, enjoyable, purposeful.* But every one
of those italicized words are nonempiric entities, being subjective
values and intentions. That is to say, a sane scientist is non-scientific
as regards his or her person.

We will, however, leave the insanity of the scientistic world view
to the psychiatrists, and concentrate instead on Whitehead's point of
unbelievability. And the empiric-scientific world view is unbelievable because it is partial, and in pretending to be total, it lands itself
in incredulity. For, among other things, the empiric-scientific
method is virtually incapable of dealing with *quality.* "Science is
primarily quantitative," says Whitehead, and one is not thinking
scientifically if one "is thinking qualitatively and not quantitatively."
For science is "a search for quantitives."[130] That is, *numbers.*

Now the problem with numbers is that, whereas one quality can be better than another, one number cannot. Love is *intrinsically* better than hate, but three is not intrinsically better than five. And thus, once you have translated the world into empiric measurement and numbers, you have a world without quality, guaranteed. Which is to say, without *value* or *meaning*. All that is left, says Whitehead, is "bare valuelessness," which "has directed attention to *things* as opposed to *values*."[130] Bertrand Russell, who probably ought to know, agrees: "The sphere of values lies outside science."[103] According to Huston Smith, science tends to miss values because "quality itself is unmeasurable. . . . Inability to deal with the qualitatively unmeasurable leads science to work with what Lewis Mumford calls a 'disqualified universe.'" In short, says Smith, "values, life meanings, purposes, and qualities slip through science like sea slips through the nets of fishermen."[110]

Empiric-analytic science cannot easily operate without measurement; measurement is essentially quantity; quantity is number; number is per se outside of values. Quality never gets in and cannot get in. L. L. Whyte nailed it: "All magnitudes have equal status before the laws of elementary arithmetic, whose operators recognize no distinction between one value and another."[131]

Notice I am not condemning empiric-analytic science for this; I am simply trying to delineate its role, so that when it steps outside of its proper sphere and tries to become a complete world view, we will be in a better position to criticize this overreach, this category error, known as empirical positivism or exclusively empirical verification, or scientific materialism.

Now the traditional view of reality had maintained that existence is hierarchically graded, that the contemplative realm is more real and more valuable than the mental realm, which in turn is more real and more valuable than the fleshy realm. All three realms were to be appreciated and used, but let there be no mistake as to their relative worth: the causal is higher than the subtle is higher than the gross—and, as Smith says, the higher is *more real* than the lower because it is more fully saturated with Being.

But as all knowledge came to be reduced to fleshy, empiric knowledge, and since the arbiter of fleshy knowledge is number, and since number is quantity without quality or value, then when science looked carefully for the great value Chain of Being, an extraordinary translation occurred, perhaps the most significant ever to appear in history. *Everything* science could see was viewed numerically, and since no number is intrinsically better than another, the whole hierarchy of value collapsed—it was reduced to simple, valueless place setters, there to take its rightful spot in the rest of nature, to become part of that dull affair, soundless, scentless, colorless; merely the hurrying of material, endlessly, meaninglessly.

The old hierarchy of value and being was thereby ditched in favor of a hierarchy of number. Certain realms could no longer be said to be *higher* or *more real* or *better* than others—they could only be said to be bigger or smaller than others. We might say that *levels of significance* were replaced by *levels of magnification*. We no longer recognized realms which were higher and more significant and more real than the ordinary—such as the contemplative heaven—we only recognized realms *bigger* than the ordinary—such as astronomical distances. And in place of lower, less significant, and less real realms than the ordinary—the subhuman, fleshy, materialistic—we found only realms *smaller* than the ordinary—such as the subatomic. Better and worse were converted into bigger and smaller, and subsequently dropped altogether.

But what could one expect from an animal that had renounced the mind's eye and the contemplative eye? The only eye left was fleshy and physical, and as it searched around, the only differences it could locate were differences in size. As the eyes of reason and contemplation closed, the eye of flesh leveled its gaze unflinchingly at the material world, and began to click off its litany of claims: 1, 2, 3, 4, 5. . . .

The Contradiction of Scientism

Now if scientism were merely unbelievable, we all might be tempted to let it go at that. But it is not merely unbelievable—nor merely insane in its quantifying madness—it is, as a world view, a formal self-contradiction.

There are many ways to approach this topic. Perhaps we might first note that scientism maintains that contemplative knowledge of the Absolute is impossible—the only knowledge admissible is fleshy knowledge, which is by all accounts *relative* knowledge. Now if the positivist simply said, "We will limit ourselves to the study of relative knowledge," then that would be quite acceptable. But he goes beyond that and says, "Only relative knowledge is valid." And that is an *absolute* statement: it says, "It is absolutely true that there is no absolute truth." As Schuon puts it: "Relativism sets out to reduce every element of absoluteness to a relativity, while making a quite illogical exception in favor of this reduction itself." He continues:

> In effect, relativism consists in declaring it to be true that there is no such thing as truth, or in declaring it to be absolutely true that nothing but the relatively true exists; one might just as well say that language does not exist, or write that there is no such thing as writing.[106]

In other words, the scientistic claim is "disproved by the very existence of the postulate itself."[106]

In a similar vein the scientician does not merely say, "The empiric proof is the best method of gaining facts in the sense realm," but goes on to say, "Only those propositions that can be empirically verified are true." Unfortunately, *that* proposition itself cannot be empirically verified. There is no empirical proof that empirical proof alone is real. Thus, as Smith says, "The contention that there are no truths save those of science is not itself a scientific truth, and thus in affirming it scientism contradicts itself."[110]

One of the other fashions of scientism is the notion that evolution by *natural selection* (mutation plus statistical-probability) is the sole explanatory agent for all of creation. Now we are not discussing whether evolution occurred; it most apparently did. We are discussing its cause or agent, in this case, chance. For it is asserted that everything, in no matter what domain, is equally a product of chance evolution. Jacques Monod, whose *Chance and Necessity* is the bible of such views, explains: "Evolution . . . the product of an enormous lottery presided over by natural selection, blindly picking the rare winners from among numbers drawn at utter random. . . . This conception alone is compatible with the facts." He is saying that, as far as we know, the concept of evolution as chance selection is *truer* than its rival theories.

But if it were true, there would be no way whatsoever to find out. If all phenomena are equally the product of blind chance, there can be no question of one thing being truer than another. A frog and an ape are equally products of statistical evolution, and we cannot say a frog is truer than an ape. Likewise, since all phenomena are results of statistical chance, *ideas* too are such products—thus it is impossible for one idea to be truer than another, for all are equally chance productions. If everything is a product of statistical necessity, then so is the idea of statistical necessity, in which case it carries no more authority than any other production.

In psychology, this type of scientism appears as the statement—almost uncontested in orthodoxy—that (to use Tart's wording of it, although he himself does not believe it) "All human experience is ultimately reducible to patterns of electrical and chemical activity within the nervous system and body."[118] But if all human activity is reducible to biochemical activity, then so is that human statement itself. So, in fact, are *all* statements equally biochemical fireworks. But there could then be no question of a true statement versus a false statement, because *all* thoughts are *equally* biochemistry. There cannot be true thoughts versus false thoughts, there can only be thoughts. If thoughts are indeed ultimately reducible to electrons firing in the nervous system, then there cannot be true thoughts and false thoughts for the simple reason that there are no true electrons versus false electrons. And so, if that statement is true then it cannot be true.

In short, as Schuon, Smith, and so many others have pointed out, the very existence of the idea of scientism proves that scientism is fundamentally incorrect.

Now it is frequently said today that scientism is dead, and so in the preceding sections I might seem to be resurrecting not only a straw man, but a very dead straw man at that. It is certainly true that the scientistic-positivistic world view has lost some of its overt persuasiveness; but I believe that it is not only still with us but also, in many ways, extending its influence. Nobody would overtly claim to be a "scientician"—the word itself sounds like a disease. But the *empiric*-scientific enterprise all too often implicitly or explicitly rejects other approaches as not equally valid. My point is that while few would claim to be scienticians, in fact, many are in effect. "Empirical verification" still rules the day in mainstream philosophy and psychology, and that means "verification by the senses or their extensions." In principle, not much else is accepted. How else explain the fact that just a few years ago, Jürgen Habermas—considered by many (myself included) the world's greatest living philosopher—had to devote an entire book to once again refuting and beating back positivism? (A book whose first paragraph contains the stinging comment, "That we disavow reflection [the mind's eye] *is* positivism.") If empirical-positivism is dead, it is a decidedly frisky corpse.

But the basic reason for examining scientism and its contradictions is simply to use it as an example of pervasive category error, so that what is involved in that fallacy can be more easily grasped. My eventual conclusion will be that an overall integral paradigm—or any comprehensive investigative paradigm—should use and integrate all three eyes, and so it is necessary, at the start, to delineate the respective roles of each. If they are not delineated, then our "comprehensive paradigm" can be opened to scientism, to mentalism, or to spiritualism, each based on category error, each deadly in effect.

But Can It Be Verified?

To escape from scientism or exclusive empiricism is simply to realize that empiric knowledge is not the only form of knowledge; there exists beyond it mental-rational knowledge and contemplative-spiritual knowledge. But if that is so, then how can these "higher" forms of knowledge be verified? If there is no empirical proof, what is left?

This seems to be a problem because we do not see that all valid knowledge is essentially similar in structure, and thus can be similarly verified (or rejected). That is, all valid knowledge—in whatever realm—consists of three basic components, which we will call injunction, illumination, and confirmation. But this topic itself is so intricate and so complex that we will actually devote an entire chapter—the next chapter—solely to it. What I would like to do here is simply introduce and outline the essentials of our argument, so we will be better prepared for the details. In essence, we will simply suggest that all *valid knowledge*—in whatever realm—consists most fundamentally of these basic components:

1. *An instrumental or injunctive strand.* This is a set of instructions, simple or complex, internal or external. All have the form: "If you want to know this, do this."

2. *An illuminative or apprehensive strand.* This is an illuminative *seeing* by the particular eye of knowledge evoked by the injunctive strand. Besides being self-illuminative, it leads to the possibility of:

3. *A communal strand.* This is the actual sharing of the illuminative seeing with others who are using the same eye. If the shared-vision is agreed upon by others, this constitutes a communal or consensual proof of *true seeing*.

Those are the basic strands of any type of true knowledge using any eye. Knowledge does become more complicated when one eye tries to match its knowledge with a higher or lower eye, but these basic strands underlie even that complication (as we will see in the next chapter).

Starting with the eye of flesh, let me give some examples. The injunctive strand, we said, is of the form, "If you want to see this, do this." In the eye of flesh, which is the simplest knowledge, injunctions can be as prosaic as, "If you don't believe it's raining outside, go look." The person looks, and there is his or her illumination, his or her knowledge (strand #2). If others repeat the same instruction ("Go look out the window"), and all see the same thing, there is the communal strand (#3), and we can say, "It is true that it is raining," and so on.

Even in the eye of flesh, however, the injunctions can be quite complex. In empirical science, for instance, we usually find highly difficult and technical instructions, such as: "If you want to see a cell nucleus, then learn how to take histological sections, learn how to use a microscope, learn how to stain tissues, learn how to differentiate cell components one from the other, and *then* look." In other words, the injunctive strand *demands* that, for whatever type of knowledge, the *appropriate eye must be trained until it can be adequate to its illumination.* This is true in art, in science, in philosophy, in contemplation. It is true, in fact, for all valid forms of knowledge.

Now if a person refuses to train a particular eye (flesh, mental, contemplative), then it is equivalent to refusing to look, and we are justified in disregarding this person's opinions and excluding him or her from our vote as to communal proof. Someone who refuses to learn geometry cannot be allowed to vote on the truth of the Pythagorean theorem; someone who refuses to learn contemplation cannot be allowed to vote on the truth of Buddha Nature or Spirit. In other words, if an individual will not take up strand #1 of knowledge, he or she will be excluded from strands #2 and #3. We say that person's knowledge is inadequate to the task. The Churchmen who *refused* to look through Galileo's telescope were *inadequate* in the eye of flesh, and their opinions can be disregarded in that realm.

Moving up to the next eye, the mind's eye, we find that the injunctive strand can be even more complex and more difficult to share. But you and I are hopefully doing so now—we are seeing eye to eye using the mind (although we might not totally agree on what we see); if not, you wouldn't be able to understand one word written. But in order to *see* the meaning of any of these words, we all had to follow certain instructions, foremost among which is, "Learn to read." And that ushered us all into a world which is *not* given to the eye of flesh all by itself. E. F. Schumacher put it nicely: "With the light of the intellect [*lumen interius*] we can see things which are invisible to our bodily senses. No one denies that mathematical and geometrical truths are 'seen' this way [i.e., with the eye of mind, not the eye of flesh]. To *prove* a proposition means to give it a form, by analysis, simplification, transformation, or dissection [the injunctive strand], through which the truth can be *seen* [the illuminative strand]; beyond this seeing there is neither the possibility nor the need for any further proof [except, I might add, *sharing* this proof with others to establish communal proof, the third strand]."[105]

One can train the mind's eye for outward philosophic seeing or for inward psychologic seeing. To the extent the mind's eye refuses to rise above the eye of flesh, it produces in philosophy nothing but positivism and in psychology nothing but behaviorism. On the other hand, to the extent the mind's eye rises to its own occasion, it produces phenomenology, linguistics, proper speculative philosophy (critical, analytical, and synthesizing), and intersubjective psychology (as we will explain in the next chapter).

Proof in this area shares the same form, the same three strands, as in the other areas: train the mental eye, personally look, and then communally compare and confirm. The communal wing of this knowledge is, of course, harder to come by than it is with fleshy knowledge, because everybody is given the same eye of flesh but different mental outlooks. This is certainly not a drawback in the mind's eye, but simply an indication of its richness.

Knowledge in the transcendent realm is gained in precisely the same way: it has an injunction, an illumination, and a confirmation. In Zen: zazen, satori, and imprimatur. There is no Zen without *all three strands;* there is, in fact, no real esoteric or transcendent knowledge without all three. One first takes up the practice of *contemplatio,* which may be meditation, zazen, mantra, japa, interior prayer, and so on. When the eye of contemplation is fully trained, then *look.* Check this direct illumination with others and, more importantly, with the teacher or master. Checking with the master is just like checking math problems with the teacher when one is first learning geometry.

This final and highest proof is ultimately a proof of God or Buddha Nature or Tao—but it is not an empiric proof, and not a rational-philosophic proof, but a contemplative proof. "Our whole business in this life," said St. Augustine, "is to restore to health the eye of the heart whereby God may be seen." To restore that eye is to train that eye, thereby becoming adequate to the knowledge "which is unto salvation."

It is sometimes said that mystic knowledge is not real knowledge because it is not public knowledge, only "private," and hence it is incapable of consensual validation. That is not quite correct, however. For the secret to consensual validation in all three realms is the same, namely: a *trained eye* is a *public eye,* or it could not be trained in the first place; and a public eye is a communal or *consensual* eye. Mathematical knowledge is public knowledge to trained mathematicians (but not to nonmathematicians); contemplative knowledge is public knowledge to all sages. Even though contemplative knowledge is ineffable, it is *not* private: it is a shared vision. The essence of Zen is: "A special transmission outside the Scriptures [that is, between Master and student]; Not dependent upon words and letters [the eye of mind]; Seeing into one's Nature [with the eye of contemplation] and becoming Buddha." It is a *direct seeing* by the contemplative eye, and it can be *transmitted* from teacher to student because it is directly *public* to that eye. The knowledge of God is as public to the contemplative eye as is geometry to the mental eye and rainfall to the physical eye. And a trained contemplative eye can *prove* the existence of God with exactly the same certainty and the same public nature as the eye of flesh can prove the existence of rocks.

A comprehensive-integral paradigm would draw freely on the eye of flesh and on the eye of reason; but it would also be grounded in the eye of contemplation. That eye embodies a valid mode of knowledge; it can be publicly shared; it can be communally validated. No more is possible, no more is needed.

SCIENCE AND RELIGION

The conflict between empirical-science and religion is, and always has been, a conflict between the pseudoscientific aspects of religion and the pseudoreligious aspects of science. To the extent that science remains science and religion remains religion, no conflict is possible—or rather, any conflict that occurs can always be shown to reduce to a category error: theologians are trying to be scientists or scientists are trying to be theologians. In the past, it was most common for the theologians to try to become scientists, and talk of Christ as a historical fact, creation as an empirical fact, the virgin birth as a biological fact, and so on, in which case they should be prepared to answer scientific questions about all that. The virgin birth as an *empirical* fact means that a person was born without a biological father; as a mental symbol it might signify the birth of one whose Father is in Heaven (i.e., one who realizes the transpersonal Self); as a contemplative insight, it might be a direct realization that one's True Self is virgin-born moment to moment. Now the virgin birth as an empiric fact is probably quite wrong; as a symbol and a realization, it is probably quite valid. The point is that when theologians talk empiric facts, they must be prepared to face scientists; when they talk mental principles, they must face philosophers or psychologists; only when they practice contemplation are they truly at home. And a comprehensive-integral paradigm should be able to embrace, charitably, all three. That makes it different from traditional religion, traditional philosophy/psychology, and traditional science—because it includes and can potentially integrate all of them.

More recently, it is the *empirical* scientists who are trying to become theologians or even prophets. This is also an unflattering stance. But when empiric-scientists attempt to become theologians or religionists, they must be prepared to face the same type of stern questioning, this time coming from the contemplatives. If, for instance, the physicist says, "Modern physics shows us that *all* things are fundamentally One, just like the Tao or Brahman," then he is making a statement, not just about the physical realm, but about all realms, about ultimates and absolutes. The religionist is therefore able to say, "That is simply an *idea* presented by the eye of mind; where is your *method* for opening the eye of contemplation? Describe to me, in injunctive language, what you must *do* in order to *see*—directly see—this Oneness. If you cannot do that, you have committed a category error: you are merely talking about the contemplative/meditative realm using only the eye of mind." Notice the Zen Master can pass that test; we are still awaiting word from the physicist. For the simple fact is that one *can* be a good physicist *without* becoming mystically or transcendentally involved. One *can* master physics without mastering enlightenment. But one *cannot* become a good Zen Master without becoming a mystic. That the in-depth and heartfelt study of physics leads some physicists (perhaps 10 percent or so) to a mystical world view tells us something nice about, not physics per se, but about those sensitive and noble physicists. Those sensitive physicists, however, often then make the category error of claiming that physical data per se prove transcendental states—an understandable but messy confusion, and one clearly refuted by the number of great physicists who are *not* mystics.

Thus, it is my feeling that the most important thing a comprehensive or integral paradigm can do is try to avoid the category errors: confusing the eye of flesh with the eye of mind with the eye of contemplation (or, in the more detailed models, such as the five-level Vedanta, avoid confusing any of the levels). When someone asks "Where is your empirical proof for transcendence?" we need not panic. We explain the instrumental methods of our knowledge and invite him or her to check it out personally. Should that person accept and complete the injunctive strand, then that person is capable of becoming part of the community of those whose eye is adequate to the transcendent realm. Prior to that time, that person is inadequate to form an opinion about transcendental concerns. We are then no more obliged to account to that person than is a physicist to one who refuses to learn mathematics.

We of today are in an extraordinarily favorable position: we can preserve the utterly unique position of possessing and championing a balanced and integrated approach to reality—a "new and higher" paradigm—one that can include the eye of flesh and the eye of reason and the eye of contemplation. And I think that the history of thought will eventually prove that to do more than that is impossible, to do less than that, disastrous.

2

The Problem of Proof

GIVEN EACH OF THE THREE modes of knowing—sensory, symbolic, and spiritual—the question naturally arises, as it certainly did in the history of philosophy, psychology, and religion, how can we be sure that the "knowledge" gained by any of these modes is valid? Or conversely—and more significantly—on what grounds may we reject any "knowledge" as likely being erroneous?

DATA AND KNOWLEDGE

By data I simply mean any *directly apprehended experience* (using "experience" in the broad sense, as prehension or awareness). As William James explained it, using as an example the perception of a piece of paper, "If our own private vision of the paper be considered in abstraction [or bracketed off] from every other event, then the paper seen and the seeing of it are only two names for one indivisible fact which, properly named, is *the datum, the phenomenon, or the experience.*"[67] And I am saying (and will try to demonstrate) that there are legitimate data—*direct apprehensions*—to be found in the realms of flesh, mind, and spirit; that is, real data in these *real* object domains, object domains that we can call *sensibilia, intelligibilia,* and *transcendelia.* It is the existence of these real object domains (sensory,

38

mental, and spiritual) and their real data that *grounds* the knowledge quest and assures its consummation.

Notice that what especially defines a datum, in any realm, is not its simplicity or atomism, but its immediate givenness, its direct apprehension. A datum is not necessarily the smallest bit of experience in any realm, but the immediate display of experience disclosed when one is introduced to that realm. Thus, for example, when James talks about data in the realm of sensibilia, he uses as examples the direct experience of a piece of paper, a tiger, the walls of a room, and so on: whatever is immediately *given* in present sensibilia. Now that sensory data may in fact be very atomistic—the dark-adapted human retina, for instance, can register a *single* photon, and in that immediate register, the photon (or whatever it is) is the sensory datum. But the datum can also be very large and fairly complex—a sunset, the sky at night, the view from a hilltop, and so on. The point is not so much size or complexity; the point is immediateness or givenness in direct experience. (Many philosophers, in fact, refer to this direct apprehension of sensibilia as *intuition*—James and Kant, for example. But this sensory intuition is not to be confused with spiritual intuition, or even mental intuition, as Kant was careful to point out. When I use "intuition" in this broad sense, it simply means direct and immediate apprehension in *any* realm, and that direct apprehension, experience, or intuition is what most defines a datum.)

Exactly the same thing applies to the data of intelligibilia and transcendelia. In the realm of intelligibilia, for instance, one's present, given, immediate mental experience, whatever its nature, is a *datum, a mental* datum (or series of them). The datum may be rather brief or atomistic—a simple image, a fleeting thought—or it may be rather complex and sustained—the understanding of the overall meaning of a sentence, the grasp of an idea, a sustained memory. In either case the mental datum is simply the immediate gestaltlike mental experience, whatever its "size" or complexity or duration. Even if you are thinking of some past event or anticipating tomorrow's actions, the thought *itself* is a *present* event immediately perceived and experienced—that is, it is a *datum*.

In the field of language, analysts often speak of the present and direct apprehension of symbols as "linguistic intuition." Once you have mastered a particular language, you simply know (or mentally "intuit") the meaning of its common words. And even when you are learning the language, you still directly experience the symbols *themselves* as and when you think them, even if you don't yet know their meaning. The point is that, either way, you see them with the mind's eye, and that "seeing" per se is direct and immediate. If meaning then follows, the perception of *that* is now the direct and immediate mental datum, and so on. Thus, whether of a letter, a word, a sentence, an idea—in each case the mental datum is simply the *immediate mental experience,* whatever it is.

Likewise, in the realm of transcendelia, a datum may be a single spiritual intuition, a mass illumination, a particular gnostic insight, or overall satori—all such transcendental data are directly perceived or intuited by the eye of contemplation. Here, too, not complexity but immediacy or givenness most defines a datum.

On further analysis or inquiry, of course, we might find that various data contain *other* data or flow into other data. For instance, James's piece of paper, itself a single sensory datum, contains four corners, each of which can become individual sensory datum (by simply looking at them), and is itself part of a larger experience of paper-desk-room, another sensory datum. Likewise, the mentally perceived symbol "tree," itself a single mental datum, is composed of four letters, each of which can be apprehended as a separate mental datum. But the important point is that, for instance, when I apprehend the meaning, the immediate datum, of the word "tree," I do *not* do so by adding up letters. The mental datum or meaning or linguistic intuition of the word "tree" is not given to me as four fast additions, *t* plus *r* plus *e* plus *e.* The mental datum "tree" is a direct, nonreducible, gestaltlike apprehension, and it is that direct apprehension or intuition, the present, immediate, given experience, whatever it is, in whatever realm, that essentially defines a datum—a sensory datum, a mental datum, a transcendental datum.

The Meaning of "Experience" and "Empiricism"

We have said that a datum is any immediate experience in any of the three realms—sensory, mental, or transcendental. But right here we are faced with an extreme semantic and philosophic difficulty, because traditionally it was the empiricists who insisted that all knowledge must be grounded in experience, and they claimed the rationalists as well as the mystics had no such grounding. And further, although empiricism in that stance is very reductionistic, many new schools of humanistic and transpersonal psychology and philosophy dearly wish and loudly claim to be empirical. Obviously, the words "experience" and "empirical" are being used in several different ways, and this has generated certain grave misunderstandings.

The core of the problem is that there is a great ambiguity in the meaning of the word "experience." It can be used to mean only sensory experience (as many empiricists do), but it can also be used to cover virtually all modes of awareness and consciousness. For instance, there is a sense in which I *experience* not only my own sensations and perceptions (sensibilia) but also my own ideas, thoughts, and concepts (intelligibilia)—I see them with the mind's eye, I *experience* my train of thoughts, my personal ideals, my imaginative displays. These are subtler experiences than a clunk on the head, but they are nonetheless experiential, or directly and immediately perceived by the mind's eye. Likewise, there is a sense in which I can *experience* spirit—with the eye of contemplation or *gnosis,* I directly and immediately apprehend and experience spirit *as* spirit, the realm of transcendelia.

In all these broader senses, "experience" is simply synonymous with direct apprehension, immediate givenness, intuition—sensory, mental, and spiritual.

Stated thus, there is indeed a sense in which all knowledge is grounded in experience (as empiricists claim)—but not in *sensory* experience (which they also claim). Thus, various *a priori* or rational truths are those I *experience* in the mental realm but not in the sensory realm (e.g., mathematics). And transcendental truths are those I *experience* in the spiritual realm but not in the mental or sensory realms (e.g., satori). And in that sense, there are all sorts of knowledge outside of sensory experience, but none that is finally outside of *experience* in general. Sensibilia, intelligibilia, and transcendelia can all be open to direct and immediate experiential apprehension or intuition, and those apprehensions constitute the data of the knowledge quest in each of those domains.

Empiricism, then, rightly claims that all valid knowledge must be grounded in experience, but it then reduces the meaning of experience solely to *sensibilia*. Empiricism wishes to derive my experience of reason solely from my experience of sensations—that is, to claim that there is no experience of reason that is not first found in my experience of sensations. And that attempt has a type of strong attraction ("We want *empirical* data!") simply because one can easily but vaguely confuse sensory experience (pure empiricism) with experience *in general*. Empiricism sounds like it's making such good sense, being so pragmatic and all, but only because it confuses two basic propositions; it says all real knowledge must be experiential, which is true enough using experience in the broad sense, but then it can't resist the temptation to say that experience is really or basically *sensory* experience—and that is the great disaster.

Let me repeat that one of the reasons that ambiguity can and does occur is that "experience" can be used in the broad sense ("direct awareness"), but then also given a common and much narrower meaning: *sensory* perceptions. By consciously or unconsciously juxtaposing those meanings, the modern-day empiricist can ridicule the idea of knowledge outside experience (so far, so good), but then *limit* experience to its sensory-empiric modes (reductionistic fallacy, category error, etc.). And to completely confound matters, many of the new humanistic and transpersonal psychologists, working mostly with intelligibilia and transcendelia, and correctly realizing that their data is indeed experiential (in the broad sense), and wishing equal recognition as "real sciences," simply *call* their endeavors and their data "empirical," only to find that strict empirical scientists simply reject their results, sometimes with undisguised mocking.

To avoid these ambiguities, I will restrict the term "empirical" to its original meaning: knowledge grounded in sensory experience (sensibilia). I suggest humanistic and transpersonal psychologists do the same. Classical empiricism was an attempt to reduce all higher knowledge and experience to sensory knowledge and experience. The emphasis on direct experience (in the broad sense) was the great and enduring contribution of the empiricists; the reduction of experience to sensory experience was their great and enduring crime.

THE VERIFICATION PROCEDURES

Each of the three modes of knowing, then, has access to real (experiential) data in their respective realms—to sensible data, intelligible data, and transcendental data—and the data in each case is marked by its immediate or intuitive apprehension. (The data might indeed be mediated, but the moment of apprehension is itself immediate.) This intuitive immediateness, as James knew, must be the defining characteristic of data and our only *starting* point, or else we end up in an infinite regress.

The problem then becomes, given my immediate apprehension or intuition of any datum, how can I be reasonably sure that the perception itself is not mistaken? And that brings us to the notion of adequate verification (or nonverification) principles for the gathering of data in each of the modes of knowing involved. But two points should be kept equally in mind as we discuss these data-gathering and verification procedures: (1) the *actual methodologies* of data accumulation and verification differ drastically in all three modes, but (2) the *abstract principles* of data accumulation and verification are essentially *identical* in each. Exactly what that means, and the reason I emphasize both, will become increasingly obvious as we proceed.

First, the abstract principles of data accumulation and verification. As we suggested in the last chapter, valid data accumulation in any realm has three basic strands:

1. *Instrumental injunction.* This is always of the form, "If you want to *know* this, *do* this."
2. *Intuitive apprehension.* This is a cognitive grasp, prehension, or immediate *experience* of the object domain (or aspect of the object domain) addressed by the injunction; that is, the immediate *data*-apprehension.
3. *Communal confirmation.* This is a checking of results (apprehensions or data) with others who have adequately completed the injunctive and apprehensive strands.

Science, of course, is often taken as the model of genuine knowledge, and the philosophy of science is now dominated by three major approaches, which are generally viewed as mutually exclusive: that of empiricism, Thomas Kuhn, and Sir Karl Popper. The strength of empiricism, as we have seen, is its demand that all genuine knowledge be grounded in experiential evidence; and if we use evidence and experience in the general sense, this a grounding that I firmly share. But evidence and data are not simply lying around waiting to be perceived by all and sundry, which is where Kuhn enters the picture.

Thomas Kuhn, in one of the greatly misunderstood ideas of our time, pointed out that normal science proceeds most fundamentally by way of what he called *paradigms* or *exemplars.* A paradigm is not merely a concept, it is an *actual practice,* an injunction, a technique taken as an exemplar for generating data. And Kuhn's point is that genuine scientific knowledge is grounded in paradigms, exemplars, injunctions, which bring forth new data. New injunctions disclose new data, and this is why Kuhn maintained *both* that science is progressive and cumulative *and* that it also shows certain breaks or discontinuities (new injunctions bring forth new data). Kuhn, in other words, is highlighting the importance of strand #1 in the knowledge quest, namely, that data are not simply lying around waiting for anybody to see, but rather are brought forth by valid injunctions.

The knowledge brought forth by valid injunctions is indeed genuine knowledge precisely because paradigms disclose data, they do not merely invent it. And the validity of this data is demonstrated by the fact that bad data can be rebuffed, which is where Popper enters the picture.

Sir Karl Popper's approach emphasizes the importance of falsifiability: genuine knowledge must be open to disproof, or else it is simply dogma in disguise. And, as we will see, the three strands fully acknowledge the falsifiability principle *in every domain,* sensibilia to intelligibilia to transcendelia.

Thus, this integral approach acknowledges and incorporates the moments of truth in each of these important contributions to the human knowledge quest (evidence, Kuhn, and Popper), but without the need to reduce these truths to sensibilia alone, as I will now try to demonstrate.

We can now give some examples of these three strands as they appear in the realms of sensibilia, intelligibilia, and transcendelia. As we do so, I will try to emphasize that although the same three abstract strands operate in each, the actual or concrete methodologies are quite different (owing to the different structures of the data or object domains themselves).

EMPIRIC-ANALYTIC INQUIRY

In the realm of sensibilia—empirical or sensorimotor occasions—if you want to know, for instance, whether the volume of hydrogen gas released by the electrolysis of water is twice that of the volume of oxygen gas, then you must (1) learn to perform electrolysis, build the equipment itself, run the experiment, collect the gases (injunctions, exemplars); (2) look at and measure the volumes of the gases collected (apprehensions); and (3) compare and confirm the data with other researchers. These mundane examples could be repeated indefinitely—the point is simply that every empirical scientist, in doing actual research (i.e., collecting data), follows *injunctions,* apprehends *data* (either directly or via extended-sensory instrumentation), and then *communally* checks his or her results. That is how the very data base of empiric-analytic science is built. And any data that is obedient to *all three strands* is provisionally accepted as valid.

The key point, however, is that those three strands contain a way to *reject* data that are apparently erroneous. For, as Karl Popper has made very clear, if there is no way whatsoever to at least theoretically disprove a datum, then that datum cannot enter cognitive status—if there is no way whatsoever to disprove a point, then there is no way to prove it either. The three strands provide a potential "disproof mechanism," and this is the key to their success.

The problem is this: Although it is the defining nature of data (in any realm) that, when they present themselves to awareness, they do so in an immediate, intuitive, and apparently self-validating fashion, nonetheless that presentation (the apprehension) depends upon a prior *injunction* or *instrument,* and it is sometimes the case that one's cognitive instruments, whether scientific, personal, or spiritual, are occasionally less than perfected. To give a simple example: If I develop cataracts, I might see two moons—the data itself is erroneous because the instrument is blurred. The data is still immediate, direct, and evident—it really looks like two moons—but it is nonetheless misleading. The three strands help correct this. In this example, I turn to friends and say, "Do you see two moons?" My empirical data, my sensibilia, are accordingly rebuffed. Thus, in empirical inquiry, a "bad" fact (such as in a poorly run experiment) will be *rebuffed,* not only by other facts, but by the community of investigators, and it is this *potential rebuff* that constitutes the falsifiability principle of Popper.

Because the same three strands operate in all modes of valid cognitive inquiry—empirical, rational, and transcendental—the same rebuff mechanism is at work in each (as we will see), and it is this rebuff mechanism that prevents the true knowledge quest, *in any domain,* from degenerating into mere dogmatism and blind-faith embrace. In other words, what specifically marks empiric-analytic inquiry is not its "superior methodology" and its supposedly unique "verification/rejection" procedure—for that, we will see, can and should be applied to *all* realms. No, what marks empiric-analytic inquiry is simply that the only *data* with which it operates is *sensibilia*—the eye of flesh or its extensions. Empiric-analytic inquiry, of course, uses mental and rational reflection, but those operations are grounded in, and always subservient to, sensibilia.

It is sometimes objected that empirical sciences, such as physics or biology, often work with objects or events that in fact cannot be experienced by the senses (or their extensions). For example, when Mendel proposed the existence of genes, the genes themselves were never seen. Likewise, the atomic/molecular theory was proposed by Dalton without his ever actually *seeing* molecules. The point, however, is as James said: "Even if science supposed a molecular architecture beneath the smooth whiteness of the paper, that architecture itself could only be defined as the stuff of a farther possible experience, a vision, say, of certain vibrating particles with which our acquaintance with the paper would terminate if it were prolonged by magnifying artifices not yet known."[67] Thus, decades after Mendel proposed the existence of genes, electron microscopes delivered actual pictures of DNA molecules. The "gene substances" were apprehended by an extended sensory eye, and the existence of genetic material became an empirical *datum* (and not just a theory). It is true that the farther we go into submolecular realms, the fuzzier become our apprehensions, but the point is that an empiric-analytic proposition has meaning only insofar as it grounds itself in sensible or potentially sensible data. That, as we saw, was the great contribution of Galileo, Kepler, and Newton, and as far as it goes, that grounding—empiric-analytic inquiry—is just right.

The problem, we have seen, is that empiric-analytic science soured into scientism by refusing to admit as real any data other than sensibilia, and that, indeed, is what is now called "the crime of Galileo" (perhaps unfairly to the man himself, who never seemed to intend such ugly reductionism). And while we certainly must make ample room for empiric-analytic inquiry, we by no means must restrict our cognition to that mode alone. For next up, in the hierarchy of the knowledge quest, is inquiry into *intelligibilia*.

MENTAL-PHENOMENOLOGICAL INQUIRY

This whole book is visually oriented as opposed to literary or feeling.

The same three abstract strands operate in the gathering of valid linguistic, noetic, or mental-phenomenological *data,* although of course the actual methodology is quite different because the object domain is that of intelligibilia, not mere sensibilia. The "things" we are looking at here are *thoughts*—their structure and their form—as they immediately display themselves to the inward mental eye.

Take, as an initial example, the field of mathematics, for there we find the same three basic strands. As G. Spencer Brown points out: "The primary form of mathematical communication is not description, but injunction [strand #1]. In this respect it is comparable with practical art forms like cookery, in which the taste of a cake, although literally indescribable, can be conveyed to a reader in the form of a set of injunctions called a recipe. . . . Even natural science [i.e., empiric-analytic] appears to be dependent on injunctions. The professional initiation of the man of science consists not so much in reading the proper textbooks [although that is also an injunction], as in obeying injunctions such as 'look down that microscope' [as in the example given in the first chapter]. But it is not out of order for men of [empirical] science, having looked down the microscope [#1], now to describe to each other, and to discuss among themselves [#3], what they have seen [with the eye of flesh; #2], and to write papers and textbooks describing it. Similarly, it is not out of order for mathematicians, each having obeyed a given set of injunctions [e.g., imagine two parallel lines meeting at infinity; picture the cross-section of a trapezoid; take the square of the hypotenuse, etc.;

#1], to describe to each other, and to discuss among themselves [#3], what they have seen [with the eye of mind; #2], and to write textbooks describing it. But in each case, the description is dependent upon, and secondary to, the set of injunctions having been obeyed first."[25] The great difference, as noted, is that in the empiric sciences, the data (or their macro effects) can be seen or experienced with the eye of flesh (or its extensions); in rational-phenomenology, including mathematics, the *data* itself is seen or experienced only with the eye of mind. The injunctions address a different object domain, that of intelligibilia, not sensibilia.

The same three strands are operative, to give another example, in classical phenomenology (e.g., Husserl). For one begins phenomenology with an *injunction,* which is to "bracket out" extraneous events and various preconceptions and thus approach a direct, immediate, and intuitive *apprehension* of the object domain of mental phenomena *as* mental phenomena, and these apprehensions are then shared and confirmed (or rebuffed) via interpersonal communication and interpretation.

The starting point for such mental-phenomenology is simply this: What is the very nature of a *mental* act, a *symbolic* occasion, a *linguistic* understanding, as it discloses itself intuitively or immediately to the mind's eye? According to phenomenology, if one directly inquires into a mental act—an image, a symbol, a word, as one actually uses it—one will find that it intrinsically possesses *intentionality* or *meaning;* it has a native form or structure; and it is semiotic or symbolic. For, unlike the objects of sensibilia—rocks, photons, trees, and so on, which do not themselves possess meaning (in the sense that they do not symbolically represent or point to something other than themselves)—the objects of intelligibilia intrinsically possess meaning, value, or intentionality (i.e., a mental symbol or act carries the power to represent or point to some other object or act). And the way you discover such *meaning* is via mental inquiry or interpretation, not sensory impact.

To give a simple example, there is no *empirical*-scientific proof for the meaning of *Hamlet.* It is a mental-symbolic production and can thus be understood or apprehended only by a mental act—sensory evidence is almost entirely worthless. *Hamlet* is not composed of electrons, molecules, wood, or zinc; it is composed of *units of mean-*

ing—mental data—which disclose themselves not as sensibilia but as intelligibilia.

Likewise, phenomenology discloses that intelligibilia are not only meaningful and intentional, they are intrinsically *intersubjective*. For example, if you issue a symbol to me (say, the word *apple*), and I intuitively understand or grasp that symbol, then the symbol—once literally "in" your head or mind—is now also literally *in* my mind: we are directly and intimately linked in an *intersubjective* occasion, an interpersonal exchange. In communication and discourse, many minds may step into the union of shared symbols, entering into each other in a way that greatly transcends mere bodily contact or intercourse. And notice that meaningful communication is no mere chaos or random babbling—it has *structure,* it has *rules,* it follows a *logic* or *form. It is a very real territory with very real data*—but data that are hidden to mere sensory apprehension.

All of that—intentionality, value, meaning, intersubjective structure—is essentially true of any mental phenomena, and *overall mental-phenomenological investigation* is simply concerned with the nature, structure, and meaning of intelligibilia—with language, syntax, communication, discourse, logic, value, intentionality, ideas, meaning, concepts, images, symbols, semiotics—as they appear in psychology, philosophy, sociology, and the "human (i.e., mental) sciences" in general. And all of that, basically, we refer to as "mental-phenomenology."

Thus, via injunctive inquiry in general mental-phenomenology, one discovers those facts or data that apply to the sphere of *intelligibilia,* the mental or subjective realm per se, and in that sense the facts are subjective facts. *But that does not mean mere individual whim,* as empiricists like to claim. First of all, these phenomenological apprehensions are not "mere values" or "just ideas" as *opposed* to "real facts," because in the mental realm, values and ideas *are* the real or immediate facts or data *directly* disclosed. Second, these phenomenological apprehensions can be *tested* by striking them against the community of other minds who have followed the proper injunctions. In that case, a "bad" phenomenological apprehension will simply not mesh with the ground of other phenomenological facts, as *embedded and disclosed in intersubjective consensus.* This "bad datum" or "poor apprehension" is thus *rebuffed* by a reality that is very real and very lawful—the domain of intelligibilia and its *intersubjective structures*—just as a bad empiric fact will not mesh with, and is rebuffed by, the ground of other sensible facts.

Let us take, as a simple example, the discovery of Egyptian hieroglyphics. What we have here is a mysterious language—some form of hidden intelligibilia—inscribed on stone tablets. Now empiric-analytic inquiry can tell us how old the stone is, what it is made of, how much it weighs, and so on. But it is of precisely no use in figuring out the intelligibilia of the hieroglyphics themselves, or what they *mean*. In order to determine that, I must follow a set of mental injunctions—I must begin to look for the inner structure of the symbols with my mind's eye; I must experiment, try out, various combinations of symbols to see if the right combination, the right injunction, leads to a meaningful apprehension of their possible meanings. If a certain combination looks correct, I still must check it with other combinations—a promising meaning might actually be rebuffed by other meanings down the line, because language does indeed possess intersymbolic structure or syntax, and a bad linguistic apprehension simply will not mesh with the other linguistic apprehensions. Finally, I must check my overall results with others similarly qualified. (And that, of course, is precisely what Jean-François Champollion and Thomas Young did with the Rosetta stone.)

The point is simply that, although we are working with a largely subjective production—a language—nonetheless that doesn't mean I can pop out any ole interpretation that suits me, because intelligibilia possess intersymbolic and intersubjective *structures* that will themselves *rebuff* erroneous claims. And that is fundamentally true of the meaning of any intelligibilia—the meaning of language, of psychological goals and drives, of logic and syntax, of intentions and values. Although the truths in these domains are not *empirically* verifiable or even obvious, nonetheless they are by no means based on wishful thinking, subjective bias, or nonverifiable opinion. In determining the truth or facts of intelligibilia, as Ogilvy so clearly explains, "not just any wild hypothesis will do. Nor will a simple negation [i.e., "there's no way to tell since it can't be empirically determined"]. Only a community of interpreters can generate the intersubjective basis for a set of criteria that might validate the truth claims forming a coherent interpretation. The moment of truth is saved from a subjective relativism that renders the idea of truth absurd. Only *some* interpretations make sense. Their sensibleness is a function of their satisfying certain rules for good interpretation, rules that in some cases are no different from the rules for good [empirical] science, e.g., elegance and simplicity, freedom from subjective bias [or, as I would put it, obedience to the three strands]."[87]

Empiricists, of course, scoff at the notion of any verification procedures not grounded in sensory evidence. They call all such non-empirical or nonsensory investigations (subjective psychology, idealistic phenomenology, ontology, etc.) by the derisive term "meta-physical," and say they are without reliable, reproducible, and verifiable grounding. But they do so only because they have overlooked the intrinsic structures of *intelligibilia* itself. This is indeed odd, because the fact that empiricists *talk* to each other, and repeatedly *understand* each other, rests precisely on the real existence of a lawful, reproducible, intersubjective realm of intelligibilia. And overall mental-phenomenology (in any of its various branches, philosophical, psychological, linguistic, sociological, etc.) is simply the science of discovering and reproducing those meanings, patterns, structures, and laws. It is indeed meta-physical or meta-empirical, but hardly in a pejorative sense.

And so, when even the empiricists frame their hypotheses, formulate their theories, organize their sensory data, and offer systematic explanations, what exactly is the mode of inquiry that guides *that* particular aspect of their endeavors? Rational-phenomenology, of course. And yet it is that very "meta-physical" mode itself that the empiricist or scientician then numbly uses to claim it has no real existence, to claim it is not "really real," not dependable, not meaningful, not verifiable, and just a bunch of metaphysical nonsense. Might as well write a dozen books claiming there is no such thing as writing.

The point is that there are mental-phenomenological facts, truths, or data, but in order to be recognized as such, they too must observe all three strands—and any apprehension failing that overall test is soundly rebuffed by the very *structure* of the intersubjective realm of intelligibilia (the other mental facts themselves and the community of interpreters). This constitutes, for intelligibilia, an *experimental test*—the accumulation and verification of data—that is just as stringent and just as demanding as the empiric test, because *both* rest on the same three strands. The difference lies not in the abstract methodology, but in the actual *territory* being mapped (sensibilia versus intelligibilia). Of course, the empiric test is considerably easier because it is performed by a subject on an object, whereas mental-phenomenology is performed by a subject (or symbol) on or with other subjects (or symbols)—much more difficult. The object domain here is *of* subjective or intersubjective "objects" (intelligibilia), not merely objective "objects" (sensibilia).

And there we can already see one of the profound differences between empiric-analytic inquiry and mental-phenomenological inquiry. In the empiric-analytic, one is using the symbolic mind to map or mirror the *pre*symbolic world. But in mental-phenomenology, one is using the symbolic mind to map or mirror the symbolic mind itself. One is using symbols to mirror or reflect other symbols, which themselves can reflect the reflection, and so on in a "hermeneutic circle" of meaning that two minds or symbols co-create whenever they inquire into each other. The most obvious example of this is simple verbal communication; when we talk, I try to grasp your meaning and you mine, and so around we go in the intersubjective circle. When one symbol probes another symbol, the latter can *respond* in a way that presymbolic objects (rocks, electrons, planets) cannot: in a *proactive* and not merely reactive fashion. Thus, mental-phenomenology is not so much a starkly objective affair as it is an intersubjective mesh, and it is that mesh that *grounds* the phenomenological knowledge quest. An empiric proposition is true if it more or less accurately mirrors the sensory, biomaterial, objective world. But a mental-phenomenological proposition is true, not if it matches any set of sensibilia, but if it meshes with an intersubjective structure of meaning (or, as in mathematics, an intersymbolic logic). Thus, for example, in mathematical theorems (i.e., hypotheses with logical injunctions), we do not look to empirical facts for proof (or disproof); the *facts* here are units of intersymbolic intelligibilia. A theorem is true if it conforms to the consensus of intersymbolic logic, not if it conforms to sensory evidence. Not mind on matter but mind on mind!

We can put all of these important differences between empiric-analytic and mental-phenomenological inquiry in several different ways:

1. Empiric-analytic inquiry is performed by a subject on an object; mental-phenomenological inquiry is performed by a subject (or symbol) on or with other subjects (or symbols).

2. In empiric-analytic inquiry, the referent of conceptual knowledge is other than conceptual knowledge; in mental-phenomenology, the referent of conceptual knowledge is the process of conceptual knowledge itself (or the structure of ideas, language, communication, intentions, etc.). More simply:

3. The *facts* (data) of empiric-analytic inquiry are things; the *facts* (data) of mental-phenomenology are thoughts.

4. In empiric-analytic inquiry, the propositions themselves are intentional (symbolic), but the data are nonintentional (presymbolic); in mental-phenomenology, *both* the propositions and the data are intentional and symbolic.

5. Empiric-analytic inquiry works predominantly with things in *nature;* mental-phenomenology works predominantly with symbols in *history.* "Among the most important premises would be the distinction between nature [disclosed in or as sensibilia] and human history [disclosed in or as intelligibilia]. For after all, is not the distinction between voluntary action [mental intention] and mechanical behavior [physical causality] another version of the distinction between human freedom and natural necessity? History is precisely the record of our escape from natural necessity. History is the chronicle of *actions* [not just reactions], intentional plots with beginnings, middles, and ends. The logic of the concepts of space, time, and mass [sensibilia] is significantly different from the logic of concepts like success, honor, and duty [intelligibilia]: their presupposed contexts are *non*natural [i.e., historical]. The inventions of reason transcend the uniform regularities of the natural laws. Where the very phenomena in question have to do not with the articulations achieved by natural evolution but by human history, the language used in formulating the creators' *intentions* plays a constituitive role; they are *historical* terms in the sense that their meanings are not *given* by nature but are instead successively constituted by the ways they are used [i.e., historically]. The criteria for satisfying such intentions are not reducible to ahistorical descriptions of natural phe-

nomena"[87]—as, for example, the historical production of Egyptian hieroglyphics cannot be reduced to its empirical sensibilia.

But perhaps the most important distinction, and certainly one of the easiest to use, is this:

6. Empiric-analytic inquiry is a *monologue*—a symbolizing inquirer looks at a nonsymbolizing occasion; mental-phenomenology, however, is a *dialogue*—a symbolizing inquirer looks at other symbolizing occasions. The paradigm of empiric-analytic inquiry is, "I see the rock"; the paradigm of mental-phenomenological inquiry is, "I talk to you and vice versa." Empiric-analytic inquiry can proceed *without talking* to the object of its investigation—no empirical scientist talks to electrons, plastic, molecules, protozoa, ferns, or whatever, because he is studying preverbal entities. But the very field of mental-phenomenological inquiry is *communicative exchange* or intersubjective and intersymbolic relationships (language and logic), and this mental-phenomenology depends in large measure on talking to and with the subject of investigation. And any science that *talks to* its subject of investigation is not empirical but phenomenological, not monologic but dialogic.

7. In short, empiric-analytic inquiry accepts as its essential data sensibilia; mental-phenomenology accepts as its essential data intelligibilia.

SOME EXAMPLES IN PSYCHOLOGY

Let me give a few examples of these different methodologies as they operate in the field of psychology. Exclusive empiric-analytic inquiry, when applied to the human being, produces classical behaviorism. In its most typical form (e.g., Skinner), behaviorism accepts as data only sensibilia, or objectively perceived occasions. The mind *as* mind, in fact, is all but dismissed, and the organism is viewed as a rather complex but totally *reactive* mechanism. And, indeed, behaviorism can and does collect all sorts of sensible-objective data—data on reinforcement timetables, conditioned responses, positive and negative reinforcements, and so on. And in its classical form, behaviorism does not even really care to *talk* to the person involved. They do talk, of course, because they are human, but in the model itself there's no ultimate reason to do so; if you want a particular response from the person—regardless of whether the person wants it—you simply start reinforcing the desired reaction. In this model, the person really has no choice but to reactively follow the reinforcement, because in this model, the person has no mind *as* mind, no free will, no pro-action, no choice. Behaviorism, that is, is basically a monologue, or a monological science—it is empiric-analytic. And this model works very well with subhuman animals (and the subhuman levels of the human animal), because animals are indeed largely presymbolic, preintentional, prehistorical, and prevolitional—all occasions that can be perceived and studied *empirically*.

But, of course, the classical behavioristic model works rather poorly with human beings, because human beings possess, *between* the sensory stimuli and the sensory response, a *mental structure,* and that structure obeys laws whose actions are not of sensibilia but intelligibilia. As classical behaviorism began to even vaguely acknowledge this fact, it tried to accommodate its model by introducing the notion of "intervening variables" (e.g., Hull)—that is, between the sensorimotor stimulus and the sensorimotor response, there exist "intervening" or cognitive variables, such as *expectation* and *value* (Hull, Tolman). While that is true enough, the empiric-analytic methodology of behaviorism was ill-equipped to investigate these intervening variables, because empiric inquiry works with objective data, yet the intervening variables—the intelligibilia—are not so much objective as intersubjective. And the moment one starts investigating intersubjective phenomena, one is immediately ushered into the realm of discourse, dialogue, communication, introspection, hermeneutics, phenomenology, and so on. And trying to handle these mental-phenomenological *data* with empiric-analytic methods—by, for instance, calling them "verbal behavior"—is about as effective as trying to discover the meaning of *War and Peace* by analyzing the objective paper and ink by which it is expressed.

This is in no way whatsoever to deny the limited usefulness of empiric-analytic inquiry in human behavior. Not only should human sensibilia be investigated empirically, but also to the extent that intelligibilia (or transcendelia) alter the objective world, those alterations can and should be investigated empirically. But empiricism alone misses the essence of even these alterations. Let me give perhaps the most difficult example, just to show that the point can be made: an artwork, a painting—say, Goya's *May 3, 1808*. By several of our criteria, the artwork can be studied empirically. For one, the composition of the paint, the date of the canvas, and so on can be empirically analyzed, and the sensibilia of the artwork itself—its colors, lines, surfaces, aesthetics—can be apprehended empirically. For another, the artwork itself is indeed an *objective* entity. And for yet another, I can look at the painting and study it *without talking* to Goya (after all, he's dead).

But if I wish also to know if Goya was trying to tell me something, to speak to me, as it were, to communicate not just sensibilia but intelligibilia, then empirical impact and study no longer avail. The canvas and paint are still "objects out there," but they are *formed* and *informed* by human intelligibilia, by the human creative mind; they embody in objective form the *intentions* of a human *subject,* and those *intentions* are not given empirically or sensorily. Even though the work now *exists* in the objective-sensory world, it cannot be *grasped* by that world.

To ascertain those intentions and meanings, then, I must try, somehow, to enter Goya's mind, to "talk" to him—I must use historic-phenomenology, hermeneutics, dialogic technique. Of course, I can't directly talk to Goya; were he alive, we could talk about the painting's meaning, share in discourse the common sentiments it evokes in the human mind and spirit. That being impossible, I must—as in historic-hermeneutic phenomenology—attempt to re-create, via the rules of good interpretation, Goya's intentions. I must look at the *historical* period and mood in which Goya painted; I must attempt to grasp and interpret his personal-subjective intentions; and I must ground these interpretations in a community of similarly skilled. Otherwise, I will know only *my* intentions as I talk to myself.

Proceeding thus historically, phenomenologically, and dialogically, several of the intelligible and not just aesthetic-sensory meanings of the painting begin unequivocally to emerge. Goya was trying to tell me something. The painting was done during the period of Napoleonic invasions, of civil war, of firing squads, all of which appalled Goya. The painting is brilliant and frenzied in its execution; it constitutes a vivid and vicious indictment of human barbarism and outrage at a world given over to war. Of course, there might be other meanings as well, and each person is free to bring personal reactions to it. But any ole meaning or interpretation will not do—this painting is *not* about the joys of war. We might not be able to determine *all* the legitimate meanings via hermeneutic-phenomenology, but we most certainly can determine some, perhaps most of them. And the empiricist who shuns such knowledge is simply one who, in this realm, would rather know nothing at all than half know much.

The point is that the human mind can indeed form and inform the *objective* world, but those objects then *embody* an *intelligibilia* that is not given to mere *sensibilia*. Thus, if we wish to understand not just sensibilia but intelligibilia, we must have recourse to a dia-logic (dialogue) science—a general mental-phenomenology. This is especially so in psychology. And thus, once again, I will give the most difficult example: Freudian psychoanalysis.

In many ways Freud began with an empiric-analytic or merely physiological approach. But, as he would later put it, even if we figured out all the physiological aspects of awareness, "it would at most afford us an exact localization of the processes of consciousness and would give us no help toward understanding them."[46] It was the *meaning* of psychological data—their intentionality and their in-terpretation (interpretation of dreams, symptoms, etc.)—that Freud most wanted to study. That is, his approach, and his territory, was almost entirely mental-phenomenological, hermeneutical, and his-torical—the *history* here simply being the history and development of the person's own self-system (past fixations, traumas, repressions, etc.). Psychoanalytic consciousness is *historical* consciousness, a re-construction and remembrance of personal history so as to under-stand its present influence. And, most importantly, psychoanalysis was a *dialogue*—it demanded *intersubjective discourse*—"the talking cure."

Further—and this, too, is central—Freud's major discovery was not a theory, but an *injunction* (an exemplar, a paradigm). The in-junction was free association, which disclosed an object domain (data) hitherto largely ignored (unconscious primary processes). Free association surpassed Bernheim and Charcot's injunction, which was simple hypnosis. So important was the free association injunc-tion that to this day it is called the "basic rule of psychoanalysis"

("Say whatever comes into your mind"). By using this injunction, Freud began to collect *data* on this new object domain, the unconscious primary process. And these data could be *checked* by anyone willing to follow the three strands: (1) take up the injunction to free associate; (2) note the resultant apprehensions or data; and (3) compare and contrast these data in a community of the similarly adequate.

Of course, one may disagree with some of Freud's interpretations and theories *about* the data (a distinction we will return to shortly), but the data itself was as generally sound as the injunctions allowed. Even Jung, who disagreed with Freud's overall theory, generally acknowledged his data. But a mental-phenomenological proposition, to be recognized as sound, must not only account for data, it must do so in a fashion capable of withstanding the fire of unrestrained communication and intersubjective discourse. The circle of subjectivity will eventually but soundly rebuff and dislodge those hypothetical forms that do not mesh with its intersubjective structures. Thus, some of Freud's theories have generally passed that test: the existence of unconscious processes, defensive or repressive mechanisms, narcissism, the importance of development, the existence of different types of psychological structures—these concepts are accepted by virtually all schools of modern psychology, regardless of the emphasis placed on them. Other of his theories have not meshed with informed intersubjective consensus and have thus dropped from the ongoing development of psychological theory—derivation of ego from id, overemphasis on sexual etiology, certain anthropological speculations, phallocentrism, and the exact nature of dreams. The same, of course, can be said for Jung, Wundt, Rank, Adler, and all the dialogical-phenomenological psychologists. Their data is not as gross (dense) as that of the empiricists or behaviorists, but neither is it "mere subjectivism," because there is an external corrective to undue subjective bias: the data *and* its discourse must be grounded in the intersubjective mesh of communicative intelligibilia.

The point is that such dialogical-phenomenological psychology, in its various forms, has today culminated in a most impressive body of sound data and sturdy theory. Among the most recent of such researchers, Piaget may especially be noted, because, again, what immediately distinguishes his system is the introduction of a new *injunction,* in this case, the "method clinique." This method is, of course, dialogical (Piaget despises mere empiricism), a method of investigating intersubjective exchange and discourse. The method clinique is basically a highly refined question-and-answer format, applied to individuals of various age groups (although it is of course altered for the preverbal age, from birth to two years, the period where the child lives mostly in the realm of sensibilia, not intelligibilia). Through this and other injunctive techniques, Piaget has accumulated a massive amount of mental-phenomenological *data,* which he has then subjected to a structural and developmental analysis. The results have largely been reproduced by others and in cross-cultural settings. Essentially the same type of dialogic approach has been used by Kohlberg, Loevinger, Broughton, Maslow, and others.

As for Freud's legacy, psychoanalysis itself has given way to psychoanalytic ego psychology, which is basically structural, developmental, and object-relations oriented (i.e., intersubjective), and *that* now meshes to a surprising degree with the general structural-developmental and cognitive schools of psychology, as many have clearly pointed out, including Piaget himself.

New injunctive techniques—projective techniques (Rorschach), thematic apperception (Murray), method clinique (Piaget), sentence completion (Loevinger), word association (Jung), moral dilemma (Kohlberg), and others—have produced a tremendous fund of phenomenological data, and there has been a marked acceleration of unrestrained communication and open discourse between different branches of psychology. The upshot of all this is that we have been steadily producing a decently coherent and fairly unified view of human psychological growth and development (at least in its personal stages), a view that is structural, developmental, phenomenological, interpersonal, and systems-functional. This view is, of course, far from complete, far from absolutely agreed upon in all details, far from proven in all aspects. The point, however, is that in a very impressive number of areas, there is a decent intersubjective consensus on fact, theory, and practice; a general and ongoing intersubjective movement of *intelligibilia* that not only produces repeatable data but rebuffs incongruent apprehensions and dislodges them

from the ongoing sweep of the knowledge quest. This potential rebuff eloquently speaks for a real object domain (intelligibilia) that
grounds inquiry and prevents the truths of the subjective realm
from becoming merely subjective.

Transcendental Inquiry

Let us now briefly return to the example of Zen and see how the
three strands apply to the accumulation and verification of transcendental data or apprehensions.

At the very heart and foundation of Zen is not a theory, a dogma,
a belief, or a proposition, but, as in any true knowledge quest, an
injunction, an exemplar. This injunctive strand—zazen or contemplation—requires years of specialized training and critical discipline
(a certified *roshi* or Zen teacher has to undergo from ten to twenty
years of training). Zazen is simply the injunctive tool for possible
cognitive disclosure, and a person must be *developmentally adequate*
to that disclosure or there is, in fact, no disclosure, just as if you
never learn to read you will never grasp *Macbeth.* We might say
that meditative awareness or contemplation is to transcendelia as
linguistic awareness or ratiocination is to intelligibilia—both the tool
and the territory of cognitive disclosure. Not surprisingly, then, the
zazen injunction is always of the form, "If you want to know
whether there is Buddha Nature, you must first do this." That is
experimental and *experiential* injunction.

After that strand is mastered, the investigator is opened to the
second strand, that of intuitive apprehension of the object domain
disclosed by the injunction, in this case, the *data* of the transcendental sphere. This intuitive apprehension—an immediate experiential
impact or perception—is known in Zen as satori or *kensho,* both
meaning, in essence, a "direct seeing into one's spiritual nature"—as
perfectly direct as looking into the microscope to see the cell nucleus,
with the all-important proviso in each case: only a trained eye need
look.

Of course, the *referent* of transcendental perception, its very data,
cannot be perceived with the mental or sensory eyes. Satori takes as
its referent, not sensory objects out there and not mental subjects in
here, but nondual spirit as such, a direct apprehension *of* spirit, *by*

spirit, *as* spirit, an apprehension that unites subject and object by disclosing that which is prior to both, and an apprehension that therefore is quite beyond the capacities of objective-empirical or subjective-phenomenal cognition. As Hegel put it, this is "Spirit's return to itself on a higher plane, a level at which subjectivity and objectivity are united in one infinite act." This transcendental apperception arises when "I am aware, not simply of myself as a finite individual standing over against other finite persons [subjects] and things [objects], but rather of the Absolute as the ultimate and all-embracing reality. My knowledge, if I attain it, of Nature as the objective manifestation of the Absolute [sensibilia; Bonaventure's *vestigium* of God] and the Absolute as returning to itself as subjectivity in the *form* of Spirit [intelligibilia; Bonaventure's *imago* of God], existing in and through the spiritual life of man in history, is a movement in absolute consciousness [transcendelia], that is, in the self-knowledge of Being or the Absolute."[31]

This direct, immediate, intuitive apprehension of Being—not by the eye of flesh, and not by the eye of mind, but by the eye of contemplation—is satori, and it is simply the second strand in the knowledge quest of Zen. (Of course, at its summit, the eye of contemplation does not reveal data, plural, but datum, singular: The Datum, as it were, which is One Spirit as One Spirit. But there are all sorts of stages and sublevels of contemplation leading up to that summit, and all sorts of real but less than ultimate apprehensions along the way, as we will see throughout this book—and for all of those reasons, we speak generally of the eye of contemplation as disclosing the facts or data, plural, of the transcendental realm.)

But, of course, any particular individual's apprehensions of the transcendental object domain may be less than sound or initially mistaken, and therefore Zen, at every stage, has recourse to the third strand, which is careful confirmation by both the Zen Master and the community of participant meditators. This is no merely automatic pat on the back and mutual agreement society; it is a vigorous *test,* and it constitutes a potentially powerful rebuff and *nonverification* of any particular apprehension suffered in strand #2. Both in private, intense interaction with the Zen Master *(dokusan)* and in exacting public participation in rigorous tests of authenticity *(shosan), all* apprehensions are struck against the community of those whose cognitive eyes are adequate to the transcendent, and such apprehensions are soundly nonverified if they do not match the facts of transcendence as disclosed by the community of like-spirited (and this includes past apprehensions once judged, by the standards of the times, to be true but now subrated or found to be partial by more sophisticated experience). It is this explicit and conscientious adherence to *all three strands* of data accumulation and verification that makes Zen—and all similarly sophisticated contemplative inquiries—a sound and valid transcendental methodology.

PROOF OF GOD'S EXISTENCE

At its summit such transcendental methodology constitutes an experimental, verifiable, repeatable proof for the existence of Godhead, *as a fact,* as a penultimate Datum, but that proof is not—indeed, could not be—merely rational or logical (let alone empirical), a truth persistently overlooked by most theologians and religious philosophers from Aristotle to Anselm to Aquinas to Descartes to Leibniz (and down to today with Mortimer Adler, Ronald Green, Alvin Plantinga, Ross et al.)—although *never* overlooked by mystics and sages, from Plotinus ("You ask, how can we know the Infinite? I answer, not by reason") to Pascal ("The heart has its reasons, which reason cannot know") to Nagarjuna (whose dialectic remains the most powerful demonstration of reason's inadequacy in the face of the Divine).

The problem with all these rational "proofs" of God's existence—the cosmological, the teleological, the ontological, the moral, and so on—is that the circle is trying to prove the sphere, the tail is trying to wag the dog, and the results in all cases are rather less than convincing, as philosophers from Russell to Mackie (not to mention Nagarjuna et al.) have amply demonstrated. I will not bore the reader with a point-by-point critique of all these rational "proofs"—able philosophers have already done so. I will simply say that, as one who does believe Spirit exists, as one *already* predisposed, I find the *rational* proofs for such, especially considering the stakes, to be anemic in the extreme (and that includes Ross's supposedly "invincible" update of Anselm-Scotus's ontic "proof"), and I think it quite true, as many philosophers have labored to show, that such arguments can be adequately shredded. The basic problem with them all is simply that they are based on a profound category error—an attempt to prove the transrational realm with merely rational operations.

Of course, reason can and does *attempt* to think about Spirit, however inadequately, and reason is perfectly free to offer various types of *plausibility arguments* for the existence of Spirit. These are by no means *proofs* but rather hints, and I have no quarrel with all that. In fact, I find them vaguely healthy and certainly engaging, and I would definitely prefer to see the (impossible) attempt to rationally prove Spirit than the (equally impossible) attempt to rationally disprove Spirit. But even the most sophisticated of such arguments have concluded, by their authors' own admissions, nothing much more substantial than, "Well, there must be some sort of a transcendental something somewhere," a conclusion that, when placed next to the direct, immediate, in-depth realization offered by the eye of contemplation, appears a pathetically lame performance.

My point is simply that, by offering solely rational "proofs" for the Absolute—proofs that can at least be as easily defeated as defended—then when that poor proof goes, that poor god goes with it. Such category errors then simply delay the realization that there *is* an instrumental proof for the existence of God, but the instrument is contemplation, not reason, and the proof is direct, not mediate. As a *supplement* to *gnosis,* such rational discussions are very useful; as a replacement for *gnosis,* they are profoundly misleading.

But Is It "Science"?

If such endeavors as Zen, Yoga, Gnostic Christianity, Vajrayana Buddhism, Vedanta, and others do in fact follow the three strands of valid data accumulation and verification (or rejection), can they legitimately be called "sciences"?

The answer, of course, depends upon what one means by "science." If by "science" one means the three strands of knowledge accumulation in any realm, then indeed the purer schools of Zen, Yoga, and so on can be called scientific. They are injunctive, instrumental, experimental, experiential, and consensual. That being so, then we could legitimately speak of "spiritual sciences" just as we now speak of social sciences, hermeneutical sciences, psychological sciences, and physical sciences (the latter being empirical, the others being phenomenological or transcendental). Many of the meditation masters themselves like to refer to the science of Yoga, the science of Being, or the science of meditation.

But there are, indeed, some problems with that, because if by "science" we mean empirical science—and that, in fact, is what is usually meant—then not only are meditative-contemplative-spiritual disciplines *not* science, neither are hermeneutics, phenomenology, introspective psychology, mathematics, psychoanalysis, interpretive sociology, and so on. Empiric-analytic inquiry cannot, as we have seen, even adequately deal with the realm of intelligibilia, and how much less so with that of transcendelia!

Thus, in the past I have been most reluctant, even harsh, in accepting the notion of a "higher science," simply because most advocates of a "higher science" have in fact implicitly attempted to expand the definition of science *without relinquishing the exclusively empiric-analytic mode.* Most of today's psychological, philosophical, and sociological theorists have long ago relinquished mere empiricism (Piaget, Whitehead, Lacan, Habermas, Gadamer, Ricoeur, Bateson, etc.), and the transcendental disciplines, for even more compelling reasons, must surely follow suit (transcending but including empiricism). And yet here were so many theorists claiming that the "new and higher" science—transpersonal, transcendental, spiritual—would be a purely *empirical discipline,* without apparently being very clear about just what they meant by "empiricism." Of course, by "empirical" they often meant experimental and experiential (in the broad sense), but they often also meant, equally and at the same time, objective-sensory data, and this ambiguity has caused much unnecessary confusion.

Let me give a few examples of the messy results that have occurred when purely empirical evidence was advanced as "proof" of higher or transpersonal or transcendental states. Begin with brain-physiological monitoring of "altered states of consciousness." Various researchers have taken advanced meditators, yogis or swamis, who claim to be able to enter a "higher state of consciousness," and, to check out this claim, have plugged them into an empiric-scientific machine, the EEG. The yogi enters his "higher state" *(samadhi)* and, sure enough, a totally unprecedented EEG pattern is produced. Which proves?

Which proves that this yogi is capable of altering his brain patterns and thus the EEG machine. It offers no proof whatsoever of a *higher* state of consciousness, only of a *different* state of consciousness. That state, in fact, might be a new form of psychosis or a new breed of catatonic schizophrenia or *whatever*. Nothing from the EEG can prove this is a *transcendent* state. To the utter contrary, *it is the yogi, using his inward contemplative eye, who alone pronounces this to be a transcendent state*. Not the EEG machine, which is an extended eye of flesh, but only the yogi, using his eye of contemplation, can even talk of higher states. That a higher state might always be correlated with a particular brain-wave pattern would be an important bit of data, but it is *proven* to be *higher* by the yogi (and the community of like-spirited contemplatives), not the machine. The *proof* is contemplative, not empiric. The empiric data is *useful;* it is just not *central*.

But the real problem is even worse than that. As we have often said, the higher leaves its footprints in the lower, and those footprints are a legitimate, if limited, field of investigation (you get the footprints, but never the beast itself). The real problem is that those who advanced empirical brain physiology as "proof" of a transcendent state soon found that the argument quickly turned on them, offering powerful evidence, in fact, of just the opposite. If these "higher states" can indeed be reckoned most fundamentally by brain physiology, then the correct conclusion is that these "higher" or "transpersonal" states are really and merely events occurring in the *personal* brain itself—they aren't really transpersonal or transcendental at all.

As soon as the transpersonal researcher (e.g., Ornstein) comes back with, "No, what's happening is that this new physiological brain state is simply allowing the brain to attune itself with higher and transpersonal energies and realms," then the empiricist merely says, "Show me the empirical evidence of these transpersonal realms." The transpersonalist cannot now point again to brain physiology, because he has just said—in order to escape the first criticism—that physiology is merely allowing *higher* realms to be perceived, and so these higher realms cannot be the same as physiology. But as for these higher realms *themselves,* he has, empirically, precisely nothing, and the empiricist knows it. The transpersonalist is now right back where he started, with the added disadvantage that the empiricist now has new ammunition: The purely empirical data, far from proving a transcendental, transindividual, transpersonal occasion, simply prove—taken in and by themselves—that the mystic is perceiving not Spirit but merely his or her own brain structure. And since the cosmos has been in existence for perhaps 15 billion years, and the human brain for only a pitiful 6 million, then *that* brain "god" is clearly not an infinite, eternal, all-pervading, and transcendental essence, but a simple neurological spark in a purely personal brain. In short, the brain physiology argument, *exactly* by trying to be empirical, now constitutes one of the greatest obstacles to an acceptance of genuinely transpersonal states.

Part of the problem, again, is that such transpersonal researchers have thoughtlessly tried to jump from empirical-sensory data straight to transcendental-contemplative data, without realizing that empiric-analytic inquiry doesn't even adequately cover the intermediate ground of intelligibilia. No amount of EEG sophistication, for instance, no amount of physiological data, can help you decide the meaning of *Macbeth,* the appropriateness of supply-side economics, the geopolitics of the Middle East situation, or the meaning of Egyptian hieroglyphics. All such *intelligibilia,* while certainly leaving their registerable footprints in the brain's physiology, nonetheless have their essence, their referent, their ground, and their *fundamental* existence in the *intersubjective* circle of mental phenomenology. Empiric-physiological studies are not useless in the understanding of intelligibilia, they are simply extremely secondary—and thus, when it comes to transcendelia, they are, one might say, extremely tertiary. Attempting to ground transcendental truth claims in brain physiology is about as useful as hooking Einstein to an EEG in order to find out if E really does equal mc^2.

My point is simply that when it comes to intelligibilia and transcendelia, empiric-analytic studies are of extremely limited and extremely secondary importance. And worse: when it is claimed that there is empiric-scientific proof for any of these states, the researcher has simply but implicitly *accepted the positivistic-reductionistic standards,* and has thus unwittingly played into the hands of the very opponents of such states, thereby hurting the advancement not only of valid rational-phenomenology but also of genuine transcendental inquiry.

Now I am not saying that the word "science" cannot be legitimately applied to phenomenological and transcendental concerns; I am not saying there can be no science of intelligibilia and transcendelia. I am saying that the methodology of monological or empiric-analytic science *cannot* be applied to those higher realms. If we are to speak of a "higher science"—and I think we can—then we must be much more cautious than past advocates of such have generally been. And there is one last caution that—although somewhat technical—cannot be overlooked. It is to that point we now turn.

Theory and Hypothesis

We have seen that each of the three general modes of knowing—sensory, mental, and spiritual—has access to direct, immediate, and intuitive apprehensions or data (sensibilia, intelligibilia, and transcendelia). Notice, however, that the very data of the *mental mode*—its words and symbols and concepts—simply because they are indeed symbolic, intentional, reflective, and referential can be used to *point* to, or *represent, other* data, from any other realm: sensibilia, intelligibilia itself, or transcendelia. We can indicate all these epistemological relationships as follows:

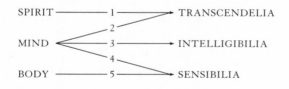

Mode #5 is simple sensorimotor cognition, the eye of flesh, the presymbolic grasp of the presymbolic world (sensibilia). Mode #4 is empiric-analytic thought; it is mind (intelligibilia) reflecting on and grounding itself *in* the world of sensibilia. Mode #3 is mental-phenomenological thought; it is mind (intelligibilia) reflecting on and grounding itself in the world of intelligibilia itself. Mode #2 can be called mandalic or paradoxical thinking; it is mind (intelligibilia) attempting to reason about spirit or transcendelia. And mode #1 is *gnosis,* the eye of contemplation, the transsymbolic grasp of the transsymbolic world, spirit's direct knowledge of spirit, the immediate intuition of transcendelia.

But notice: Whereas the *data* in *any* realm is itself immediate and direct (by definition), the *pointing* by *mental* data to *other* data (sensory, mental, or transcendental) is a mediate or intermediate process—it is a *mapping, modeling,* or *matching* procedure. And this mapping procedure—the use of mental data (symbols and concepts) to explain or map *other* data (sensory, mental, or transcendental)—simply results in what is known as *theoretical knowledge.*

We come, then, to a crucial point. Neither the sensorimotor realms per se, nor the spiritual realms per se, form theories. They can be the *object* of theories, but do not themselves produce theories. The one is presymbolic, the other, transsymbolic, and theories are, above all else, symbolic or mental productions. There is valid experience, valid knowledge, valid apprehensions in the spiritual and sensible realms but not symbolic or theoretical experience. We will return to this important point shortly; for the moment, let us look more closely at the nature of *mental theories* themselves, because they are crucial in deciding on what we mean by the word "science."

A theory or hypothesis is basically a set of *directly apprehended mental data* used to intermediately map, explain, or organize *other directly apprehended data.* For example, take the empirical hypothesis, "The back side of the moon is made of green cheese." Regardless of the truth or falsity of the proposition, notice that you nevertheless directly understand the *meaning* of that proposition itself, because the proposition per se is a *mental datum,* a direct and immediate apprehension of intelligibilia by the mind's eye. The question *then* arises, does the *mental* datum accurately model or represent the *physical* datum about the moon? In order to find out once and for all, we send a person (or instruments) to the moon and we *look*—that gives us the *direct* and immediate physical datum, and then we discover that the *intermediate* or mapping proposition is false.

Now I emphasize the apparently trivial point that the hypothesis *itself* is a directly apprehended *mental datum,* because without that understanding the status of the mind itself, in the hands of the empiricists, is in great jeopardy. For mind then starts to look like "nothing but" a gross or physical-reflecting entity, "nothing but" an "arid abstraction" that somehow isn't as real as the "concrete territory" of good ole sensibilia, overlooking the fact that the mind it-self—the realm of intelligibilia—is an *experiential territory* every bit as (or more) real than sensibilia. Even William James fell into this pernicious reductionism. "There are two ways of knowing things," he says, "knowing them immediately or intuitively [data], and knowing them conceptually or representatively [which would include map-theory]. Although such things as the white paper before our eyes can be known intuitively [he doesn't mean spiritually, he means directly and immediately], most of the things we know, the tigers now in India, for example [i.e., objects outside our present sensory awareness], are known only representatively or symbolically."[67] And, according to James, the symbol-map, such as the image or concept "tiger," mediates or points to the real tiger, but it is *only* the *sensory experience* of the real tiger that constitutes direct and immediate knowledge. Incredibly, James overlooks the fact that the symbol per se, the word-image "tiger," is itself, by itself, directly and immediately experienced or apprehended by the mind's eye, *just as* the physical tiger can be directly apprehended by the eye of flesh. And, indeed, the mental-phenomenological sciences—linguistics, for instance—take as their *concrete territory* the native and intuitive experience and grasp of mental symbols and words themselves! Thus, in no sense does "real territory" mean just physical sensibilia; there is sensory territory, mental territory, and spiritual territory— *all* being real and experiential object domains. And in no sense does "map" take on the derogatory epithet, "just a mere abstraction," for the abstraction per se is itself part of a very real territory, the territory of intelligibilia.

A theory or hypothesis, then, is an *immediately* apprehended mental datum (or gestalt of data) used to *mediately* point to, map, or logically systematize, other *immediately* apprehended data (sensory, mental, spiritual). But if a theory is a mental map, nonetheless the map may be wrong, and what distinguishes a theory or hypothesis from a merely dogmatic formulation is its call to experiential or data-based verification. A hypothesis is not just a formulation of present data; it is a formulation of present data in an attempt to create a map that will not be surprised by future data. And the only way to see if a map is surprised by future data is to actually gather future data.

And we have already seen the means for doing so: the three strands of data accumulation and verification—injunction, apprehension, and confirmation. With hypotheses, there is simply the *extra step* of *intermediate mapping:* the readjustment (or sometimes total rejection) of the hypothesis or map in light of the newly acquired data. A hypothesis, then, is a tentative map *plus* suggested injunctions.

Thus, for example, Freud gathered his data—various images, symbols, dream displays, free associations, abreactions, and so on; he formed various theories; then checked the theories against new data; then reformulated his theories, and so on. The same applies whenever we are discussing not just *direct experiential apprehension* (data in any realm) but the systematic *mental mapping* of that data (from any realm)—that is, it applies (or can apply) to empiric-analytic inquiry (#4), to mental-phenomenological inquiry (#3), and to mandalic inquiry (#2; e.g., mental cartographies, however limited, of the higher and transmental realms).

I think most of this is fairly self-evident. I am simply emphasizing the fact that the maps, theories, or hypotheses *themselves,* regardless of their referents (sensory, mental, or transcendental), and regardless of their eventual truth or falsity, are still themselves part of the realm of *mental data:* produced by mind and directly apprehended by mind.

But this makes a "spiritual science" or genuinely "transcendental science" doubly difficult. For unlike sensibilia or intelligibilia, transcendelia cannot be easily or adequately described in mental terms or maps. Spiritual *data* themselves are transmental and transconceptual, and thus they resist, even defy, conceptual, rational, theoretical mapping and codification. We saw, in fact, that when the *mind* attempts to look at or think about spirit, it produces paradoxical results. The mind can adequately look at and map sensibilia because it transcends sensibilia; it can adequately look at and map intelligibilia because that is its own backyard; but it cannot adequately look at or map spirit because spirit transcends *it.* And when spirit *is* described in mental terms, it is not in the nice, commonsensical, down-to-earth categories of empiric-analytic thought or even in the subtler symbolic logic; it is in the slippery, paradoxical, poetical terms of mandalic reason. Understand that spiritual knowledge itself—

gnosis, #1—is the most direct, clearcut, impactful knowledge imaginable—it simply transcends conceptualization and therefore resists neat hypothetical categorizations and mental mappings.

The point is that one of the standard definitions of any sort of science is "theoretical consistency." Even Charles Tart accepts that as a criterion of a "spiritual," "state specific," or "higher science." But it is useless to demand theoretical consistency from transtheoretical states. Of course, Hinduism, Buddhism, and others can speak logically and consistently, it is just a great mistake to think that their hearts can be poured into concepts. As Watts put it: "Zen does not attempt to be intelligible, that is to say, capable of being understood by the intellect." Yogananda put it thus: "Reason is powerless to understand transcendental truth. Man's highest faculty is not reason but intuition [*gnosis*]: apprehension of knowledge derived immediately and spontaneously from the soul, not from the fallible agency of the senses or of reason." As Kaplan explains: "Esotericists see the theory-building activity of the mind as a lower-state-specific function—one which is left behind with the attainment of those altogether different but [valid] cognitive functions of the mind, which result in esoteric [spiritual] knowledge. Esotericists insist that esoteric knowledge per se is not a matter of theory, which means that this [criterion of science] has no applicability to esoteric knowledge."[69]

So What Do We Mean by "Science"?

And so, for all the above-mentioned reasons, I have in the past been very reluctant to speak of a "higher science"—a science not just of sensibilia but of intelligibilia and transcendelia. But there is, admittedly, something of a "political" or perhaps "public relations" problem with saying that a discipline is "not scientific," no matter how carefully the definitions are arranged, because "not scientific" has come to mean, for reasons good and bad, "not verifiable," "not really real," or "not cognitively valid."

Accordingly, if by "not scientific" we mean "not amenable to direct observation and verification," then by "scientific" we must mean the opposite: open to direct experiential observation and consensual validation. If that is so, then by science we cannot mean

But what about hope, envy, pride, joy, understanding? What is the length of a concept? How much does insight weigh? What is the width of an idea? For what characterizes intelligibilia is not so much their *extension* as their *intention*—their meaning, their value, their intersubjective understanding. Physical space-time no longer quite applies to them, and thus *physical* measurement and quantification are of rather limited use.

This is not to say, however, that some types of measurement or quantification are not applicable to intelligibilia; nor is it to deny that intelligibilia have their own subtler forms of space-time. For the mental realm does indeed have a form of time, but it is not merely natural time or seasonal time—it is *historical time* or history: the mode of time marked not just by its extension but also and mostly by its *intention*. It is *narrative* time, the time that marks the history of one's own life story or self, the time that carries and creates hopes and ideals, plans and ambitions, goals and visions; the *subtle* time that can speed up or slow down, expand or collapse, transcend or concentrate, according to its *interest,* whereas poor ole physical time just clicks along, stuck in the passing present, mindlessly, monotonously, causally.

In other words, historical time *transcends* physical time: not stuck in the simple moment-to-moment time of sensibilia, historical time can span and scan the past and future, anticipate and remember, reminisce and envision, and thus allow mind to escape its bondage to the merely passing present of bodily sensations and perceptions and thereby enter the larger span of consciousness called historical perspective. Thus, this *subtler* form of time is also a more encompassing and transcendent mode of time. As you are now reading these words, following my intentions, grasping my symbolic points, your body is existing in physical time, clicking away in the present, but your mind is moving in historical time, speeding up, slowing down, looking forward, looking backward—the time that is the movement not of things but of thoughts, the time that stretches beyond the naive present and marks *its* pace with vision and intention.

Likewise, the realm of intelligibilia has a *subtle* form of space, exactly the space that today's jargon calls "psychological space." It is the space of self-identity; also the space of imagination, the space of dreams, the space of vision, the inward space created by mind in its formal operations. It is a *narrative* space, the space of stories and intentions and choices, not merely the physical space of extensions and collisions and causalities. This space, being *subtler* than physical space, can transcend physical space. My "psychological space" can expand to include, in the very circle of myself, my friends, my family, even my country. I can do all this without even moving in physical space. This mode of mental space, and its *correlative* mode of time (history), characterize intelligibilia and its dynamics.

Look now at transcendelia: for here, space-time has become so subtle, so transcendent, so expansive, so all-encompassing that we can either say (paradoxically!) that time and space cease to exist entirely, or that all time and space exist simultaneously, now, in the eternal moment (what the mystics call the *nunc stans,* which they are very careful to point out should not be confused with the *nunc fluens,* the simple passing present of mere sensibilia). We are here in the realm of the Timeless that is All Time, the Spaceless that is All Space.

And so here is the point about *measurement:* It is not that space and time exist *only* in the gross realm of sensibilia. It is that in the physical realm, space and time are the densest, the grossest, the most head-knockingly concrete. As we move up the spectrum of consciousness, space and time become subtler and subtler (and therefore more encompassing or transcendent), but, accordingly, measurement becomes subtler and thus infinitely more difficult to perform, until it becomes, finally, completely meaningless.

Measurement, then, most easily and most essentially characterizes the gross realm of sensibilia. In the realm of intelligibilia, measurement, if used, switches from a gauge of extension to a gauge of intention. We speak, for instance, of the *intensity* of a value, *how much* we love someone, the *degree* of ambition, and the *measure* of intelligence. And we can also use number-measures as a marker of *relative* values (as, for instance, a person does when he or she subjectively judges a member of the opposite sex on the scale of "one to ten"). In the field of social phenomenology itself, there has been much work done on the quantification of mental intention (not extension). And even in transcendelia, there is a sense in speaking of the *degree* of spiritual progress and understanding (the ten stages of enlightenment, for example).

All of which is fine; measurement, in the broadest sense, simply means "more" or "less" of a datum, and *all* realms have their data. But we ought to be very careful not to confuse what we mean by measurement of *extension* with measurement of *intention* with measurement of *transcension* (or degree of specific transcendence). And *the* problem with empirical scientism was that, by measurement, it meant the easiest and most objective form of measurement: measurement of extensive gross-realm sensibilia. Since it is much harder to measure subjective intelligibilia (let alone spiritual transcendelia), the scienticians simply dismissed data that could not be forced into physical measurement dimensions—and that was the horrendous crime that led to the "disqualified universe." All of this can be avoided if we simply remember that measurement in the monological sciences is primarily of extension; measurement in the dialogical sciences is primarily of intention; and measurement in the gnostic sciences is primarily of transcension.

Summary and Conclusion: The *Geist* Sciences

The Germans have a beautiful concept for our larger science: *Geisteswissenschaften. Geist* itself is a fortunate word because it means both mind and spirit, and simply signifies all realms not merely physical or empirical. Wilhelm Dilthey, who first introduced the idea, simply pointed out that alongside the *natural sciences* there has grown up the *Geisteswissenschaften,* the mental and spiritual sciences, which include "history, national economy, the sciences of law and the state, the science of religion, the study of literature and poetry, of art and music, of philosophical world views, systems, and finally psychology."[31]

It was Dilthey's genius to point out that although the natural sciences deal with the purely objective, natural world, and the geist-sciences with the cultural, historical, and spiritual world, nonetheless *Geist* itself—the human mind and spirit—can and does form and inform, mold and alter, the objective world of material sensibilia. We already gave an example of this with Goya's painting, or sensibilia formed and informed by intelligibilia. But of course the same is true of transcendelia—it can form and inform its junior levels: intelligibilia (as mandalic reason, mystical poetry, etc.) and sensibilia (as art, sculpture, temples, etc.). *Geist* (mind and spirit) everywhere *objectifies* itself, and part of geist-science is *not only dealing with the higher realms in and as themselves* but also in grasping and understanding the meaning and intent of their particular *objectifications* in their junior realms, the intermediate realms of culture and history, and the lower realms of nature and physical material.

According to Dilthey, there are two essential ingredients necessary for "decoding" these objectifications of *Geist*. The first he called *Erlebnisse,* which means my own personal and *lived experience* in the realm which issued the objectification. This is similar to the notion of *adequatio*—if I am to grasp any objectification of mind or spirit, I must, in my own personal lived experience, my own *Erlebnisse,* be *adequate* to the realm that produced the objectification, or else, as the biblical wisdom has it, we are casting pearls before swine.

Using *Erlebnisse* as a base, I must then attempt to understand (*verstehen*), or grasp from within, the mind or spirit that formed and informed the objectification of itself. "And to understand a phase of objective spirit means relating its phenomena to an inner structure which finds expression in these phenomena."[31] That is, where the original objectification or expression was a movement from the inside to the outside, my *understanding* of it is the reverse: a movement from the outside to the inside, an attempt to re-create its inner life and meaning. Thus, the geist-sciences " 'rest on the relation of *lived experience, expression,* and *understanding.*' Expresion is required because the underlying spiritual structure is grasped only in and through its external expressions. Understanding is a movement from the outside to the inside. And in the process of understanding a spiritual object rises before our vision . . . ,"[31] a vision-insight given only by the mental and/or contemplative eye.

The point is that the higher realms everywhere leave their footprints in the lower. The higher realms form and inform, create and mold, produce and alter, all manner of forms in the lower realms. But those productions cannot be grasped *by* the lower realms nor reduced *to* them. And it is that double understanding—the higher *as* higher and the higher as objectified, expressed, and embodied in the lower—that will announce the new and truly higher sciences.

3

A Mandalic Map of Consciousness

W E H A V E S E E N T H E N E E D for a comprehensive paradigm to include monological, dialogical, and translogical sciences. When applied to psychology, such an integral approach would produce a broad-spectrum map or model of consciousness on the whole—its development, its structures, its levels—stretching from material and sensory stages to mental and verbal stages to transcendental and spiritual stages. In this chapter we will examine one such possible model.

THE NATURE OF DEVELOPMENT

Everywhere we look in nature, said the philospher Jan Smuts,[111] we see nothing but *wholes*. And not just simple wholes but hierarchical ones: each whole is a part of a larger whole which is itself part of a larger whole. Fields within fields within fields, stretching through the cosmos, interlacing each and every thing with each and every other.

Further, said Smuts, the universe is not a thoughtlessly static and inert whole—the cosmos is not lazy but energetically dynamic and even creative. It tends to produce higher- and higher-level wholes, ever more inclusive and organized. This overall cosmic process, as it unfolds in time, is nothing other than evolution. And the drive to ever higher unities, Smuts called *holism*.

If we continued this line of thinking, we might say that because the human mind or psyche is an aspect of the cosmos, we would expect to find, in the psyche itself, the same hierarchical arrangement of wholes within wholes, reaching from the simplest and most rudimentary to the most complex and inclusive. In general, such is exactly the discovery of modern psychology. As Werner put it, "Wherever [psychological] development occurs it proceeds from a state of relative globality and lack of differentiation to a state of increasing differentiation, articulation, and hierarchical integration."[127] Jakobson speaks of "those stratified phenomena which modern psychology uncovers in the different areas of the realm of the mind,"[64] where each stratified layer is more integrated and more encompassing than its predecessor. Bateson points out that even learning itself is hierarchical, involving several major levels, each of which is "meta-" to its predecessor. As a general approximation, then, we may conclude that the psyche—like the cosmos at large—is many-layered ("pluridimensional"), composed of successively higher-order wholes and unities and integrations.

Now the holistic evolution of nature—which produces everywhere higher and higher wholes—shows up in the human psyche as development or growth. The same force that produced humans from amoebas produces adults from infants. That is, a person's growth, from infancy to adulthood, is simply a miniature version of cosmic evolution. Or, we might say, psychological growth or development in humans is simply a microcosmic reflection of universal growth on the whole and has the same goal: the unfolding of ever higher-order unities and integrations. And that is one of the major reasons that the psyche is, indeed, stratified. Very like the geological formation of the earth, psychological development proceeds stratum by stratum, level by level, stage by stage, with each successive level superimposed upon its predecessor in such a way that it transcends but includes it ("envelopes it," as Werner put it).

Now in psychological development, the whole of any level becomes merely a part of the whole of the next level, which in turn becomes a part of the next whole, and so on throughout the evolution of consciousness (what Koestler nicely called a "holon"—an entity which, looking down, is whole, looking up, is part). Take, as but one example, the development of language: The child first learns babbling sounds, then wider vowel and consonant sounds, then simple words, then small phrases, then simple sentences, and then extended sentences. At each stage, simple parts (e.g., words) are integrated into higher wholes (e.g., sentences), and as Jakobson points out, "new additions are superimposed on earlier ones and dissolution begins with the higher strata."[64]

Modern developmental psychology has, on the whole, simply devoted itself to the exploration and explanation of the various levels, stages, and strata of the human constitution—mind, personality, psychosexuality, character, consciousness, and object-relations. The cognitive studies of Piaget and Werner, the works of Loevinger and Arieti and Maslow and Jakobson, the moral development studies of Kohlberg—all subscribe to the concept of stratified stages of increasing complexity, integration, and unity.

Having said that much, we are at once entitled to ask, "What, then, is the *highest* stage of unity to which one may aspire?" Or perhaps we should not phrase the question in such ultimate terms, but simply ask instead, "What is the nature of some of the higher and highest stages of development? What forms of unity are disclosed in the most developed souls of the human species?"

We all know what the "lower" stages and levels of the psyche are like (I am speaking in simple, general terms): they are instinctual, impulsive, libidinous, id-ish, animal, apelike. And we all know what some of the "middle" stages are like: socially adapted, mentally adjusted, egoically integrated, syntactically organized, conceptually advanced. But are there no "higher" stages? Is an "integrated ego" or "autonomous individual" the highest reach of consciousness in human beings? The individual ego is a marvelously high-order unity, but compared with the Unity of the cosmos at large, it is a pitiful slice of holistic reality. Has nature labored these billions of years just to bring forth this egoic mouse?

The problem with that type of question lies in finding examples of truly higher-order personalities—and in deciding exactly *what* constitutes a higher-order personality in the first place. My own feeling is that as humanity continues its collective evolution, this will become very easy to decide, because more and more "enlightened" personalities will show up in data populations, and psychologists will be forced, by their statistical analyses, to include higher-order profiles in their developmental stages. In the meantime, one's idea of "higher-order" or "highly developed" remains rather philosophic. Nonetheless, those few gifted souls who have bothered to look at this problem have suggested that the world's great mystics and sages represent some of the very highest, if not the highest, of all stages of human development. Bergson said exactly that; and so did Toynbee and Tolstoy and James and Schopenhauer and Nietzsche and Maslow and Hegel.

The point is that we *might* have an excellent population of extremely evolved and developed personalities in the form of the world's great mystic-sages (a point which is supported by Maslow's studies). Let us, then, simply assume that the authentic mystic-sage represents some of the very highest stages of human development—as far beyond normal-and-average humanity as it itself is beyond apes. This, in effect, would give us a sample which approximates the "highest state of consciousness," a type of "superconscious" state. Furthermore, most of the mystic-sages have left rather detailed records of the stages and substages of their own transformations into the upper reaches of consciousness. That is, they tell us not only of the highest level of consciousness and superconsciousness but also of all the intermediate levels leading up to it. If we take these higher stages and add them to the lower and middle stages and levels which have been so carefully described and studied by Western psychology, we would then arrive at a fairly well-balanced and comprehensive model of the spectrum of consciousness. I have attempted this type of synthesis in a series of books.[133, 137, 139] As a very general and simplistic outline, here is what we find:

THE LOWER REALMS

It is generally agreed, by Eastern and Western psychology alike, that the lowest levels of development involve simple material and biological functions and processes. That is, the lowest levels involve somatic processes, instincts, simple sensations and perceptions, and emotional-sexual impulses. In Piaget's system, these are the sensorimotor realms; Arieti refers to them as instinctual, exoceptual, and protoemotional; Loevinger calls them presocial, symbiotic, and impulsive. In Vedanta, this is the realm of the *annamayakosha* and *pranamayakosha,* the levels of food, hunger, and emotional sexuality. The Buddhist calls them the lower five *vijnanas* or the realm of the five senses. The Yoga *chakra* psychology refers to them as the lower three *chakras:* the *muladhara* or root material and pleromatic level; the *svadhisthana* or emotional-sexual level; and *manipura* or aggressive-power level. This is also the lower three *skandhas* in the Theravadin Buddhist system of psychology: the physical body, perception-sensation, and emotion-impulse. And it is Maslow's lowest two needs, the physiological and safety needs. All of this simply goes to point up one of Freud's major ideas: "The ego," he said, "is first and foremost a body-ego."[44]

Now the body-ego or body-self tends to develop in the following way: It is generally agreed, by virtually all schools of modern psychology, that the infant initially cannot distinguish self from not-self, subject from object, body from environment. That is, the self at this earliest of stages (the first four to eight months of life) is largely one with or confused with the physical world. As Piaget put it, "During the early stages the world and the self are one; neither term is distinguished from the other. . . . The self is still material, so to speak."[93] That initial stage of *material oneness,* which Piaget called "protoplasmic," Neumann calls "pleromatic" and "uroboric." "Pleromatic" is an old gnostic term meaning the material universe—the *materia prima* and *virgo mater.* "Uroboros" is a mythic symbol of a serpent eating its own tail, and signifies "wholly self-absorbed" and "not able to recognize an other" (autistic and narcissistic); it also refers to alimentary-reptilian drives and the crudest forms of sensations and rudimentary perceptions.

It is out of this primordial fusion state that the separate self emerges, and as Freud said, the self emerges first as a body, a body-self. The infant bites a blanket, and it does not hurt; he bites his thumb, and it hurts. There is a difference, he learns, between the body and the not-body, and he gradually learns to focus his awareness *from* the pleroma *to* the body. Thus, out of primitive material unity emerges the first real self sense: the body-ego. The infant *identifies* with the newly emergent body, with its sensations and emotions, and gradually learns to differentiate them from the material world at large.

Notice that the body-ego, by differentiating itself from the material environment, actually *transcends* that primitive state of fusion and embeddedness. The body-ego transcends the material environment, and thus can perform physical operations upon that environment. Toward the end of the sensorimotor period (around age two), the child has differentiated the body-self and the material environment to such a degree that he has a fairly stable image of "object constancy," and so he can muscularly coordinate physical operations on those objects. He can coordinate a physical movement of various objects in the environment, something he could not easily do as long as he could not differentiate himself *from* those objects.

Let us note that triad: by *differentiating* the self from an object, the self *transcends* that object and thus can *operate* upon it (using *as tools* the *structures* of the self at that level—at this stage, the sensorimotor body).

At this body-self stage(s), then, the self is no longer bound to the material-pleromatic environment—but it is bound to, or identified with, the biological body. The self, as body-ego, is dominated by instinctual urges, impulsiveness, the pleasure principle, involuntary urges and discharges—all the id-like primary processes and drives described so well by Freud and others. For this reason, we also call the body-self the "typhonic self"—the typhon, in mythology, was half human, half serpent (uroboros).

THE INTERMEDIATE REALMS

Eventually, however, true *mental* or conceptual functions begin to emerge out of, and differentiate from, the body-self. As language develops, the child is ushered into the world of symbols and ideas and concepts, and thus is gradually raised above the fluctuations of the simple, instinctual, immediate, and impulsive body-ego. Among other things, language carries the ability to picture things and events which are not *immediately* present to the body senses. "Language," as Robert Hall put it, "is the means of dealing with the nonpresent world."[137]

By the same token, then, language is the means of transcending the simply present world (language, in the higher realms of consciousness, is itself transcended, but one must go from the preverbal to the verbal in order to get to the transverbal; we are here talking about the transcendence of the preverbal by the verbal, which, although only half the story, is an extraordinary achievement). Through language one can anticipate the future, plan for it, and thus gear one's present activities in accordance with tomorrow. That is, one can delay or control one's present bodily desires and activities. This is, as Fenichel explains, "a gradual substituting of actions for mere discharge reactions. This is achieved through the interposing of a time period between stimulus and response."[39] Through language and its symbolic, tensed structures, one can postpone and channel the otherwise immediate and impulsive discharges of simple biological drives. One is no longer totally dominated by instinctual demands but can to a certain degree *transcend* them. And this simply means that the self is starting to differentiate from the body and emerge as a mental or verbal or syntactical being.

Notice again: As the mental-self emerges and *differentiates* from the body (with the help of language), it *transcends* the body and thus can *operate* upon it using its own mental structures as tools (it can delay the body's immediate discharges and postpone its instinctual gratifications using verbal insertions). At the same time, this allows a sublimation of the body's emotional-sexual energies into more subtle, complex, and evolved activities.

Thus, a fairly coherent mental-ego eventually emerges (usually between ages four and seven), differentiates itself from the body (after the Oedipal stage), transcends the simple biological world, and therefore can to a certain degree operate on the biological world (and the earlier physical world), using the tools of representational thinking. This whole trend is consolidated with the emergence (around age seven) of what Piaget calls "concrete operational thinking"—thinking that can *operate* on the concrete world and the body using concepts.

By the time of adolescence, another extraordinary differentiation begins to occur. In essence, the self simply starts to differentiate *from* the concrete thought process. And because the self starts to differentiate itself from the concrete thought process, it can to a certain degree *transcend* that thought process and therefore *operate* upon it. It is thus not surprising that Piaget calls this—his highest stage—"formal operational," because one can operate on one's own thought (i.e., work with linguistic objects as well as physical ones), a detailed operation which, among other things, results in the sixteen binary propositions of formal logic. But the only point I wish to emphasize here is that this can occur because consciousness differentiates itself from concrete thought, thus transcends it, and hence can operate upon it—something it could not do when it *was* it. (Actually, this process is just beginning at this stage—it intensifies at the higher stages—but the overall point seems fairly clear: Consciousness is *starting* to transcend the verbal ego-mind.)

This overall verbal ego-mind is known in Mahayana Buddhism as the *manovijnana* (*mano* means "mind"; same root), in Hinduism as the *manomayakosha,* in Hinayana Buddhism as the fourth and fifth *skandhas* (words and thoughts); it is also the fourth and fifth *chakras,* the latter, the *visuddha-chakra,* being the lower of verbal-rational mind. It is basically Freud's mature ego and secondary process, Arieti's language and conceptual levels, Loevinger's conscientious and individualistic stages, Sullivan's syntaxic mode, Maslow's belongingness and self-esteem needs, and so on. These are all very general but adequate correlations. (For a more precise alignment, see chapter 9.)

Now as consciousness begins to transcend the verbal ego-mind, it can integrate the ego-mind with all the lower levels. That is, because consciousness is no longer identified with any of these elements to the exclusion of any others, all of them can be integrated: the body and mind can be brought into a higher-order holistic integration. This stage has been referred to as the "integration of all lower levels" (Sullivan, Grant, and Grant), "integrated" (Loevinger), "self-actualized" (Maslow), "autonomous" (Fromm, Riesman). My favorite descriptive phrase comes from Loevinger's statement of Broughton's work: his highest stage, stage 6, is one wherein "mind and body are both experiences of an integrated self."[78] This integrated self, wherein mind and body are harmoniously one, we call the "centaur." The centaur: the great mythological being with animal body and human mind existing in a state of at-one-ment.

As I mentioned, both Eastern and Western psychology are in general agreement as to the nature of these lower levels, from pleroma to body to ego-mind to centaur. But the West has contributed a rather exact understanding of a phenomenon that is only vaguely understood in the East: namely, the process of dynamic repression. For what Western psychology discovered is that as higher-order levels of consciousness *emerge* in development, they can *repress* the lower levels, with results that range from mild to catastrophic.

In order to take into account this process of dynamic repression, we simply use the Jungian terms "shadow" and "persona." The shadow is the personal unconscious, a series of "feeling-toned complexes." These complexes are images and concepts which become "contaminated" by the lower levels—in particular, the emotional-sexual (typhonic)—and thus are felt, for various reasons, to be threatening to the higher-order structure of the ego-mind. These complexes are thus split off from consciousness (they become shadow), a process which simultaneously distorts the self-concept (the ego), and thus leaves the individual with a false or inaccurate self-image (the persona). If the persona and shadow can be reunited, then the higher-order integration of the total ego can be established. That, in very general terms, is the major aim of most orthodox Western psychotherapy.

So far, then, we have these major levels of increasing integration and transcendence: the simple and primitive fusion-unity of the pleroma; the next higher-order unity of the biological body-self; then the mental-persona, which, if integrated with the shadow, yields the higher-order unity of the total ego; and finally the centaur, which is a higher-order integration of the total ego with all preceding and lower levels—body, persona, and shadow.

THE HIGHER REALMS

With the exception of transpersonal psychology, the centaur level is about the highest level of consciousness taken seriously by Western psychology. The existence of levels above or higher than the centaur is thus viewed by Western psychology with a somewhat jaundiced eye. Western psychologists and psychiatrists either deny the existence of any sort of higher-order unities, or—should they actually confront what seems to be a higher-order level—simply try to pathologize its existence, to explain it by diagnosis. Thus, for indications as to the nature of any higher levels of consciousness, beyond the ego and centaur, we have to turn to the great mystic-sages and perennial philosophers, East and West. It is somewhat surprising, but very significant, that most of these sources agree almost unanimously on the nature of the "farther reaches of human nature" (hence, indeed, the title *"perennial* philosophy"). There are in fact, these traditions tell us, higher levels of consciousness—as far above the ego-mind as the ego-mind is above the typhon. And they look like this:

Beginning with (to use the terms of yogic *chakra* psychology) the sixth *chakra,* the *ajna chakra,* consciousness *starts* to go transpersonal or genuinely transcendental. It begins to enter what is called the "subtle sphere." This process quickens and intensifies as it reaches the highest *chakra*—the *sahasrara*—and then goes supramental as it enters the seven (some say ten) higher stages of consciousness within and beyond the *sahasrara.* The *ajna,* the *sahasrara,* and the seven or so sublevels are, on the whole, referred to as the subtle realm (although the exact wording is a matter of semantic choice).

For convenience sake, we speak of the "low-subtle" (or "psychic") and the "high-subtle." The low-subtle is epitomized by the *ajna chakra,* the "third eye," which is said to include and dominate psychic events and certain lower forms of mysticlike experiences. Patanjali has an entire chapter of his Yoga Sutras devoted to this plane and its structures (called *siddhis*). According to some texts, this level can tend to display actual paranormal events but does not *have* to do so; it is *defined* simply by its intensification of consciousness and the beginning of the opening of the eye of contemplation. We call it "psychic" simply as a reminder that even if paranormal events might more easily occur here, they are said to reach *no higher* than this, the lowest of the transcendental realms.

The high-subtle begins at the *sahasrara* and extends within and beyond to various subphases of extraordinarily high-order transcendence, differentiation, and integration. I am not going to present an exhaustive breakdown of this realm and its various (seven to ten) subphases. Besides, the *surface structures* of this realm are naturally different from culture to culture and tradition to tradition. The *deep structure* of this overall realm, however, is simply that of *archetypal form;* it is marked by transmental *illumination, intuition,* and beginning *gnosis,* which brings a profound insight into the fundamental or Archetypal Forms of being and existence itself. It is not *Formless,* however, or radically transcendent, but rather expresses insight into the subtlest forms of mind, being, deity, and manifestation.

In Theravadin Buddhism, this is the realm of the four *"jhanas* with form," or the four stages of concentrative meditation into archetypal "planes of illumination" or "Brahma realms." In *vipassana* or insight meditation, this is the stage-realm of initial or pseudonirvana, the realm of illumination and rapture and initial transcendental insight. This is the realm of *nada* and *shabd* yoga, of high religious intuition and literal inspiration; of *bija-mantra*; of symbolic visions; of blue, gold, and white light; of audible illuminations and brightness upon brightness; it is the realm of angelic forms, *ishtadevas,* and *dhyani*-buddhas, all of which—as we will soon explain—are simply high archetypal forms of one's own being (although they initially and necessarily appear "other"). It is the realm of *Sar* and *Sat Shabd,* of Brahma the Controller, of platonic Forms and Demiurgos. Dante sang of it thus:

> Fixing my gaze upon the Eternal Light
> I saw within its depths,
>> Bound up with love together in one volume,
>> The scattered leaves of all the universe. . . .
> Within the luminous profound subsistence
>> Of that Exalted Light saw I three circles
>> Of three colors yet of one dimension
> And by the second seemed the first reflected
>> As rainbow is by rainbow, and the third
>> Seemed fire that equally from both is breathed.

Keep in mind that this is what Dante *saw,* literally, with his eye of contemplation. He is not simply waxing poetic, but using mandalic poetry to sing of what he saw.

The psychiatrist Dean, pioneer in the new field of metapsychiatry, reports this:

> An intellectual illumination occurs that is quite impossible to describe. In an intuitive flash, one has an awareness of the meaning

and drift of the universe, an identification and merging with creation, infinity and immortality, a depth beyond depth of revealed meaning—in short, a conception of an over-self, so omnipotent . . .[33]

In Hinduism, this general realm is called the *vijnanamayakosha*; in Mahayana Buddhism, this is the *manas*; in Kabbalah, it is *Gevurah* and *Hesed*. Aspects of this subtle realm have been called the "over-self" or "over-mind"—as in Aurobindo and Emerson. The point is simply that consciousness, in a rapid ascent, is differentiating itself entirely from the ordinary mind and self, and thus can be called an "over-self" or "over-mind"—almost like calling the ego an "over-body" or "over-instincts," since the mental-ego transcends and reaches over the simple feelings and perceptions of the typhon. The over-mind simply embodies a transcendence of all lower mental forms, and discloses, at its summit, an intuition of That which is above and prior to mind, self, body, and world—something which, as Aquinas would have said, all men and women would call God.

But this is not God as an ontological other, set apart from the cosmos, from humans, and from creation at large. Rather, it is God as an archetypal summit of one's own Consciousness. John Blofeld quotes Edward Conze on the Vajrayana Buddhist viewpoint: " 'It is the emptiness of everything which allows the identification to take place—the emptiness [which means "transcendental openness" or "nonobstruction"] which is in us coming together with the emptiness which is the deity. By visualizing that identification 'we actually do become the deity. The subject is identified with the object of faith. The worship, the worshipper, and the worshipped, those three are not separate.' "[16] At its peak, the soul becomes one, literally one, with the deity-form, with the *dhyani*-buddha, with (choose whatever term one prefers) God. One dissolves into Deity, *as* Deity—that Deity which, from the beginning, has been one's own Self or highest Archetype. In this way only could St. Clement say that he who knows himself knows God. We could now say, he who knows his over-self knows God. They are one and the same.

Now all of this might sound rather "far out," of course, to the skeptical scientist, the empiricist, the rationalist. But I would like you to simply consider the implications of the *possible existence* of the subtle realm. What *if* the mystic-sages are right?

The whole point would be that in the subtle realm—and especially the high-subtle—a very high-order differentiation and transcendence is occurring. Mediated through high-archetypal *cognitive forms*—those that lie immediately beyond formal-operational in the developmental sequence—consciousness is following a path of transformation-upward which leads beyond the gross body-mind and merely rational ego. This transformation-upward, like *all* the others we have studied, involves the *emergence* of a higher-order deep structure, followed by the shifting of *identity* to that higher-order structure, and the differentiation or *dis-identification* with the lower structures (in this case, the ego-mind and centaur). This amounts to a *transcendence* of the lower-order structures, which thus enables consciousness to *operate* on and *integrate* all of the lower-order structures, an integration that, at this high level, simply leads to various forms of *samadhi* or mystical union or identity. Viewed thus, the "super-natural" is simply the next *natural* step in overall or higher development and evolution.

Lex Hixon has described one form of the subtle deep-structure called an *ishtadeva*. The *ishtadeva* is simply a high-archetypal form of cognition evoked in certain meditations on the path of form—a type of inner cognitive vision, directly perceived with the eye of contemplation. I realize that some people would say that the *ishtadeva* is "just a mental image" and doesn't *really* exist—but that is to simultaneously reduce *all* mental productions: might as well say that mathematics is just a mental production and therefore doesn't really exist. No, the *ishtadeva* is real—more than real—in its emergence and perception.

Hixon describes it thus: "The Form of Presence of the *ishtadeva* appears as vibrantly alive, composed from the radiance of Consciousness. We are not projecting the *ishtadeva*. The primal radiance which assumes the form of the *ishtadeva* is actually projecting us and all the phenomena that we call the universe."[61] This high archetypal cognitive form eventually mediates the ascension of consciousness to an *identity* with that Form: "Gradually we realise that the Divine Form or Presence is our own archetype, an image of our own essential nature."[61]

This, however, is not a *loss* of consciousness but an *intensification* of consciousness through a higher-order development, evolution, transcendence, and *identification:* "The *ishtadeva* does not disappear into us; we as individuals disappear into the *ishtadeva*, which now remains alone. Yet there is no loss of our individual being as we blend into the object of our contemplation, for it has been our own archetype from the beginning, the source of this fragmentary reflection we call our individual personality."[61]

The whole point is that the rational ego has not simply swallowed or introjected the high Archetypal Form, but that the prior *nature* of the ego is revealed to *be* that Form, so that consciousness reverts to, or remembers, its own prior and higher identity: "We remain now as a transcendental center of consciousness expressed through the Form or Presence of the *ishtadeva*. We are now experiencing the life of the *ishtadeva* from within. We are consciously meeting and becoming [via higher identification] ourselves in our archetypal and eternal nature."[61]

Now that is, as I said, simply one particular description of development in the subtle realm, and thus its surface structures will naturally be different from other descriptions (and experiences) of the same realm (just as, for example, all mature egos have access to the same basic type of secondary process thinking but don't therefore think the same thoughts). But the realm itself, its actual *deep structures,* appear universally the same. State it in terms of saintly mystical insight or the *jhanas* of Form or *vipassana* pseudonirvana or absorption in the Zen *koan* or *nada-shabd* identity or simple transcendental illumination—the *essential* deep structure of the subtle realm everywhere announces itself: insight into, and absorption as, Archetypal Essence.

THE ULTIMATE REALMS

As the process of transcendence and integration continues, it discloses even higher-order unities, leading, consumately, to Unity itself.

Beyond the high-subtle lies the causal region, known variously as the *alaya-vijnana* (Yogacara Buddhism), the *anandamayakosha* (Hinduism), *pneuma* (Christian mysticism), *karana-sharira* (Vedanta),

Binah and *Hokhmah* (Kabbalah), *Dharmakaya* (Mahayana), and so on. Again, for convenience, we divide it into the low-causal and the high-causal.

The low-causal, which classically is revealed in a state of consciousness known as *savikalpa samadhi,* represents the pinnacle of God consciousness (or Archetypal-Formal absorption), the final and highest abode of Ishvara, the Creatrix of all realms. This represents the *culmination* of events which began in the high-subtle. In the high-subtle, recall, the self was dissolved or reabsorbed into Archetypal deity, *as* that deity—a deity which from the beginning has always been one's own Self and highest Archetype.

Now at the low-causal, that deity-Archetype itself condenses and dissolves into final-God, which is variously described as an extraordinarily subtle audible illumination or *bija-mantra* or point source from which the individual *ishtadeva, yidam,* or Archetype emerged in the first place. Final-God (by whatever name and under whatever surface structure appearance) is simply the ground or essence of all the archetypal, pseudonirvanic, and lesser-god manifestations which were evoked—and then identified with—in the subtle realms. In the low-causal, all of these Archetypal Forms and illuminations simply reduce to their Source in final-God, and thus, by the very same token and in the very same step, one's own self is here shown to *be* that final-God, and consciousness itself thus transforms upward into a higher-order identity with that Radiance. In Theravadin Buddhism, this is the culmination of the fourth *jhana* (the highest *jhana* of form) and the beginning of the fifth and sixth *jhanas* (the lowest *jhanas* without form); in *vipassana,* this is the great transition insight from the pseudonirvana of subtle-form to the cessation, nirvanic, or formless state of the high-causal; in Zen, this is the seventh of the ten "ox-herding" stages to enlightenment: the transition from formal consciousness to formless consciousness.

Beyond the low-causal, into the high-causal, all manifest forms are so radically transcended that they no longer need even appear or arise in Consciousness. This is total and utter transcendence and release into Formless Consciousness, Boundless Radiance. There is here no self, no God, no final-God, no subjects, and no thingness, apart from or other than Consciousness as Such.

Note the overall progression of the higher-unity structures: In the subtle realm, the self dissolves into archetypal deity (as *ishtadeva, yidam, dhyani*-buddha, audible-illuminations, etc.). In the low-causal, that Deity-Self in turn disappears into final-God, which is its Source and Essence. Here, in the high-causal, the final-God Self is reduced likewise to its own prior Ground: it dissolves into Formlessness, or Infinite and Unobstructed Consciousness. Each step is an increase in consciousness and an intensification of Awareness until all forms return to perfect and radical release in Formlessness.

John Blofeld describes beautifully one form of this general progression from the Vajrayana Buddhist view: "As the rite progresses, this deity [cf. *ishtadeva*] enters the adept's body and sits upon a solar-disc supported by a lunar-disc above a lotus in his heart [these are visualizations used to train concentration]; presently the adept shrinks in size until he and the deity are coextensive [the beginning of the subtle]; then, merging indistinguishably [becoming *one* with deity-form in the high-subtle], they are absorbed by the seed-syllable from which the deity originally sprang [the low-causal]; this syllable contracts to a single point [final-God]; the point vanishes and deity and adept in perfect union remain sunk in the *samadhi* of voidness [the high-causal]."[16]

We already heard Lex Hixon, representing the Hindu view, describe the progression into the subtle realm. But he naturally continues the account into the causal: After the *ishtadeva*-archetype has emerged and one has identified with it (in the high-subtle), then "that Archetype dissolves into its own essence, or ground [the causal]. . . . There is now perfect release into the radiance of formless Consciousness. There is no *ishtadeva*, no meditator, and no meditation, nor is there any awareness of an absence of these. There is only radiance."[61]

Precisely the same sequence is described by Zen texts on *koan* study. After the initial stages of concentrating on the *koan* (this is equivalent to visualizing the *ishtadeva* or *dhyani*-buddha), a point is reached where the individual dissolves into the *koan*—he becomes *one* with the *koan* in a superabundance of consciousness: not a loss of awareness but an extraordinary intensification of it. This is called "the man forgotten"—that is, the separate subject is forgotten in union with the *koan*, which now alone is. This is the subtle state. As this process intensifies, the *koan* itself is forgotten—that is, it dissolves itself into its own prior ground of Formlessness. This is called "the *dharma* (the *koan*) forgotten" or "both man and *dharma* forgotten"—and this is the high-causal of formless *samadhi*. This overall process is so consistently and similarly described by all the traditions which reach this high realm that we can now be quite certain of its general (deep structure) features. They are unmistakable.

Let us note that this state itself—the high-causal of "both man and *dharma* forgotten"—is known as *nirvikalpa samadhi* (Hinduism), *jnana samadhi* (Vedanta); it is the seventh *jhana* (Theravada); the stage of effortless insight and beginning *nirodh/nirvana (vipassana);* and it is the eighth of the ten ox-herding stages in Zen.

Passing through *nirvikalpa samadhi,* Consciousness totally awakens as its Original Condition and Suchness *(tathata),* which is, at the same time, the condition and suchness of all that is, gross, subtle, or causal. That which witnesses, and that which is witnessed, are only one and the same. The entire World Process then arises, moment to moment, as one's own Being, outside of which, and prior to which, nothing exists. That Being is totally beyond and prior to anything that arises, and yet no part of that Being is other to what arises.

And so: as the center of self was shown to be Archetype; and as the center of Archetype was shown to be final-God; and as the center of final-God was shown to be Formlessness—so the center of Formlessness is shown to be not other than the entire world of Form. "Form is not other than Emptiness, Emptiness is not other than Form," says the most famous Buddhist Sutra ("The Heart Sutra"). At that point, the extraordinary and the ordinary, the supernatural and the mundane, are precisely one and the same. This is the tenth Zen ox-herding picture, which reads: "The gate of his cottage is closed and even the wisest cannot find him. He goes his own way, making no attempt to follow the steps of earlier sages. Carrying a gourd, he strolls into the market; leaning on his staff, he returns home."

This is also *sahaja samadhi,* the *Turiya* state, the *Svabhavikakaya*— the ultimate Unity, wherein all things and events, while remaining perfectly separate and discrete, are only One. By the same token, this is the radically perfect integration of all prior levels—gross, subtle, and causal, which, now of themselves so, continue to arise moment to moment in an iridescent play of mutual interpenetration.

This is the final differentiation of Consciousness from all forms in Consciousness, whereupon Consciousness as Such is released in Perfect Transcendence, which is not a transcendence from the world but a final transcendence as the World. Consciousness henceforth *operates,* not on the world, but only as the entire World Process, integrating and interpenetrating all levels, realms, and planes, high or low, sacred or profane.

And this, finally, is the ultimate Unity toward which all evolution, human and cosmic, drives. And, it might be said, cosmic evolution—that holistic pattern—is completed in and as human evolution, which itself reaches ultimate unity consciousness and so completes that absolute gestalt toward which all manifestation moves.

4

Development, Meditation, and the Unconscious

THE FORM OF DEVELOPMENT

OVERALL, THE PROCESS of psychological development—which is the operation, in humans, of cosmic or universal evolution—proceeds in a most articulate fashion. As we saw in the last chapter, at each stage of development, a higher-order structure—more complex and therefore more unified—emerges through a differentiation of the preceding, lower-order level. This higher-order structure is introduced to consciousness, and eventually the self *identifies* with that emergent structure. For example, when the body emerged from its pleromatic fusion with the material world, consciousness became a body-self: identified with the body. The self was then no longer *bound* to the pleromatic fusion, but it *was* bound to the body. As language emerged in consciousness, the self began to shift from a solely biological body-self to a syntaxic ego—the self eventually identified itself with language and operated *as* a syntaxic self. It was then no longer bound exclusively to the body, but it *was* bound to the mental-ego. Likewise, in advanced evolution, the deity-Archetype emerges, is introduced to consciousness (in the sub-

tle), the self then identifies with and as that Archetype, and operates from that identification. The self is then no longer exclusively bound to the ego, but it *is* bound to its own Archetype, and so on.

The point is that as each higher-order structure emerges, the self eventually identifies with that structure—which is normal, natural, appropriate. As evolution proceeds, however, each level in turn is differentiated from the self, or "peeled off," so to speak. The self, that is, eventually *dis-identifies* with its present structure so as to *identify* with the next higher-order emergent structure. More precisely, we say that the self detaches itself from its *exclusive* identification with that lower structure. It doesn't throw that basic structure away, it simply no longer exclusively identifies with it. The point is that because the self is differentiated from the lower structure, it *transcends* that structure and can thus *operate* on that lower structure, using as tools the newly emergent structure.

Thus, when the body-self was differentiated from the material environment, it could operate on the environment using the tools of the body itself (such as the muscles). As the ego-mind was then differentiated from the body, it could operate on the body and world with *its* tools (concepts, syntax). As the subtle self was differentiated from the ego-mind, it could operate on the mind, body, and world using its structures (*siddhi,* intuition), and so on.

Thus, at each point in psychological growth, we find: (1) a higher-order structure emerges in consciousness; (2) the self identifies its being with that higher structure; (3) the next-higher-order structure eventually emerges; (4) the self dis-identifies with the lower structure and shifts its essential identity to the higher structure; (5) consciousness thereby transcends the lower structure; and (6) becomes capable of operating on that lower structure from the higher-order level; so that (7) all preceding levels can be integrated in consciousness. We noted that each successively higher-order structure is more complex, more organized, and more unified—and evolution continues until there is only Unity, ultimate in all directions, whereupon the force of evolution is exhausted, and there is perfect release in Radiance as the entire World Flux.

A few technical points: Using the terms of linguistics, we say that each level of consciousness consists of a *deep structure* and a *surface structure.* The deep structure is the *defining form* of a level, which embodies all of the potentials and limitations of that level. Surface structure is simply a *particular* manifestation of the deep structure. The surface structure is constrained by the form of the deep structure, but within that form it is free to select various contents. To use a simple example, take a ten-story building: each of the floors is a deep structure, whereas the various rooms and objects on each floor are surface structures. All body-selves are on the second floor; all verbal ego-minds are on the fifth floor; all subtle archetypes are on the eighth floor; the causal is on top and the building itself is Consciousness as Such. The point is that although all verbal egos are quite different, they are all on the fifth floor: they all share the same deep structure.

Now the movement of surface structures we call *translation*; the movement of deep structures we call *transformation*. Thus, if we move furniture around on the fourth floor, that is a translation; but if we move up to the seventh floor, that is a transformation. Thus, each transformation upward marks the emergence in consciousness of a new and higher level, with a new deep structure, within which new translations or surface structures can unfold and operate.

Every time a higher-order deep structure emerges, the lower-order structures are subsumed, enveloped, or comprehended by it. That is, at each point in evolution or development, what is the *whole* of one level becomes merely a *part* of the higher-order whole of the next level. We saw, for example, that the body is, during the earlier stages of growth, the *whole* of the self-sense—that is, the body-ego. As the mind emerges and develops, however, the sense of identity shifts to the mind, and the body becomes merely one aspect, one part of the total self. Similarly, as the subtle level emerges, the mind and body—which together had constituted the whole of the self-system—become merely aspects or parts of the new and more encompassing self.

In precisely the same way, we can say that at each point in evolution or development, a *mode* of self becomes merely a *component* of a higher-order self (e.g., the body was *the* mode of self before the mind emerged, whereupon it became merely a component of self). This can be put in several different ways, each of which tells us something important about development, evolution, and transcendence: (1) what is *identification* becomes *detachment*; (2) what is *con-*

text becomes *content* (that is, the context of cognition and experience of one level becomes simply a content of the cognition and experience of the next); (3) what is *ground* becomes *figure* (which releases higher-order ground); (4) what is *subjective* becomes *objective* (until both terms become meaningless); and (5) what is *condition* becomes *element* (e.g., the mind, which is the *a priori* condition of egoic experience, becomes merely an element of experience in the subtle).

Each of those points is, in effect, a definition of *transcendence*. Yet each is also a definition of a stage of *development*. It follows that the two are essentially identical, and that evolution, as has been said, is actually "self-realization through self-transcendence."

THE TYPES OF THE UNCONSCIOUS

Many accounts of "the unconscious" simply assume that it is there, either as process or as content, from the start, and then proceed to describe its layers, levels, grounds, modes, or contents. But I believe that approach must be supplemented by developmental or evolutionary concerns on the one hand, and dynamic factors on the other.

Let me give a few examples of the problem itself: Transactional Analysis speaks of unconscious (or preconscious) script programming, containing *verbal* commands such as "feel guilty" or "collect anxiety." The job of the script analyst is to discover these commands, make them explicit and conscious, and thus release the client from their compulsive power. For simplicity's sake, let's call this the "verbal-script unconscious."

Let us now note a rather simple point: A preverbal child cannot have a verbal-script unconscious. Rather, language itself will have to *emerge* developmentally, then be loaded with script commands which will then have to sink back below the ordinary threshold of consciousness—at which point, and not before, we may speak of the unconscious script. In the same way, a child in the prephallic stage cannot have a phallic fixation, the preegoic infant doesn't possess unconscious ego-character structure, and so on.

Clearly, what exists in "the" unconscious depends in large measure on developmental concerns—*all* of the unconscious, in all its forms, is not just given at the start. Yet, to continue the story, many writers seem to assume that there is a "transpersonal unconscious" that is present but repressed from the beginning, whereas—if it is like verbal programming, character structure, mental capacity, abstract thinking, and higher structures in general—it is not yet repressed because it has not yet developmentally had the chance to emerge. It is not yet repressed from awareness because it has not yet even tentatively emerged in awareness in the first place.

With this developmental and dynamic, as opposed to static and given, viewpoint in mind, I will now outline five basic types of unconscious processes. These are *types* of unconscious processes, not *levels* of the unconscious (although I will mention those as well). This outline is meant to be neither exhaustive nor definitive, but simply indicative of concerns I feel psychology in general, and contemplative psychology in particular, must address.

1. *The Ground-Unconscious.* By "ground" I intend an essentially neutral meaning; it is not to be confused with "Ground of Being" or "Open Ground" or "Primal Ground." Although in a certain sense it is "all-encompassing," it is basically a developmental concept. The fetus "possesses" the ground-unconscious; in essence, it is *all the deep structures existing as potentials ready to emerge at some future point.* All the deep structures given to a collective humanity—pertaining to every level of consciousness from the body to mind to soul to spirit, gross, subtle, and causal—are enfolded or enwrapped or undifferentiated in the ground-unconscious. All of those structures are unconscious, but they are *not* repressed because they have not yet entered consciousness. Development or evolution consists of a series of hierarchical transformations, unfoldings, or differentiations of the deep structures out of the ground-unconscious, starting with the lowest (matter and body) and ending with the highest (causal and ultimate). When—and if—*all* of the ground-unconscious has emerged, then there is *only* consciousness: all is conscious *as* the All. As Aristotle put it, when all potential has been actualized, the result is God.

Notice that the ground-unconscious is largely devoid of surface structures, for these are basically *learned* during the unfolding of deep structures. This is similar to Jung's idea of the archetypes as "forms devoid of content." As Jung put it, an archetype (deep structure) "is determined as to its content [surface structure] only when it becomes conscious and is therefore filled out with the material of conscious experience."[48] Everyone "inherits" the *same* basic deep structures; but everybody learns *individual* surface structures, which can be quite similar or quite dissimilar from those of other individuals and especially other cultures (but still within the constraints of the deep structures themselves). This is also very similar to Hartmann's conception of an "undifferentiated matrix" or "in-born apparatuses," a concept accepted by virtually all modern schools of psychoanalytic ego psychology. In the words of Blanck and Blanck, "As we presently know it, then, the undifferentiated matrix contains potential ego, id, drive, affect, psyche, soma, and still more to be discovered."[13] I would simply add that that "more to be discovered" includes all the higher levels we have discussed; and that the undifferentiated matrix contains basically only the *deep structures* of all these components and levels, for the surface structures are individually learned and culturally molded, and thus can vary from person to person. This sum of native deep structures, then, we call the ground-unconscious.

Now all of the following types of the unconscious can be defined in relation to the ground-unconscious. This gives us a concept of unconscious processes that is at once structural and dynamic, layered and developmental.

2. *The Archaic-Unconscious.* Freud's initial pioneering efforts in psychoanalysis led him to postulate two basically distinct psychic systems: the system-unconscious, as he called it, and the system-conscious. The unconscious was, he felt, *generated* by repression: certain impulses, because they were dynamically resisted by the system-conscious, were forcefully expelled from awareness. "The unconscious" and "the repressed" were basically the same.

Eventually, however, Freud came to speak, not so much of the system-conscious and the system-unconscious, but rather of the ego and the id, and these two formulations did not overlap very clearly. That is, the ego was *not* the same as the system-conscious, and the id was not the same as the system-unconscious. First of all, parts of the ego (the superego, the defenses, and the character-structure) were *unconscious*; and parts of the id were unconscious *but not repressed*. In his words, "We recognize that the *Ucs.* does not coincide with the repressed; it is still true that all that is repressed is *Ucs.*, but not all that is *Ucs.* is repressed."[44]

Not all that is unconscious is repressed because, as Freud came to see, some of the unconscious simply finds itself unconscious from the start—it is not first a personal experience which is then repressed, but something that, as it were, *begins* in the unconscious. Freud had once thought that the symbols in dreams and phantasies could be traced back to real life personal experiences, but he came to see that many of the symbols found in dreams and in phantasies could not possibly have been generated by personal experience. "Whence comes the necessity for these phantasies and the material for them?" we hear him ask. "There can be no doubt about the instinctual sources; but how is it to be explained that the same phantasies are always formed with the same content? I have an answer to this which I know will seem to you very daring. I believe that these *primal phantasies* . . . are a phylogenetic possession. In them the individual . . . stretches out . . . to the experiences of past ages."[47] This phylogenetic or "archaic heritage" included, besides instincts, "abbreviated repetitions of the evolution undergone by the whole human race through long-drawn-out periods and from pre-historic ages." Although Freud differed profoundly from Jung on the nature of this archaic heritage, he nevertheless stated that "I fully agree with Jung in recognizing the existence of this phylogenetic heritage."[48]

For Jung, of course, the "phylogenetic heritage" consisted of the instincts and the mental-forms or images associated with the instincts, which he eventually (and unfortunately) termed the *archetypes*. For Jung, instinct and archetype were intimately related—almost one. As Frey-Rohn explains it, "The connection between instinct and archetypal image appeared to [Jung] so close that he drew the conclusion that the two were coupled. . . . He saw the primordial image [the "archetype"] as the self-portrait of the instinct—in other words, the instinct's perception of itself."[48] As for these archaic-images themselves:

> Man inherits these images from his ancestral past, a past that includes all of his human ancestors as well as his prehuman or animal ancestors. These racial images are not inherited in the sense that a person consciously remembers or has images that his ancestors had. Rather they are predispositions or potentialities for experiencing

and responding to the world in the same ways that his ancestors did [they are, that is, archaic deep structures].[58]

Such is the archaic-unconscious, which is simply the most primitive and least developed structures of the ground-unconscious—the pleroma (physical matter), the uroboros (alimentary drives), the typhon (emotional-sexual energies), and various primitive mental-phantasmic forms. They are initially unconscious but unrepressed, and some tend to remain unconscious, never clearly unfolded in awareness. Self-reflexive awareness is out of the question with these structures, so they always retain a heavy mood of unconsciousness, *with* or *without* repression (which is a significant point). The "prevailing quality of the id," said Freud, "is that of being unconscious,"[46] and that is the *nature* of the id, not something *created* by repression.

Incidentally, I do not share Jung's enthusiasm over the archaic images; and I do not equate the archetypes, which are highly advanced structures lying in the high-subtle and low-causal, with the archaic-images, which are, as Jung himself said, instinctual or typhonic counterparts. I agree with most everything Jung says about the archaic images as archaic images, but I do not equate them with the archetypes per se. (See chapter 7.)

At any rate, following both Freud and Jung, we can say in general that the somatic side of the archaic-unconscious is the id (instinctual, limbic, typhonic, pranic); the psychic side is the phylogenetic phantasy heritage. On the whole, the archaic-unconscious is not the product of personal experience; it is initially unconscious but not repressed; it contains the earliest and most primitive structures to unfold from the ground-unconscious, and, even when unfolded, they tend toward subconsciousness. They are largely preverbal and most are subhuman.

3. *The Submergent-Unconscious.* Once a deep structure has emerged from the ground-unconscious and taken on various surface structures, those surface structures, for various reasons, can be returned to a state of unconsciousness. That is, once a structure has emerged, it can be submerged, and the total of such structures we call the submergent-unconscious. The submergent-unconscious is that which was once conscious, in the lifetime of the individual, but is now screened out of awareness.

Now the submergent-unconscious can include, in principle, every structure that has emerged, whether collective, personal, archaic, subtle, and so on. It can contain collective elements that have clearly and unequivocably emerged and then been suppressed, or it can contain personal elements molded and learned in this lifetime and then suppressed, or it can contain a mixture of both. Jung has written extensively on just that subject, and we needn't repeat him here. But we should notice that even Freud was aware of the difference between the archaic-unconscious id and the submergent-unconscious id, even if it is occasionally hard to perfectly differentiate them. "In the course of this slow development certain contents of the id were . . . taken into the ego; others of its contents remained in the id unchanged, as its scarcely accessible nucleus. During this development, however, the young and feeble ego put back into the unconscious state some of the material it had already taken in, dropped it, and behaved in the same way to some fresh impressions it might have taken in, so that these, having been rejected, could leave only a trace in the id. In consideration of its origin, we speak of this latter portion of the id as *the repressed* [in contrast to the first part which was simply unconscious from the start: the archaic-unconscious]."[46] There is the difference, or rather one of them, between the original archaic-unconscious and the repressed or submergent-unconscious. But, as Freud says: "It is of little importance that we are not always able to draw a sharp line between these two categories of contents in the id. They coincide approximately with the distinction between what was innately present originally [the archaic-unconscious] and what was acquired in the course of the ego's development [the submergent-unconscious]."[46] Notice that Freud arrives at these conclusions on the basis of developmental thinking: "in consideration of its *origin*. . . ."

The submergent-unconscious becomes unconscious for various reasons, and these reasons lie along a *continuum of inattention*. This continuum ranges from simple forgetting through selective forgetting to forceful/dynamic forgetting (the latter alone being repression proper). Of the *personal* submergent-unconscious, Jung states:

> The personal unconscious . . . includes all those psychic contents which have been forgotten during the course of the individual's

life. Traces of them are still preserved in the unconscious, even if all conscious memory of them has been lost. In addition, it contains all subliminal impressions or perceptions which have too little energy to reach consciousness. To these we must add unconscious combinations of ideas that are still too feeble and too indistinct to cross over the threshold. Finally, the personal unconscious contains all psychic contents that are incompatible with the conscious attitude.[68]

Simple forgetting and lack of threshold response constitute the *subliminal submergent-unconscious.* Dynamic or forceful forgetting, however, is repression proper, Freud's great discovery. The *repressed submergent-unconscious* is that aspect of the ground-unconscious which, upon emerging and picking up surface structures, is then forcefully repressed or returned to unconsciousness due to an incompatibility with conscious structures (for which, see the next section).

The personal aspect of the repressed submergent-unconscious is the *shadow.* Once rendered unconscious, the shadow can be strongly influenced by the archaic-unconscious (following primary process laws and the pleasure principle, which dominate the typhonic realms), although this is definitely a relative affair. I agree with Jung, for instance, that the shadow *can* be verbal and highly structured (similar in structure and content to the ego/persona). Actually, there seems to be a continuum of unconscious structure, ranging from the highly structured verbal components of the unconscious (e.g., scripts) all the way down to the primal chaos of the unstructured or barely structured *materia prima,* the pleromatic fusion base of the archaic-unconscious. Needless to say, one of the major reasons for repressing the shadow is that it becomes a vehicle for the archaic-unconscious: loaded with instinctual impulses which are felt to be incompatible with the ego.

4. *The Embedded-Unconscious.* We come now to that aspect of the unconscious which most puzzled Freud, but which is nonetheless one of his greatest discoveries. Recall that Freud abandoned the conscious-unconscious model in favor of the ego-id model because "we recognize that the *Ucs.* does not coincide with the repressed; it is still true that all that is repressed is *Ucs.,* but not all that is *Ucs.* is

repressed." Besides the archaic-unconscious, which was unconscious but unrepressed, Freud found that "it is certain that much of the ego is itself unconscious." At the same time, he began to locate the *origin* of repression in the ego, because "we can say that the patient's resistance arises from his ego. . . ."[43]

The point was this: Repression *originates* in some part of the ego; it is some aspect of the ego that represses the shadow-id. But Freud then discovered that part of the ego was itself unconscious, *yet it was not repressed*. He simply put two and two together and concluded that the *unrepressed* part of the ego was the *repressing* part. This part he called the superego: it was unconscious, unrepressed, but repressing. "We may say that repression is the work of this superego and that it is carried out either by itself or by the ego in obedience to its orders . . . portions of the both of them, the ego and the superego themselves, are unconscious."[45] But *not* repressed.

Before we try to make sense of this unrepressed but repressing structure, I must briefly recap my general theory of repression, a theory based on the works of Piaget, Freud, Sullivan, Jung, and Loevinger. In essence, we have this: The process of *translation,* by its very nature, tends to screen out all perceptions and experiences which do not conform to the basic limiting principles of the translation itself. This is normal, necessary, and healthy, and forms the basis of "necessary and normal defense mechanisms"—it prevents the self-system from being overwhelmed by its surroundings, internal or external. This is normal "inattention," and—in contrast to a plethora of theories which maintain that such "filtering" is reality corrupting—it is absolutely essential for normal equilibration.

Should, however, binds arise in the translation process of any level, then the individual mistranslates his self and his world (which means that he distorts or deletes, displaces or condenses, aspects of the deep structure that could just as well exist correctly as surface structures). This can occur in any number of ways, and for any number of reasons—and it can be expressed in terms of "energy thresholds" or "informational distortions." The essential point is that the individual is now selectively inattentive or forcefully restrictive of his awareness. He no longer simply translates his self and world (via "normal inattention"), he translates *out,* or edits, any aspects of his self and world which are threatening (via forced and *selective* inattention). This mistranslation results in both a *symptom* and a *symbol,* and the job of the therapist is to help the individual retranslate ("the interpretation") his symbolic symptoms back into their original forms by suggesting *meanings* for the symbol-symptoms. ("Your feelings of anxiety are really feelings of masked rage.") Repression is simply a form of mistranslation, but a mistranslation that is not just a mistake but an *intentional* (even if unconscious) editing, a dynamic repression with vested interests. The individual does not just forget: he doesn't want to remember.

We saw that at each level of development, the self-sense identifies with the newly emergent structures of that level. When the body emerged from the pleroma, the self identified with it; when the verbal-mind emerged, the self identified with it; and so on. Further, it is the nature of an exclusive identification that one does not and cannot realize that identification without *breaking* that identification. In other words, all exclusive identification is unconscious identification—by definition and fact. At the moment the child realizes that he *has* a body, he no longer is *just* the body: he is aware of it; he transcends it; he is looking at with his mind and therefore he cannot be *just* a body any longer. Likewise, at the point the adult realizes he has a mind, he is no longer just a mind—he is actually starting to perceive it from the subtle regions beyond mind. Prior to those points, the self was more or less exclusively identified with those structures and therefore *could not realize it.* The self could not see those structures because the self *was* those structures.

In other words, at each level of development, one cannot totally see the seer. No observing structure can observe itself observing. One uses the structures of that level as something with which to perceive and translate the world—but one cannot perceive and translate those structures *themselves,* not totally. That can occur only from a higher level. The point is that each translation process sees but is not seen; it translates but is not itself translated; *and it can repress but is not itself repressed.*

The Freudian superego, with the defenses and the character-structure, is those aspects of the ego level with which the self is unconsciously *identified,* so much so that they cannot be *objectively* perceived (as can the rest of the ego). They translate without being translated—they are repressing but unrepressed. This fits very well with Freud's own thoughts on the matter, because he himself felt that (1) the superego is created by an *identification* ("identifications replace object-choices"), and (2) one of the aims of therapy is to make the superego conscious—to see it as an object and thus cease using it as something through which to see and (mis) translate the world. This is simply one instance of the overall evolution process we earlier described, where—once one has identified with a newly emergent structure, which is necessary and desirable—one *then* becomes free of that structure by dis-identifying with it, later to integrate it in a higher-order unity. I should quickly mention that, according to Freud, the superego is frequently severe and "masochistic" because contaminated (regressively) by the archaic-unconscious.

Anyway, the superego is simply one instance of what we call the *embedded-unconscious:* because it is embedded *as* the self, the self cannot totally or accurately see it. It is unconscious, but *not* repressed. It is that aspect of the ground-unconscious which, upon emergence, emerges *as* the self-system and so remains essentially unconscious, possessing the power to send other elements to the repressed-submergent-unconscious. Again, it is unrepressed but repressing. This can and does occur at every level of consciousness, although the specifics naturally vary considerably, because the tools of resistance are simply the structures of the given level, and each level has quite different structures (for example, when the body-ego *was* the embedded-unconscious, it used not repression but introjection and projection as the modes of mistranslation, because introjection and projection are part of the primary process structure which dominates the typhonic-body realms). However, this whole process assumes its most violent, pathological, and characteristic forms with the mental-egoic level(s). All stages of development possess their own embedded-unconscious, but those lower than the mental-egoic are not really strong enough to generate fierce repression (the archaic-id is originally unrepressed *and* unrepressing), and those higher than the mental-egoic become so transcendent and integrated that repression—as we ordinarily think of it—tends to fade out. The higher realms do possess their own forms of resistances, generated by their respective embedded-unconscious, but this is a matter for a separate study (see chapter 9).

5. *The Emergent-Unconscious.* Let us now examine someone who has evolved from the pleroma to the body-self to the ego-mind. There still remain in the ground-unconscious the deep structures of the subtle and causal realms. These structures have not yet emerged; they cannot, as a rule, emerge in consciousness until the lower structures have emerged and consolidated. At any rate, it is certainly ridiculous to speak of realizing the transpersonal until the personal has been formed. The transpersonal (the subtle and causal) realms are not yet repressed—they are *not* screened out of awareness, they are not filtered out—they simply have not yet had the opportunity to emerge. We do not say of a two-year-old child that he or she is resisting the learning of geometry, because the child's mind has not yet developed and unfolded to the degree that he or she could even begin to learn mathematics. Just as we do not accuse the child of repressing mathematics, we do not accuse him of repressing the transpersonal . . . not yet, that is.

At *any* point on the developmental cycle, those deep structures which have not yet emerged from the ground-unconscious are referred to as the *emergent-unconscious.* For someone at the ego (or centaur) level, the low-subtle, the high-subtle, the low-causal, and the high-causal are emergent-unconscious. They are unconscious, *but not repressed.*

Now supposing that development is not arrested at the ego-centaur realm—which is usually the case at this point in history—the subtle will of itself begin to emerge from the ground-unconscious. It is not really possible to set timetables for these higher realms and stages, because a collective humanity has only evolved to the ego level, and thus only levels leading up to that have been determined as to emergence. In general, however, the subtle *can* begin to emerge after adolescence, but rarely before. And for all sorts of reasons, the emergence of the subtle can be resisted and even, in a sense, repressed. For the ego is strong enough to repress not only the lower realms but also the higher realms—it can seal off the superconscious as well as the subconscious.

That part of the ground-unconscious whose emergence is resisted or repressed, we call, appropriately enough, the *emergent-repressed unconscious.* It is that part of the ground-unconscious which— *excluding developmental arrest*—remains unconscious *past* the point at which it could just as well become conscious. We are then justified in looking for reasons for this lack of emergence, and we find them in a whole set of defenses, actual defenses, against transcendence. They include rationalization ("Transcendence is impossible or pathological"); isolation or avoidance of relationship ("My consciousness is supposed to be skin-bounded!"); death terror ("I'm afraid to die to my ego; what would be left?"); desacralizing (Maslow's term for refusing to see transcendent values anywhere); substitution (a lower structure is substituted for the intuited higher structure, with the pretense that the lower *is* the higher); and contraction (into forms of lower knowledge or experience). Any or all of these defenses simply become part of the ego's translation processes, such that the ego merely continues to translate when it should in fact begin tranformation.

Because psychoanalysis and orthodox psychology have never truly understood the nature of the emergent-unconscious in its higher forms, then as soon as the subtle or causal begins to emerge in awareness—perhaps as a peak experience or as subtle lights and bliss—they are all in tithers to explain it as a breakthrough of some archaic material or some past repressed impulses. Since they do not know of the emergent-unconscious, they try to explain it in terms of the *submergent*-unconscious. They think the subtle, for example, is not a higher structure emerging but a lower one reemerging; not the transtemporal coming down but the pretemporal coming back up. And so they trace *samadhi* back to infantile breast-union; they reduce transpersonal unity to prepersonal fusion in the pleroma; God is reduced to a teething nipple and all congratulate themselves on explaining the Mystery. This whole enterprise is starting to fall apart, of its own weight, because of the ridiculous number of things psychoanalysis is forced to attribute to the infant's first four months of life in order to account for *everything* that subsequently emerges.

At any rate, with an understanding of these six types of the unconscious (the ground-unconscious, archaic-unconscious, submergent-unconscious, embedded-unconscious, emergent-unconscious, and emergent-repressed-unconscious), as well as of translation/transformation and the stages of development presented in the last chapter, we can now turn to a quick study of meditation and the unconscious.

MEDITATION AND THE UNCONSCIOUS

Most of the accounts of meditation and the unconscious suffer from a lack of concern with developmental or evolutionary factors. They tend simply to assume that the unconscious is *only* the submergent-unconscious (subliminal, filtered, screened, repressed, or automated), and thus they see meditation as a way to *reverse* a nasty state of affairs created in this lifetime: they see it as a way to force entry into the unconscious. Meditation is pictured as a way to lift the repression, halt the filtering, deautomate the automating or defocalize the focalizing. It is my own opinion that those issues, however significant, are the most secondary aspects of all types of meditation.

Meditation is, if anything, a sustained instrumental path of transcendence. And since—as we saw—transcendence and development are synonymous, it follows that meditation is simply *sustained development* or growth. It is not primarily a way to reverse things but a way to carry them on. It is the natural and orderly unfolding of successively higher-order unities, until there is only Unity, until all potential is actual, until all the ground-unconscious is unfolded as Consciousness.

Meditation thus occurs in the same way all the other growth/emergences did: one translation winds down and fails to exclusively dominate consciousness, and transformation to a higher-order translation occurs (a higher-order deep structure emerges, which then underlies and creates new surface structures). There is differentiation, dis-identification, transcendence, and integration. Meditation *is* evolution; it *is* transformation—there is nothing really special about it. It seems quite mysterious and convoluted to the ego because it is a development beyond the ego. Meditation is to the ego as the ego is to the typhon: developmentally more advanced. But the same process of *growth* and emergence runs through the whole sequence—the way we got *from* the typhon to the ego is the same way we go from the ego to Spirit. We grow, we don't dig back.

My first point is that most accounts of meditation assume that the transpersonal realms—the subtle and causal, by whatever names—are parts of the submergent-unconscious or repressed-submergent-unconscious, and that meditation means lifting the repression. And I am suggesting that the transpersonal realms are really part of the emergent-unconscious and meditation is just speeding up the emergence.

However—and this is what has so confused the picture—when a person (say, a young adult) begins meditation, all sorts of different things begin to happen, many of which are only incidentally and remotely related to the actual growth and transcendence process itself, and this greatly complicates the overall picture of meditation. With that problem in mind, I would first like to discuss the nature of the meditative stance itself, and then its general and complete course.

To begin with, we note that every *transformation* in development necessitates the surrendering of the particular present *translation* (or rather, the exclusiveness of that translation). For the average person, who has already evolved from the pleroma to the typhon to the ego, transformation into the subtle or causal realms demands that egoic-translation wind down and be surrendered. These egoic-translations are usually composed of verbal thoughts and concepts (and emotional reactions to those thoughts). Therefore meditation consists, *in the beginning,* of a way to *break conceptual translating* in order to open the way to subtle-level transformation.

In essence, this means *frustrate* the present translation and encourage the new transformation. As explained in *No Boundary,* this frustration/encouragement—on *any* level, typhon to ego to subtle to causal—is strategically brought about by *special conditions,* and these special conditions—again, on *any* level—simply embody a set of activities or functions characteristic of the next higher or sought-after level.[136] Psychoanalysis, for instance, speaks of the *selective frustrations* needed to help the infant move from a typhonic-impulsive body-self to a delayed and controlled mental-egoic self (the same type of selective frustrations the analyst must use in helping a neurotic *fixated* at infantile levels move to more channeled and mature responses); in this case: *"Put it into words, not impulses!"*

Just so, in moving *from* the ego-mind to the subtle or causal realms, selective frustrations *of* the ego-mind by the special conditions of meditative practice are necessary. In principle, this is no different than asking a child to put into words something he would rather act out typhonically. We are asking the ego to go one step further and put into subtle forms that which it would rather think about conceptually or verbally. Growth occurs by adopting higher translations until one can actually transform to that higher realm itself.

For example, the *yidam* or *ishtadeva:* individuals are shown a symbol of the *yidam*-deity, a symbol which, precisely because it embodies a higher state, corresponds to nothing in this present reality. They construct or translate this symbol into their own consciousness, to the point that the subtle-*yidam* actually emerges from the ground-unconscious into full awareness. Individuals eventually *identify* (as we explained with *all* development) with this higher structure, which breaks their lower translation as ego and raises them to a higher structure.

The Master (guru, roshi, etc.) simply continues to frustrate the old translations, to undermine the old resistances, and to encourage the new transformation by enforcing the special conditions (in this case, visualization of the *yidam*). This is true in *all* forms of meditation—concentrative or receptive, mantric or silent. In concentrative meditation, the special condition has a defined form; in receptive meditation, it is "formless"—both are enforced special conditions, however, and the individual who drops his formless or defocal awareness is chastised just as severely as the one who drops his *koan*.

Since some of the major characteristics of the higher realms include trans-temporal timelessness, love, no avoidances or attachments, total acceptance, and subject-object unity, these are most often the *special conditions* of meditation—"Stay in the Now always"; "Recognize your avoidances of relationship"; "Be only Love in all conditions"; "Become one with your meditation and your world"; "Accept everything since everything is Brahman"; and so on. Our parents helped us move from the first floor of consciousness to the fifth floor by imposing the special conditions of language and egoic self-control. Just so, the Master helps us move from the fifth floor to the higher floors by imposing the special conditions of the higher upon us as practice.

It does not, in essence, matter whether the special conditions are a concentrative-absorptive or a receptive-defocal mode of meditation. The former breaks the lower and egoic translation by halting it, the latter by watching it. What they both have in common is what is essential and effective about both: jamming a translation by concentration or watching a translation by defocalizing can only be done from the next highest level. They both accomplish (eventually) the same goal, the breaking of a lower-order translation resulting in a higher-order transformation. Both are also intensely *active* processes. Even "passive receptivity" is, as Benoit said, activity on a higher plane. (This is not to say, however, that the receptive-defocal mode and the concentrative-absorptive mode are identical, or that they produce the same secondary results. This will become obvious when we outline the course of a typical meditation.)

Before discussing what transpires in meditation, however, it is important to realize that not all schools of meditation aim for the same general realm of consciousness. Rather, as we have already suggested in the previous chapters, the transpersonal and superconscious realms really break down into several different levels (low- and high-subtle, low- and high-causal, etc.). Very few religions are aware of all of these distinctions, and thus many have more or less "specialized" in one level or another. Hence, meditative practices themselves break down generally into three major classes (cf. Free John).

The first is the Nirmanakaya class, which deals with bodily or typhonic energies and their transmutation or transformation into the low-subtle region, culminating at the *sahasrara*. This includes *hatha* yoga, *kundalini* yoga, *kriya* yoga, and particularly all forms of tantric yoga. The goal of the Nirmanakaya class, as I mentioned, is the *sahasrara,* the crown *chakra,* and it is exemplified by Patanjali.

The second is the Sambhogakaya class, which deals with the high-subtle regions, and aims for the seven (to ten) subphases of subtle growth and audible illuminations secreted within and beyond the *sahasrara*. This includes Nada yoga and Shabd yoga, and is exemplified by Kirpal Singh.

The third is the Dharmakaya class, which deals with the causal regions. It operates through neither tantric energy manipulation (the first five or six *chakras*) nor subtle light and sound absorption (the seventh *chakra* and the higher subphase *chakras* beyond), but rather through inquiry into the causal field of consciousness itself, inquiry into the root of I-ness or the separate self-sense, even in and through the Transcendent Witness of the causal region, until all forms of subject-object dualism are uprooted. This class is exemplified by Sri Ramana Maharshi, Maha-Ati Vajrayana, Zen Buddhism, and Vedanta Hinduism. At the terminal point of each path, one *can* fall into the prior Suchness of all realms, the Svabhavikakaya, although this is both easier and more likely the higher the path one initially adopts.

Let us now assume that a young adult takes up the practice of Zen in either its concentrative-*koan* or receptive-*shikantaza* form. Both of these are Dharmakaya practices, and so we will expect to see, if carried through to completion, not only a higher-causal culmination, but all sorts of lower-level manifestations in the intermediate stages.

To start with, the meditation practice begins to break to the present egoic-translation by either halting it (*koan*) or watching it (*shikan*). Washburn has given an excellent account of some of the specifics of this process.[123] (His "reduction of intensity threshold" and "immobilization of psychic operations" are two ways of describing the winding down of a level's translations, which is prerequisite for both lower-level derepression and upward-transformation.) As the present egoic-translation begins to loosen, then the individual is first exposed to the *subliminal-submergent unconscious* (the nonrepressed-submergent-unconscious in general), which includes, among other things, the "innumerable unnoticed aspects of experiences, aspects tuned out due to habit, conditioning, or exigencies of the situation."[123] All sorts of odd memories float up, screen memories, insignificant memories, memories that are not repressed, merely forgotten or preconscious. Months can be spent "at the movies," watching the subliminal-submergent reemerge in awareness and dance before the inward eye.

As meditation progresses, however, the more resistant aspects of the egoic-translation are slowly undermined and dismantled in their exclusiveness. That is, the *embedded-unconscious* is jarred loose from its unconscious identification with the self and thus tends either to emerge as an actual object of awareness or to at least lose its hold on awareness. Washburn states that psychic immobilization (the halting of egoic-translation) "brings unconscious psychic operations into awareness by interfering with their normal functioning," so that "one can begin to look *at* it, rather than, as hitherto had been the case, merely looking *through* it."[123] I think that is an important point, but I would add that it applies basically to the embedded-unconscious (and parts of the repressed-submergent-unconscious); but we don't bring, for example, the emergent-unconscious into awareness by "interfering with it" but rather by allowing it to emerge in the first place, just as we don't bring mathematics into awareness by interfering with it but by first learning it.

At any rate, the embedded-unconscious, by being "interfered with," starts to shake loose its habitual hold. Now recall that the embedded-unconscious translations were the unrepressed but re-pressing aspects of the self-system of a given level. Naturally, then, as the repressor is relaxed, the repressed tends to emerge. That is to say, the *repressed-submergent-unconscious* now tends to float—or sometimes erupt—into awareness. The individual confronts his shadow (and, on occasion, primal or archaic phantasies from the archaic-unconscious). An individual can spend months or even years wrestling with his shadow, and this is where orthodox therapy can certainly complement meditation. (Incidentally, notice that what is released here is the repressed-submergent-unconscious, and not *nec-essarily* the subtle or causal emergent-unconscious, unless they are part of the emergent-repressed-unconscious screened out by the *same* defenses wielded against the shadow. This is indeed possible and even probable to a certain degree, but on the whole the defenses against the repressed shadow and those against an emergent God are of a different order, and up to this point in meditation, we are basically working with the former.)

Thus, what has happened, up to this stage in meditation, is that the individual—through the loosening of the egoic-translation and its embedded-unconscious—has "relived" his life up to that point. He has opened himself to all the traumas, the fixations, the com-plexes, the images, and the shadows of all the prior levels of con-sciousness which have so far emerged in his life—the material-pleromatic, the alimentary-uroboric, the typhonic emotional-sexual, the verbal, and the mental-egoic. All of that is up for review, in a sense, and especially up for review are the "sore spots"—the fixa-tions and repressions that occurred on the first five floors of his being. All of that occurring, and notice: *none* of it is yet of the *central* meditative state.

Incidentally, Washburn has suggested that only receptive medita-tion leads directly and immediately to the unconscious, whereas absorptive meditation "is so immersed in its object that all else, including messages from the unconscious, is unavailable to awareness; and for this reason confrontation with the unconscious can occur only after the object has been discarded, or after the practice has been concluded."[123] Again, I think that is quite true, but it applies to only some aspects of the developmental unconscious, particularly the archaic-, submergent-, and embedded-unconscious. While the concentrative practice is fully active, none of those aspects of the unconscious can "squeeze in." However, it does not apply to, for example, the subtle emergent-unconscious, because in the state of subtle absorption in the *yidam, mantram,* or *nada,* one *is* directly in touch with that previously unconscious state. Even if one doesn't cognize it as an object, which one doesn't, one is still intuitively alive to the subtle as the subtle. The concentrative path *disclosed* this subtle-realm aspect of the emergent-unconscious in a perfectly direct and immediate way, *during* the practice itself.

But while in the subtle, concentratively absorbed (*jhana*), it is true that no *other* objects tend to arise in awareness, and that would include, for example, the shadow. The subtle meditation does help to break the egoic-translation, however, so that when one ceases subtle absorption, one is indeed open to shadow-influx, just as Washburn describes. With receptive meditation, of course, one is open to whatever arises whenever it arises, and so one "sees" the shadow on the spot as it de-represses.

At any rate, as the subtle itself begins to emerge from the ground-unconscious, various high-archetypal illuminations and intuitions occur. I described the subtle realm earlier, and so needn't repeat it here. The point is that subtler and subtler translations emerge, are eventually undermined, and transformation to new and subtler translations occurs. This is nothing more than *development* in the subtle realm.

> It is the strongest impulses that are affected first, and as they dim, the meditator begins to discern more subtle ones—just as the setting of the sun brings the stars into view. But these more subtle impulses themselves wane, which allows even more subtle ones to be discriminated. Interestingly, this is not an absolutely continuous process, for during sitting meditation there occur interludes or vir-

tual silence during which, it seems, one passes through some kind of psychic "membrane" that divides the present level from the next, subtler level. Once this divide has been passed, psychomental activity resumes . . . ; but its character is now much finer and more rarefied.[123]

The "membranes" are simply the translation processes of each level, which screen out the other levels and divide the present level from the rest; the "passing of this divide" is simply transformation to a higher, subtler, and "more rarefied" translation. "The new threshold [the new translation] that is established in this way can itself be reduced [transformed] by continued meditation, and this one too, and so on. In each case a new spectrum of lower-intensity, subtler objects becomes accessible to the meditator's inner sight."[123]

Although these subtle sounds and illuminations are the goal of the Sambhogakayas, they are all viewed as *makyo* (or inferior productions) by the Dharmakayas. Thus, if meditation continues into the causal realm, all prior objects, subtle or gross, are reduced to gestures of Consciousness as Such, until even the transcendent witness or I-ness of the causal realm is broken in the Great Death of Emptiness, and the unparalleled but only Obvious state of *sahaj* is resurrected. This is called *anuttara samyak sambodhi*. It is without recourse. At this final transformation, there are no longer any exclusive translations occurring anywhere; the translator "died." The mirror and its reflections are the same.

And so proceeds meditation, which is simply higher development, which is simply higher evolution—a transformation from unity to unity until there is simple Unity, whereupon Brahman, in an unnoticed shock of recognition and final remembrance, grins silently to itself, closes its eyes, breathes deeply, and throws itself outward for the millionth time, losing itself in its manifestations for the sport and play of it all. Evolution then proceeds again, transformation by transformation, remembering more and more, unifying more and more, until every soul remembers Buddha, as Buddha, in Buddha—whereupon there is then no Buddha and no soul. And that is the final transformation. When Zen Master Fa-ch'ang was dying, a squirrel screeched on the roof. "It's just this," he said, "and nothing more."

5 _____

Physics, Mysticism, and the New Holographic Paradigm

I N THE PRECEDING CHAPTERS we have seen that there might indeed exist the possibility of a "new and higher" or comprehensive-integral paradigm, one that at least attempts to include monological sciences, dialogical sciences, mandalic sciences, and contemplative sciences. I have not really presented such a paradigm in anything resembling a fully completed version; I have simply suggested and outlined what some of its central features might be. But I hope I have done so with enough persuasion to suggest that such a paradigm is at least a genuine *possibility,* grounded in a spectrum of solid methodologies, and open at every point to consensual review. At the very least, we have seen the disastrous consequences of trying to base such a paradigm on only *one* of the various modes of knowing available to the soul.

In the past few years, however, one such paradigm—generally called the "holographic paradigm"—has received much enthusiastic and international attention. And yet, for all its good intentions, it is based almost solely on empirical physics and empirical brain physiology and, indeed, claims to ground mystical states themselves in empirical data. As Lawrence Beynam eulogized this new theory:

"We are currently undergoing a paradigm shift in science—perhaps the greatest shift of its kind to date. It is for the first time that we have stumbled upon a comprehensive model for mystical experiences, which has the additional advantage of deriving from the forefront of contemporary physics."[11]

While we all can certainly appreciate the fact that certain physicists are no longer *denying* the reality of mystical-transcendental states, we must nonetheless look with suspicion on this particular "new paradigm," simply because, in the final analysis, it seems shot through with profound category errors. In this chapter, then, we will look carefully and critically at each point of the holographic paradigm, pointing out exactly the problems involved. In the next chapter, I will present an interview (originally given for *ReVision Journal*) that simplifies and summarizes not only the critique of this chapter, but also the overall topics we have discussed thus far.

THE PERENNIAL PHILOSOPHY

In order to understand how the new holographic paradigm fits into the overall scheme of things, it is necessary to have an overall scheme of things to begin with. The perennial philosophy has always offered such a scheme, and for purposes of convenience, it is one I will use here.

In what follows, I will summarize the *philosophia perennis*—leaving, however, enough details to work with—and then apply this philosophy to an elucidation and critique of both the "holographic paradigm" and the "new physics," touching briefly on each of the key points involved.

The most striking feature of the perennial philosophy/psychology is that it presents being and consciousness as a hierarchy of dimensional levels, moving from the lowest, densest, and most fragmentary realms to the highest, subtlest, and most unitary ones. In Hinduism, for example, the lowest level is called the *annamayakosha,* which means the level made of food—that is, the physical body and the material cosmos. The next level is *pranamayakosha*—the sheath made of biological functions, life-breath, emotions, bioenergy, and so on. Both of these levels, in Mahayana Buddhism, are referred to as the five *vijnanas*—the realm of the five senses and their physical objects.

The next highest level, according to Hinduism, is the *manomaya-kosha,* "the sheath made of mind." In Buddhism, this is called the *manovijnana*—the mind that stays (myopically) close to the five senses. This is approximately the level we in the West would call intellect, mind, mental-ego, secondary process, operational thinking, and so on.

Beyond conventional mind, according to Hinduism, is the *vijna-namayakosha* (what Buddhists call *manas*). This is a very high form of mind, so high, in fact, that it is better to refer to it by a different name—the most common being "the subtle realm." The subtle is said to include archetypal processes, high-order insights and visions, ecstatic intuition, an extraordinary clarity of awareness, an open ground-consciousness that reaches far beyond the ordinary ego, mind, and body.

Beyond the subtle lies the causal realm (Hinduism: *anandamaya-kosha;* Buddhism: tainted *alayavijnana*). This is a realm of perfect transcendence, so perfect that it is said to reach beyond the conception, experience, and imagination of any ordinary individual. It is a realm of formless Radiance, of radical insight into all of manifestation, blissful release into infinity, the breaking of all boundaries, high or low, and of absolutely panoramic or perfectly mirrorlike wisdom and awareness.

Passing through the causal realm, consciousness reawakens to its absolute abode. This is Consciousness as Such, and not only is it the infinite limit of the spectrum of being, it is the nature, source, and suchness of each level of the spectrum. It is radically all-pervading, one without a second. At this point—but not before—all levels are seen to be perfect and equal manifestations of this ultimate Mystery. There are then no levels, no dimensions, no higher, no lower, no sacred, no profane, so matter-of-factly so that Zen describes it thus:

> As the wind sways the willows
> Velvet beads move in the air.
> As the rain falls on the pear blossoms
> White butterflies lilt in the sky.

The above summary would give us approximately six major levels—physical, biological, mental, subtle, causal, and ultimate (listed below). Now many traditions greatly subdivide and extend this model (the subtle, for instance, is said to consist of seven levels). But aside from that it is important to understand that *all* major perennial traditions agree with that general hierarchy, and most of them agree right down to details. Further, this hierarchy is not a nicety of philosophical side issues; for these traditions, it is the fundamental core of the perennial wisdom insofar as it can be stated in words. It is fair to say, then, that any account of the mystic's "world view" that leaves out this type of hierarchy is seriously inadequate.

According to the perennial traditions, each of these various levels has an appropriate field of study. The study of level-1 is basically that of physics and chemistry, the study of nonliving things. Level-2 is the realm of biology, the study of life processes. Level-3 is the level of both psychology (when awareness is "turned in") and philosophy (when it is "turned out"). Level-4, the subtle, is the realm of saintly religion; that is, religion which aims for visionary insight, halos of light and bliss, angelic or archetypal intuition, and so on. Level-5, the causal, is the realm of sagely religion, which aims not so much for higher experiences as for the dissolution and transcendence of the experiencer. This sagely path involves the transcendence of all subject-object duality in formless consciousness. Level-6, the ultimate, awaits any who push through the final barriers of levels 4 and 5 so as to radically awaken as ultimate consciousness.

1. Physical—nonliving matter/energy
2. Biological—living, sentient matter/energy
3. Psychological—mind, ego, logic, thinking
4. Subtle—archetypal, transindividual, intuitive
5. Causal—formless radiance, perfect transcendence
6. Ultimate—consciousness as such, the source and nature of all other levels

Notice that these different disciplines, like the levels which they address, are hierarchic. That is, just as each level of the spectrum transcends but includes its predecessor, so each higher study envelops its junior disciplines—but not vice versa. Thus, for example, the study of biology uses physics, but the study of physics does not use biology.

That is another way of saying that the lower levels do not and cannot embrace the higher levels. The primary dictum of the perennial philosophy is that the higher cannot be explained by the lower or derived from the lower. (In fact, as we will see, the lower is created from the higher, a process called "involution.")

Even though the various dimensional-levels are hierarchic, this does not mean they are radically separate, discrete, and isolated from each other. They are indeed *different* levels, but different levels *of* Consciousness. Therefore, it is said that the various levels mutually interpenetrate one another. Here is an excellent description:

> These "worlds" [or dimensional-levels] are not separate regions, spatially divided from one another, so that it would be necessary to move in space in order to pass from one to another. The higher worlds completely interpenetrate the lower worlds, which are fashioned and sustained by their activities.
>
> What divides them is that each world has a more limited and controlled level of consciousness than the world above it. The lower consciousness is unable to experience the life of the higher worlds and is even unaware of their existence, although it is interpenetrated by them.
>
> But if the beings of a lower world can raise their consciousness to a higher level, then that higher world becomes manifest to them, and they can be said to have passed to a higher world, although they have not moved in space.[109]

The various levels, then, are mutually interpenetrating and interconnecting. *But not in an equivalent fashion.* The higher transcends but includes the lower—*not* vice versa. That is, all of the lower is "in" the higher, but not all the higher is in the lower. As a simple example, there is a sense in which all of the reptile is in man, but not all of the man is in the reptile; all of the mineral world is in a plant but not vice versa, and so on. "The more highly evolved," explains Wachsmuth, "always contains in itself the attributes of the earlier, yet always develops as a new entity, an activity clearly distinguishable from that of the other."[109]

Thus, when the mystic-sage speaks of this type of mutual interpenetration, he or she means a *multidimensional interpenetration with nonequivalence.*

The explanation, by the mystic-sages, of this multidimensional interpenetration forms some of the most profound and beautiful literature in the world.* The essence of this literature, although it seems almost blasphemy to try to reduce it to a few paragraphs, is that "in the beginning" there is only Consciousness as Such, timeless, spaceless, infinite, and eternal. For no reason that can be stated in words, a subtle ripple is generated in this infinite ocean. This ripple could not in itself detract from infinity, for the infinite can embrace any and all entities. But this subtle ripple, awakening to itself, *forgets* the infinite sea of which it is just a gesture. The ripple therefore feels set apart from infinity, isolated, separate.

This ripple, very rarefied, is the causal region (level–5), the very beginning, however slight, of the wave of selfhood. At this point, however, it is still very subtle, still "close" to the infinite, still blissful.

But somehow not really satisfied, not profoundly at peace. For in order to find that utter peace, the ripple would have to return to the ocean, dissolve back into radiant infinity, forget itself and remember the absolute. But to do so, the ripple would have to die—it would have to accept the death of its separate self-sense. And it is terrified of this.

Since all it wants is the infinite, but since it is terrified of accepting the necessary death, it goes about seeking infinity in ways that prevent it. Since the ripple *wants* release and is *afraid* of it at the same time, it arranges a *compromise* and a *substitute*. Instead of finding actual Godhead, the ripple pretends itself to be god, cosmocentric, heroic, all-sufficient, immortal. This is not only the beginning of narcissism and the battle of life against death, it is a *reduced* or *restricted* version of consciousness, because no longer is the ripple *one* with the ocean, it is trying itself to *be* the ocean.

Driven by this Atman-project—the attempt to get infinity in ways that prevent it and force substitute gratifications—the ripple creates ever tighter and ever more restricted modes of consciousness. Finding the causal less than perfect, it reduces consciousness to create the subtle (level–4). Eventually finding the subtle less than ideal,

*What follows is, approximately, a combination of the *Lankavatara Sutra, The Tibetan Book of the Dead,* and Western existentialism. For a more detailed account, see *The Atman Project.*[137]

it reduces consciousness once again to create the mental (3). Failing there, it reduces to the pranic, then material plane, where, finally, exhausting its attempt to be god, it falls into insentient slumber.

Yet behind this Atman-project, the ignorant drama of the separate self, there nonetheless lies Atman. All of the tragic drama of the self's desire and mortality was just the play of the Divine, a cosmic sport, a gesture of Self-forgetting so that the shock of Self-realization would be the more delightful. The ripple *did* forget the Self, to be sure—but it was a ripple *of* the Self, and remained so throughout the play.

Thus, this movement from the higher into the lower—which is involution—is at once an act of pure creation and effulgent radiance (on the part of Atman), and a tragic tale of suffering and epic unhappiness (on the part of the self-ripple attempting the Atman project). The ultimate aim of evolution—the movement from the lower to the higher—is to awaken *as* Atman, and thus retain the glory of the creation without being forced to act in the drama of self suffering.

During the course of our universe's history (and science helps us here), we have evolved from level–1 (which began approximately fifteen billion years ago with the Big Bang) to level–2 (which occurred several billions of years later when matter awakened into some realization of life) to level–3 (which so far has been reached fully by humans only). Evolution is, as it were, half completed. "Mankind," said Plotinus, "is poised midway between the gods and the beasts."

But in the past course of human history, some men and women, through the evolutionary discipline of higher religion, succeeded in pushing their own development and evolution into level–4: that of saintly religion and the first intuition of a transcendental reality, one in essence, lying above and beyond the ordinary mind, self, body, and world. This "beyond" was poetically called heaven; this oneness was called the one God. This intuition did not fully occur until around 3000 B.C., with the rise of the first great monotheistic religions. (Prior to that time, there were only polytheistic realizations—a god of fire, a god of water, etc. This was really sympathetic magic, stemming from a simple manipulation of level–2, emotional-sexual energies and rites.) By the time of 500 B.C., however, certain evolutionary souls pushed their development into the causal—Christ, Buddha, Krishna, the great axial sages. Their insights were drawn out and extended to produce what the Tibetans called the *Svabhavikakaya* path—the path of level–6, or already realized Truth, the path of Zen, Vajrayana, Vedanta. What remains is for the world to follow suit, via evolutionary or process meditation, into the higher realms themselves.

According to the perennial philosophy, not only does this whole process of involution and evolution play itself out over centuries, it repeats itself moment to moment, ceaselessly and instantaneously. In this moment and this moment and this, an individual starts out at infinity. But in this moment and this moment and this, he contracts away from infinity and ends up reduced to the level of his present adaptation. He *involves* to the highest point he has yet *evolved*—and all the higher realms are simply forgotten, rendered unconscious. This is why all meditation is called remembrance or recollection (Sanskrit *smriti,* Pali *sati,* as in *satipatthana,* Plato's *anamnesis,* Sufi *zikr*—all are precisely translated as "memory" or "remembrance").

This whole panoply of higher levels generating the lower moment to moment, and of the dazzling interpenetrating of each level with the others, and of the extraordinary dynamics between the levels, all occurring in a field of effulgent radiance—all this is meant when the mystic-sage speaks of multidimensional interpenetration with nonequivalence.

The fact that the mystic-sages speak so often of the difference between levels, and emphasizes those differences, does not mean they neglect the relationships between the elements on a *given* level. In fact, the mystics are precise in their understanding of the community of elements constituting each level. Since all of the elements are "made of" the same density of consciousness—since they are all *of* the same level—they are all perfectly interpenetrating and mutually interdependent, in an *equivalent* fashion. That is, no element of any *given* level is higher, or more real, or more fundamental than the others, simply because they are all made of the "same stuff" (which means, same density of consciousness).

Thus, on the physical plane, no elementary particle is "most fundamental" (they all seem to bootstrap). On the nutritional plane, no vitamin is ultimately more essential (take away any one and you're equally dead). In the moral sphere, no virtue is greater than another—they all seem to involve each other (as Socrates knew and as Maslow discovered for B-values). In the subtle, all archetypes are equivalent reflections of the Godhead, just as all *Sambhogakayas* are equivalent reflections of the *Dharmakaya*.

The point is that all the elements of a given level are roughly equivalent in status and mutually interpenetrating in fact. All in one and one in all—holographically, as it were. But, by virtue of hierarchy, any element from a senior level is higher in ontological status than any element of a junior dimension (e.g., the virtue of compassion is not equivalent with vitamin B_{12}). This mutual interconnectivity of the elements of any *single* level is *one-dimensional interpenetration with equivalence.* It is a type of *heterarchy* existing within each level of *hierarchy.* Heterarchy means that no element is superior to another; it means that there is an *equivalence* of all parties in a unitary pattern. "Holographic" is simply the strong version of heterarchy, where each part is so equivalent that they actually contain each other. For our simpler and general purposes, we will use "holography" and "heterarchy" interchangeably, since the important point is that both are non-hierarchical. Thus, the simplest way to summarize the mystic's world view would be:

1. Heterarchy within each level
2. Hierarchy between each level

With this background information, we come to the new paradigm.

PHYSICS AND MYSTICISM

One of the frequently mentioned doctrines of mysticism is that of "mutual interpenetration," as presented, for instance, in the Kegon school of Buddhism, Meher Baba's *Discourses,* the Five Ranks of Soto Zen, and so on. By "mutual interpenetration" the mystic means *both* forms of interpenetration discussed above: one-dimensional and multidimensional, heterarchic and hierarchic, horizontal and vertical.

Think of the six levels of consciousness as a six-story building:

the mystic means that all the elements on each floor harmoniously interact, *and* most importantly, each of the floors interacts with each other. As for this multileveled interaction, the mystic means that the physical elements interact with the biological elements which interact with the mental which interact with the subtle which interact with the causal which pass into infinity, each level superseding its predecessor but mutually interpenetrating with it. And thus, speaking of *all* these levels the mystic says, to use Meher Baba's words, "They all interpenetrate one another and exist together."

Now it happens that modern-day physicists, working with the lowest realm—that of material or nonsentient and nonliving processes—have discovered the *one-dimensional* interpenetration of the material plane: they have discovered that all hadrons, leptons, and so on are mutually interpenetrating and interdependent. As Capra explains it:

> Quantum theory forces us to see the universe not as a collection of physical objects, but rather as a complicated web of relations between the various parts of a unified whole. . . . All [physical] particles are dynamically composed of one another in a self-consistent way, and in that sense can be said to "contain" one another. In [this theory], the emphasis is on the interaction, or "interpenetration," of all particles.[30]

In short, speaking of these subatomic particles and waves and fields, the physicist says, "They all interpenetrate one another and exist together." Now a less than cautious person, seeing that the mystic and the physicist have used precisely the same words to talk about their realities, would thereby conclude that the realities must also be the same. And they are not.

The physicists, with their one-dimensional interpenetration, tell us that all sorts of atomic events are interwoven one with the other—which is itself a significant discovery. But they tell us, and can tell us, nothing whatsoever about the interaction of nonliving matter with the biological level, and of that level's interaction with the mental field—what relationship does ionic plasma have with, say, egoic goals and drives? And beyond that, what of the interaction of the mental field with the subtle, and of the subtle with the causal, and the reverse interaction and interpenetration all the way back down through the lower levels? What can the new physics tell us of that?

I suggest that the new physics has simply discovered the one-dimensional interpenetration of its own level (nonsentient mass/energy). While this is an important discovery, it cannot be equated with the extraordinary phenomenon of multidimensional interpenetration described by the mystics. We saw that Hinduism, as only one example, has an incredibly complex and profound theory of how the ultimate realm generates the causal, which in turn generates the subtle, which creates the mind, out of which comes the fleshy world and, at the very bottom, the physical plane. Physics has told us all sorts of significant things about that last level. Of its predecessors, it can say nothing (without turning itself into biology, psychology, or religion). To put it crudely, the study of physics is on the first floor, describing the interactions of its elements; the mystics are on the sixth floor describing the interaction of all six floors.

Thus, as a blanket conclusion, even as an approximation, the statement that "The world views of physics and mysticism are similar" is a wild overgeneralization and is based, as one physicist recently put it, "on the use of accidental similarities of language as if these were somehow evidence of deeply rooted connections."[10]

Further, physics and mysticism are not two different approaches to the same reality. They are different approaches to two quite different levels of reality, the latter of which transcends but includes the former. That is to say, physics and mysticism do not follow Bohr's complementarity principle. It is not generally understood that *complementarity*, as used in physics, means two *mutually exclusive* aspects of, or approaches to, one interaction. Physics and mysticism are not a complementarity because an individual can be, at the same time and in the same act, a physicist *and* a mystic. As we said, the latter transcends but includes the former, not excludes it. Physics and mysticism are no more two mutually exclusive approaches to one reality than are, say, botany and mathematics.

This whole notion of the complementarity of physics and mysticism comes from ignoring levels 2 through 5. It then appears that physics (level–1) and mysticism (level–6) are the only two major approaches to reality. From this truncated view of reality springs the supposed "complementarity" of physics and mysticism. This claim is not made for sociology and mysticism, nutrition and mysticism, or botany and mysticism; no more so physics and mysticism. They can all *complement* each other, it is true, but they are *not* a *complementarity* as defined by physics.

What *is* new about the new physics is not that it has anything to do with higher levels of reality. With a few minor exceptions (which we will soon discuss), it does not even attempt to explain or account for level–2 (let alone 3–6). Rather, in pushing to the extremes of the material dimensions, it has apparently discovered the basic holography of level–1, and that, indeed, is novel. There, at least, physics and mysticism agree.

Yet even here we must be careful. In the rush to marry physics and mysticism, using the shotgun of generalization, we tend to forget that quantum reality has almost no bearing whatsoever in the actual world of macroscopic processes. As physicist Walker puts it, in the ordinary world of "automobiles and basketballs, the quanta are inconsequential." This has long been clearly recognized by physicists. The quantum level is so submicroscopic that its interactions can for all practical purposes be ignored in the macro world. The intense interactions between subatomic mesons, which sound so mystical, are not observed at all between macro-objects, between rocks and people and trees. As Capra carefully explains it, "The basic oneness of the universe . . . becomes apparent *at the atomic level* and manifests itself more and more as one penetrates deeper . . . into the realm of *subatomic particles*" (italics mine).[30]

But it is precisely in the *ordinary* realm of rocks and trees that the mystic *sees* his mutual interpenetration of all matter. His basic oneness of the universe does not "start at the atomic level." When the mystic looks at a bird on wing over a cascading stream and says, "They are perfectly one," he does not mean that if we got a super microscope out and examined the situation we would see bird and stream exchanging mesons in a unitary fashion. His unitary vision is an immediate impact expressing his personal realization that "All this world in truth is Brahman."

That is to say, even the agreement between mystic and physicist on level–1 must be looked upon either as somewhat tenuous or as a fortunate coincidence. Ask almost any physicist if the connections between, say, a macroscopic tree and river are as intense and unitary as those between subatomic particles, and he will say no. The mystic will say yes.

That is a fundamental issue and shows, in fact, that the physicist and mystic aren't even talking about the same world. The physicist says: "The ordinary Newtonian world is, for all practical purposes, separate and discrete, but the subatomic world is a unified pattern." The mystic says, "The ordinary Newtonian world is, as I directly perceive it, one indivisible whole; as for the subatomic realm, I've never seen it."

The issue here is crucial, because, as Jeremy Bernstein, professor of physics at the Stevens Institute, explains, "If I were an Eastern mystic the last thing in the world that I would want would be a reconciliation with modern science."[10] His point is that it is the very *nature* of empiric-scientific discoveries that they ceaselessly change and alter, that last decade's scientific proof is this decade's fallacy, and that no major scientific fact can escape being profoundly altered by time and further experimentation. What *if* we said that Buddha's enlightenment just received corroboration from physics? What then happens when, a decade from now, new scientific facts replace the current ones (as they must)? Does Buddha then lose his enlightenment? We cannot have it both ways. If we hitch mysticism to physics now, mustn't we ditch it then? What does it mean to confuse temporal scientific facts with timeless contemplative realms? "To hitch a religious [transpersonal] philosophy to a contemporary science," says Dr. Bernstein, "is a sure route to its obsolescence."

THE IMPLICATE ORDER

The same types of difficulties surround the popular use of the concept, introduced by David Bohm, of an "implicate order" of matter. The public at large, and many psychologists in particular, look upon the implicate realm as if it transcended physical particles and reached somehow into a higher state of transcendental unity and wholeness. In fact, the implicate realm does not transcend matter—it "subscends" matter and expresses a coherence, unity, and wholeness of the entire physical plane, or level–1. It does indeed go beyond explicate matter, but in a subscending or underlying man-

ner, not a transcending one. As a matter of fact, the concept explicitly *excludes* any higher realms such as mind and consciousness.

This is made very clear by Bohm himself. First of all, Bohm is
clearly opposed to trying to introduce mind or consciousness into
the formalism of quantum mechanics (QM), as some physicists
would like to do. As he and Hiley put it in a recent paper, "We
show that the introduction of the conscious mind into physics . . . is
motivated by certain quite general considerations that have little to
do with quantum mechanics itself. This approach is contrasted with
our own investigations using the quantum potential. . . . Our aim is,
in fact, to *describe this order without bringing in the observer in any
fundamental role*" (italics mine).[18] The conclusion of Bohm's work is
that there seem to be certain quantum phenomena that "present us
with a new order or a new structure process, that does not fit into
the Newtonian scheme."[18]

This new order, in general terms, is the implicate (holographic or
holomovement) realm. Bohm's theory is that explicate matter rests
upon a sea of implicate physical energy of extraordinary magnitude
and potential, and that the equations of quantum mechanics "are
describing that [implicate order]."[17] In one sense, then, the implicate
realm goes way beyond explicate matter: "Matter is like a small
ripple on this tremendous ocean of energy. . . . This implicate order
implies a reality immensely beyond what we call matter. Matter
itself is merely a ripple in this background."[17]

But in the final analysis, this implicate sea, although "finer" than
explicate matter, is still of the realm of *physis* or nonliving mass/
energy in general. This is obvious because (1) Bohm has already
excluded higher realms such as mental consciousness, from quantum
mechanics, and (2) the equations of QM are said to "describe the
implicate order." The unfolding from the implicate realm is, he
says, "a direct idea as to what is meant by the mathematics of [quan-
tum mechanics]. What's called the unitary transformation or the
basic mathematical description of movement in quantum mechanics
is exactly what we are talking about."[17] Now QM equations do not
define biological life, or level–2; they do not describe mental life, or
level–3; they do not describe subtle or causal or absolute realms
either. They describe something going on in the realm of *physis* and

nowhere else. Besides, Bohm clearly states that "the implicate order is still matter."[17]

It is to Bohm's credit that, in his theoretical writings, he makes it very clear that he is not trying to introduce consciousness or mind into the QM formalism, or trying thereby to "prove" higher states of being with equations that are clearly descriptive not even of animal life (level–2) but rather of nonsentient processes. For it is certainly true that if the implicate realm rests on an interpretation of the facts generated by QM, then it just as certainly has no fundamental *identity* with any of the levels of 2 through 6. In short, the implicate order, as I would state it, *is the unitary deep structure (holography) of level–1,* which subscends or underlies the explicate surface structures of elementary particles and waves.

At the same time, Bohm himself is perfectly aware that the notion of a nonlocal implicate order of *physis* is still far from the only possible interpretation of QM, and far, in fact, from being the absolute case anyway: "At present," he says, "it is necessary to resist the temptation to conclude that everything [in the physical realm] is connected to everything else regardless of space and time separations. The evidence to date indicates that the nonlocal effects [what the public has come generally to call "holographic" or "implicate order" events] arise under very special conditions and any correlations that have been established tend to be broken up rather quickly so that our traditional approach of analysing systems into autonomous subsystems is, in general, quite valid."[18]

The important point is that the mystic's insight does not rest on what these physicists finally decide.*

---

*I am, in this chapter, leaving out the most radical and pervasive difference between mysticism and any sort of physical or holographic paradigm, because it is also the most obvious. Namely (1) the comprehension of holographic principles is an act of mind, whereas the comprehension of mystical truth is an act of transmental contemplation, and (2) if holographic theories are actually said to describe transcendent truths, or to be the same as actually transcending, a violent fallacy known as category error occurs. Some have even suggested that a simple learning of the holographic paradigm would be the same as actual transcendence, in which case these hypothetical theories are not just wrong, they are detrimental.

Mind and Quantum Mechanics

Unlike David Bohm, and unlike the great majority of physicists, there are a handful of avant-garde physicists who not only want to inject "mind" into the equations of QM, but insist on it as well. Wigner, Walker, Muses, and Sarfatti are producing elaborate mathematical explanations that purport to show the crucial role of consciousness in the formulations of QM. It is these types of formulations, above all else, that have brought the physicist wandering into the backyard of the mystic—or at least the parapsychologist.

The impetus for these formulations lies in what is called the "measurement problem," and the measurement problem is shorthand for some very sophisticated and elaborate mathematical equations and certain paradoxes they generate.

The problem itself concerns this type of dilemma: the mathematics of QM can determine, with great precision, the *probability* that a certain quantum event will occur in a certain environment (at a certain place or at a certain time), but it can never predict *the* precise environment itself. It can say, for instance, that the chance of finding a quantum particle in area A is 50 percent, in area B, 30 percent, and in area C, 20 percent. But it cannot, under any circumstances, say that a particular event *will* occur in area A (given the above probability distribution). Thus, the particular event is not looked upon as a single entity or occurrence, but rather as a "tendency to exist," which, in this example, would be *defined* by an equation (or probability amplitude) that says, in effect: 50 percent A/30 percent B/20 percent C.

Now the odd thing is that the event, when it occurs, *does* occur in just *one* area. It is almost (not quite) as if a statistician were trying to predict which of three doors you are likely to walk through, and, for various reasons, he winds up with the results: 50 percent chance of door A, 30 percent door B, 20 percent door C. He cannot predict exactly which door it will be, just the percentages. But when you finally walk through the door, you go through only *one*—50 percent of you doesn't go through door A, 30 percent through B and 20 percent through C.

But beyond that, the analogy breaks down. The statistician has reasons to believe that you exist before you walk through any of the doors—he can go look at you, for one. But the physicist has no such assurances about his quantum particles, because there is *no way* he can go look at the particle (for our less than accurate purposes, let's just say it's too small to see perfectly). The *only* way he can look at the particle is by using certain instruments—that is, by *measuring* it in some sense. But to measure the particle he has, as it were, to get it through the doors of his instruments. And there is the problem: to find out what's behind the door, the physicist has to use a door. In all cases, his phenomena can be detected only as they walk through various doors, and the equations describing these "walks" are purely probabilistic: say, 50/30/20.

The physicist therefore faces a conceptual problem: prior to measurement, *all* he can say about a quantum event is that it *is* (not has) a certain tendency to exist (e.g., 50/30/20). The event itself, if left alone (not measured) will "propagate through space-time" according to the Schroedinger wave function, which, if squared, gives the probability of finding the event in a certain environment (50/30/20). But prior to the actual measurement, there is *no way whatsoever* to know precisely in which region the particle will occur. Yet, when it is finally detected, it does occur in *one* region only (say *B*) and does not spread out through the three doors. This is called the collapse of the state vector or wavepacket, because when measurement determines that the particle is in *B,* the probability of its being in *A* or *C* collapses to zero. The collapse of the state vector means that the event *jumped* from being a "tendency to exist" (50*A*/30*B*/20*C*) to a "real occurrence (*B*)."

Hence the problems. Does measurement itself "cause" the collapse of the wavepacket? Does the actual particle even exist at all prior to measurement? If we say it does exist (which seems common sense), how can we know for sure, since there is *no* way to tell, and since our mathematical equations, which otherwise describe perfectly this realm, tell us only 50/30/20? If we deny the equations, how can we deny the fact that they otherwise work so well?

Aside from a large number of philosophers who maintain (not without certain justifications) that what collapses the wavepacket is not mind or matter but bad metaphysics, there are several different schools of thought on this "measurement problem," offered by the physicists themselves:

1. *The Copenhagen Interpretation.* The vast number of physicists follow this school, which maintains that the collapse of the wave-packet is at bottom purely random. There is no need for an explanation. Since there is no way to get behind the door, there is no behind the door.* QM is a complete explanation as it stands, and there is no need or possibility to "look behind the scenes" and try to figure out whether the event is there or not prior to measurement. In all fairness, it should be said that there are many good, if not absolute, reasons for adopting this view. It should also be said, as is often pointed out, that Einstein himself violently rejected this view (with the exclamation "God does not play dice with the universe!"), even though every objection he forwarded to this interpretation was brilliantly parried by Bohr and others, using Einstein's own theories. At the same time, I repeat that this (and the following) are species of extremely popularized explanations. But within that disclaimer, the Copenhagen Interpretation says that the probability 50/30/20 is all we can know and all there is to know; which door the particle goes through is purely random.

2. *The Hidden Variable Theories.* These theories maintain that there are indeed specifiable factors lying "behind the scenes" of the collapse of the wavepacket. These subquantal processes are described by presently hidden variables, but it is possible that they will eventually become technically accessible. In the crudest of terms, this theory says that quantum events are not purely random, and that the particle goes through a particular door for a "hidden" reason, a reason that the particle "knows" and that we should be able to find out. Bohm and his colleagues, working with the quantum potential (and implicate order), belong to this school. Bell's theorem, which has received much popular attention, is often used by some advocates of this school to point to the apparent nonlocal (not confined to a local region of space causality) "transfer" of information between widely isolated regions of space. Bell's theorem is generally taken to mean that, if QM is otherwise correct, and if there are some sort of hidden variables, then those hidden variables are nonlocal—a

*This is crudely stated, but it is also the basis of the charge of bad metaphysics.

type of "instant" causality not separated by time or space. Bohm and his colleages take this as an example of a possible implicate order; Sarfatti takes it as an example of faster-than-light "communication"; others (such as Einstein) take it as nonsense.

3. *The Many Worlds Hypothesis.* This is proposed by Everett, Wheeler, and Graham (EWG). According to the Copenhagen Interpretation (theory #1), when the $50A/30B/20C$ particle is measured and is found to occur in region *B,* then the other two possibilities (*A* and *C*) collapse—they simply do not occur (just as, for instance, if you toss a coin and it comes up heads, the possibility of it being tails collapses to zero). Now according to EWG, *all* of the mutually exclusive possibilities contained in the wave function *do* occur, but in different branches of the universe. At the moment the particle hits *B* in this universe, two other universes branch off, one of which contains the particle hitting *A,* and one of which contains the particle hitting *C.* Or, as soon as I catch "heads" in this universe, I *also* catch "tails" but in an entirely different universe. Neither "I" knows the other. This has been developed in a very sophisticated mathematical fashion.

It's easy, upon hearing that type of theory, to sympathize with François Mauriac: "What this professor says is far more incredible than what we poor Christians believe." But the real point is that it is already obvious that what is called the "new physics" is far from a consensus as to the nature of subatomic reality, a fact that will eventually lead us to certain suggestive conclusions. In the meantime, we move on to the fourth major theory generated by the "measurement problem."

4. *The Matter/Mind Connection.* This theory has many different forms, but in keeping with our popularized presentation, we can say that the theory in general suggests the following: If measurement itself collapses the wavepacket, then isn't measurement in some way *essential* to the manifestation of this material event? And *who* is doing the measurement? Obviously, a sentient being. Is not *mind,* then, an influence on—or even creator of—matter?

This general view, in one form or another, is held by Wigner, Sarfatti, Walker, and Muses. "In my opinion," says Sarfatti, "the quantum principle involes *mind* in an essential way . . . mind creates matter."[104] Walker equates the hidden variables, assuming they are there, with consciousness; Muses plugs consciousness into the quantum vacuum potential. But Beynam sums it all up as: "It is consciousness itself that collapses the state vector." It is this theory we want now to examine, because this is said to be *the* connection between physics and parapsychology/mysticism.

To begin with, is there anything in the perennial philosophy which would accord with the general statement, "Mind creates matter"? The first-approximation answer is definitely affirmative. Matter is held, by all traditional philosophies, to be a precipitate in the mental field. But they express it more precisely. It is not directly mind (level–3) which creates matter (level–1), but prana (level–2) which does so. Mind creates prana; prana creates matter.

Thus, the physicists would be more precise, according to tradition, if they said not "mind" but "prana," "bioenergy," or "biological sentience" was directly senior to matter. Von Weizsacker has already done so explicitly (using the word "prana"), and so have several others. This would not be a problem for these physicists, because the characteristics they already ascribe to "mind" as being necessary for the wavepacket collapse are actually characteristics of prana. That is, these physicists usually don't say "concepts," "ideas," or "logic" collapses the state vector. Rather, they use such terms as "biological systems" (Sarfatti), "sentient being" (Walker), "sensation" (Wigner), and these are distally characteristic of mind but proximally characteristic of prana (or any living system). Mind could also collapse the vector, but via prana. This would also fit Sarfatti's suggestions, because all biological systems would contribute to random quantal Brownian movement, but a disciplined mind (not present in animals) might *control* it.*

All of which sounds as if this version of QM is right in accord

---

*It should be said that, while I will end up disagreeing with this school of QM as to the nature of the *generation* of matter from mind, I do not rule out that they may have some important and brilliant things to say about the *influence* of mind on matter, *after the fact* of matter's generation from mind. This is a very dilute agreement, but an agreement nonetheless, and certain very select areas of parapsychology (not mysticism at large) might find resonance with these theorists.

with the mystic view, at least as far as levels 1 and 2 are concerned (i.e., level–2 creates level–1). Yet again we must be very precise here, because premature conclusions are much too easy to draw.

First of all, when the mystic says that matter is created by prana, he does not mean that prana itself must be present in a manifest fashion (and from this point on, for ease of recognition, I will use "mind" instead of "prana," remembering the important qualifications given above). That is, mind does *not* create matter by perceiving it, or sensing it, or "measuring" it—which is, as we saw, the form of the theory held by the QM physicists under discussion. Rather, matter simply precipitates out of mind whether mind is paying attention or not. In fact, during involution, mind generates matter and then "disappears" from the scene altogether. It doesn't stay around to watch matter and thereby generate it.

In this fashion, the traditional philosophy avoids entirely the otherwise ridiculous dilemma: if mind creates matter by perception or actual contact (as participator-observer), then what occurred, say, 10 billion years ago when there was only matter and no minds? Science is rather certain that biological life appeared only billions of years *after* matter. Prior to that time, there was no life, no mind. If mind has to measure or observe matter in order for the latter to exist (or have its wavepacket collapsed), we arrive at absurdity.

This view—that mind generates matter by the effect of the "participator-observer"—is like saying the chicken (mind) *sees* the egg (matter) and thereby creates it. No chicken to see the egg, no egg. The traditional view says that the chicken (mind) lays or gives birth to the egg (matter) and thereby creates it; what the chicken does after that is its own business—the egg continues to exist, perceived or not. In fact, during involution, the chicken is, well, buried. What it leaves behind is a reduced version of chicken-ness, a reduced version of mind called matter (the egg). But the egg-matter has enfolded in it the potential to actualize ("hatch") a new chicken, or mind itself, which is just what happens in evolution. But in no case does the chicken create the egg by watching it.

It is for similar reasons that most physicists themselves reject this version of the QM interpretation. As David Bohm himself explains: "The introduction of the conscious mind into physics by Wigner is motivated by certain quite general considerations that have little to do with quantum mechanics itself." And speaking of this tendency to hastily conclude that observation by mind is needed to produce matter (measurement), Bohm answers succinctly: "Indeed this is often carried to such an extreme that it appears as if nothing ever happens without the observer. However, we know of many physical processes, even at the level of quantum phenomena, that do occur without any direct intervention of the observer. Take for example the processes that go on in a distant star. These appear to follow the known laws of physics and the processes occur, and have occurred, without any significant intervention on our part."[18]

In short, the perennial philosophy would agree that matter is created out of mind (prana), but through an act of precipitation and crystallization, not perception and measurement. But QM can account, *if* at all, for *only* the latter theory, and therefore the agreement of QM and mysticism on this point is purely coincidental. Should, therefore, this particular interpretation of QM prove incorrect (and I agree with Bohm and others that it will), it would not affect one way or the other the world view of the mystic-sage.

But my point does not concern whether any of the above four QM interpretations is right or wrong. And there are even others we haven't really discussed at all—superluminal connections, simple statistical interpretations, quantum logic interpretations. These issues are extremely complex and difficult, and it will take decades to work out their implications. However, what we can do now is reach certain immediate conclusions:

1. The "new physics" is far from a grand consensus as to the nature of even subatomic reality. To hook transpersonal psychology/mysticism to the consensus of the new quantum physics is not possible, because there is no consensus. Those connections that have been drawn between physics and mysticism are of the pick and choose variety. The actual details of the various QM interpretations are, as we have seen, largely mutually exclusive. Simply to take a detail from one interpretation, then another, a little bootstrap here, a little implicate order there, is, in the words of physicist Bernstein, "a travesty and a disservice" to the theories involved.

2. Even if we could draw several tight parallels, to hook transpersonal psychology to physics is still "the surest route to oblivion." To

paraphrase Eckhart, if your god is the god of today's physics, then when that physics goes (tomorrow), that god goes with it.

3. The most important point is that no matter which version of QM theory is finally accepted, this will not profoundly affect the mystic's vision or world view. First of all, in no case could it *invalidate* the mystic world view. When Newton's "fractured world view" was "truth," this did not invalidate the mystic vision. If the Copenhagen Interpretation is the "truth," this will not invalidate the mystic vision. If *any* of the QM interpretations are true, this will not invalidate the mystic vision. And therefore, as any epistemologist will tell us, in no case could an interpretation *validate* the mystic world view. If there is no conceivable physical test that would disprove the mystic view, and there isn't, then there is no conceivable one which could corroborate it either.

4. It is sometimes said that the new physics at least *accords* with the mystic world view. I think we can easily agree that certain aspects of some interpretations of mathematical quantum formalisms, when placed into everyday English, sound similar to aspects of the mystic's view, not of the world (levels 1–6), but of level–1. The mystic's insight, however, does not find its validation nor explanation in that possible accord. But if this accord helps "legitimize" mysticism in the public's eye; if it at least does not cause its proponents to radically deny mystical states as hallucinatory; if it opens the way to a fuller acceptance of mystical experience—then, by all accounts, we will indeed have the new physics to thank.

Beyond that point, however, take Bernstein's warning with you: thank the new physics for agreeing with you, but resist the temptation to build your transpersonal models upon the shifting sands of changing level–1 theories.

THE HOLOGRAPHIC BRAIN

While the holographic/implicate theories of physics deal unequivocably with level–1, the theories of holographic brain processes deal, apparently, with level–3, or mind and memory. In tandem, then, these theories would cover, more or less, levels 1–3.

But beyond that, it is suggested by some that *if* the mind were holographic, then this could also account for higher, transpersonal experiences via the mind melting down into the holographic blur beyond explicit distinctions. This holographic blur is called a "frequency realm," where, supposedly, objects in space and time "do not exist." The holographic blur or frequency realm is described as: "No space, no time—just events (or frequencies)."

Let us pass by the difficulties of having *events* existing without *any sort* of space or time; let us also ignore the fact that physical objects (space-time *things*) are needed to produce holograms in the first place. Aside from that, how might this holographic-mind fit with the perennial philosophy?

To start with, it is fundamentally the storage of memory-information that is said to occur on the principles of optical holography. The mechanisms of holography are explained by mathematical transforms, one of whose intriguing properties is that—in mathematical terms anyway—space and time seem at one stage to be left out, and the desired temporal results are retrieved through a readout function of frequency information. This has led to the notion of a frequency realm—the notion that space/time objects come out of "no space, no time frequencies."

I have no doubt that that is basically true—that memory is holographically stored, just as is said. I also think that the research demonstrating this is brilliant. But beyond that, how this relates in any fashion to transcendent states is far from clear. To be sure, there are similarities of language—the holographic blur ("no space, no time") sounds like a mystical state. It also sounds like passing out. There is a world of difference between pretemporal consciousness, which has no space and no time, and transtemporal consciousness, which moves beyond space and time while still embracing it. "Eternity," after all, "is in love with the productions of time." This in no way proves that the holographic blur is not a transcendent state; it demonstrates that one cannot judge so on the basis of language correlations.

Nonetheless, it is said that a shift to a "perception of the holographic blur" would produce transcendent states. Since it is memory which is holographically stored,* what would it actually mean to

---

*The "perception" of the physical frequency realm is discussed later in conjunction with William Tiller's critique of the holographic paradigm.

shift to a perception of the storage bin of personal memory? Would this be nirvana, a direct consciousness which transcended but included all manifestation?

By the accounts of the theory itself, I do not see that it would or could result in anything but an experience of one's own memory storage bin, properly blurred and without benefit of linear read-out. How one could jump from a blur of one's own memory to a crystal consciousness that transcends mind, body, self, and world is not made clear at all. It is a wild theoretical leap to move from "personal memory is holographically stored" to "therefore all minds are part of a transpersonal hologram."

I think instead that we are allowing certain superficial similarities of language to rule the day of reason. The above is example enough, perhaps, but beyond that there exists the whole notion of a "transcendent frequency realm beyond space and time"—which is said to be the implicate holographic blur. This notion, it seems to me, gains credence only from the oddities of the mathematics involved, which translate "things" into "frequencies" and thus allow a slip of language to pass for transcendent truths. The "frequency realm" transforms are assumed to refer to experiential realities in a way that is not only unbelievable, but frankly self-contradictory.

The transform of "things" into "frequencies" is not a transform of space/time into "no space, no time," but a transform of space/time objects into space/time frequencies. Frequency does not mean "no space, no time"; it means cycles/second or space per time. To read the mathematics otherwise is more than a quantum leap; it is a leap of faith.

This "theory has gained increasing support and has not been seriously challenged. An impressive body of research in many laboratories has demonstrated that the brain structures see, hear, taste, smell and touch by sophisticated mathematical analysis of temporal and/or spatial frequencies [hence the primacy of frequency realm]."[98] I do not challenge the theory; I repeat, and mean, that I am straightforwardly impressed. I am not impressed, however, by speculations that call "*temporal* and/or *spatial* frequencies" by the name "no space, no time." And it is in just that semantic slip that this theory *sounds* transcendentally alive.

Needless to say, this semantic sleight-of-hand, which replaces personal blur with transpersonal unity, helps neither the brilliant work of these brain researchers—Pribram for example—nor the difficult task of transpersonalists attempting to explain transcendence.

Aside from the above, we have still another strand of argument which has been proposed. For this strand, let us assume anyway that the mind *in general* is holographic in its operations. Would this fit with the perennial philosophy, and beyond that, would it possibly account for higher levels of consciousness?

I am afraid that, even given this generous lead, we fare no better. First of all, the fact that the deep structure of the mental field is holographic would not in itself account for transpersonal levels, or levels 4–6. The reasons, according to the perennial traditions, are that (1) *every* level is a holography, not just mind, and (2) the experience of any level's holography does not take one *beyond* that level, but merely opens up deeper insights *into* that level. Just as the holography of level–1 does not imply nor demand level 2, 3, 4, 5, or 6, so the holography of level–3 doesn't automatically account for any of the levels above it (levels 4, 5, or 6).

Likewise, the actual experience of the holography of level–3 would not necessarily—nor even likely—involve levels 4, 5, or 6. The ordinary surface mind (level–3) experiences itself as separate and somewhat isolated from other minds. To experience the holography of level–3 would be, at most, to experience a strong resonance with, and even overlapping of, other minds. It would produce a direct experience of actual interpersonal empathy.

But interpersonal empathy is not transpersonal identity. In states of transpersonal awareness (beyond certain introductory practices), whether mind is present or not, explicit or implicit, standing out or holographically blurred—all of this is irrelevant. The higher realms transcend but can easily include mind, and whether mind itself arises doesn't matter. The *existence* of higher states cannot be explained in terms of something that may or may not happen to a lower state, whether that state is unfolded and projected or enfolded and blurred. You might as well say you can explain level–2 by sufficiently blurring level–1. This disguised reductionism led Willis Harman to comment, "These holographic theories still would interpret the primary datum, consciousness, in terms of something else ultimately quantifiable [i.e., in terms of lower physical level measurements]. These theories are not yet of the new science, but rather of the old, in which the attempt is made to explain away consciousness rather than to understand it."[98]

Finally, we might heed William Tiller's suggestions: "The holographic [theory of brain perception] has focused largely on the sensor apprehension of this representation at the physical level of consciousness [level–1]. [We might do better] to opt for a multidimensional [hierarchical] representation of consciousness and possible structures of the universe for its manifestation. Without such an extension beyond the purely physical perception frame, the scope of any 'new paradigm' will be severely limited."[98]

Tiller hints at two points. First, the "frequency realm" said to be so transcendent is really prescendent: it's just the chaotic "blooming buzz" of physical level–1 frequencies before the brain can sort them into higher-order organization. An actual experience of that "primary reality" would be, in fact, pure regression, not transcendence. Second, holography cannot account for hierarchy, and thus the whole theory, as a paradigm, falls flat in the most important area of explanation.*

CONCLUSIONS AND ASSESSMENTS

There are several beneficial repercussions coming from the "new physics" and the "holographic paradigm," even if we conclude, as I

---

*I am not questioning the fact that perception and memory occur as suggested in this hypothesis. I am not challenging the hypothesis on that ground at all. I am questioning whether, beyond that, this hypothesis could have anything to do with transcendent realities. My tentative, personal conclusion is that it only *appears* to have something to do with actual transcendence because of the oddities of the math involved and because of a less than precise manipulation of language. Particularly questionable is the jump from "each personal memory is equally distributed in every cell of the individual brain" to "therefore each individual mind is part of a transpersonal hologram." The holographic paradigm is described as "one in all and all in one"—where "one" means "individual memory/cell" and "all" means "all individual brain cells." From that accurate statement a quick substitution is made: "One" comes to mean "one individual" or "one person" and "all" comes to mean, not all other personal brain cells, but all other persons, period.

think we must, that the latter constitutes nothing close to a comprehensive or even adequate paradigm. But among the benefits are:

1. The interest of influential physicists in metaphysics. This has taken two different forms. First, the willingness to postulate unmeasurable and undetectable orders of *physis* lying behind or subscending explicate energy/mass. This is Bohm's quantum potential/implicate order. Second, the willingness of physicists to acknowledge the necessity of ultimately including references to levels higher than *physis* in their accounts of *physis*. As Wheeler put it, "No theory of physics that deals only with physics will ever explain physics."[104] And Sarfatti: "Therefore, *meta* physical statements are absolutely vital for the evolution of physics,"[104] whereupon Sarfatti introduces the notion of "mind creating matter." But even if that were true in the fashion proposed by Sarfatti, the perennial philosophy would remind him to add: "And you then need meta-mental to explain mind, which brings you to the subtle; and you then need meta-subtle to explain that, and so on in such fashion until, like an asymptotic curve that approaches an axis but never reaches it until infinity, you arrive at Consciousness as Such."

2. The reductionistic fury of mechanistic science seems to be finally winding down, and physics is opening itself—and by impact of authority, many other fields as well—to open systems of unending novelty and creativity. This is especially evident in the work of I. Prigogine, whose theory of dissipative structures is as beautiful as it is profound. Dissipative structures are simply a mathematical way to *allow* for the evolution of higher, more organized states from less complex structures. Dissipative structures are not actually explanations of life or mind, as is sometimes said, but rather descriptions of what has to happen to matter in order for higher realms to unfold. To actually identify the essence of a higher level as simply being a dissipative structure is like saying the *Mona Lisa* is simply a concentration of paint.

3. The whole movement of new physics and new paradigm at least demonstrates that there is profound, serious, and rapidly growing interest in perennial concerns and transcendent realities, even among specialists and fields that a decade ago could not have cared less. No matter that some of what is said is premature, *that* it is said is extraordinary.

4. Books such as the *Tao of Physics* and *The Dancing Wu-Li Masters* and publications such as Marilyn Ferguson's *Brain/Mind Bulletin* are introducing vast numbers of people not only to the intrigue of Western science and physics, but also to aspects of Eastern wisdom and thought, and in ways that simply would not have been possible before.

My point, therefore, in criticizing certain aspects of the new paradigm is definitely *not* to forestall interest in further attempts. It is rather a call for precision and clarity in presenting issues that are, after all, extraordinarily complex and that resist quick generalization. And I say this with a certain sense of urgency, because in our understandable zeal to promulgate a new paradigm, which somehow touches bases with physics at one end and mysticism at the other, we are liable to alienate both parties—and everybody in between.

From one end of the spectrum: already certain mystically or transpersonally oriented researchers—Tiller, Harman, W. I. Thompson, Eisenbud—have expressed disappointment in or total rejection of the new paradigm.

From the other end: already many physicists are furious with the "mystical" use to which particle physics is being subjected. Particle physicist Jeremy Bernstein recently unleashed a broadside on such attempts, calling them "superficial and profoundly misleading."[10] And no less an authority than John Wheeler—whose name is always mentioned in the "new paradigm" and in a way he finds infuriating—recently released two scathing letters wherein, among several other things, he brands the physics/mysticism attempts as "moonshine," "pathological science," and "charlatanism." "Moreover," he states, "in the quantum theory of observation, my own present field of endeavor, I find honest work almost overwhelmed by the buzz of absolutely crazy ideas being put forth with the aim of establishing a link between quantum mechanics and parapsychology"[51]—and transpersonal psychology, for that matter. He has asked, and Admiral Hyman G. Rickover has joined him, to have all sanctions of the American Association for the Advancement of Science removed from any endeavor tending toward transpersonalism, a sanction that Margaret Mead, years ago, fought so hard to obtain.

The work of these scientists—Bohm, Pribram, Wheeler, and all—is too important to be weighed down with wild speculations on mysticism. And mysticism itself is too profound to be hitched to phases of empirical scientific theorizing. Let them appreciate each other, and let their dialogue and mutual exchange of ideas never cease. But unwarranted and premature marriages usually end in divorce, and all too often a divorce that terribly damages both parties.

6

Reflections on the New Age Paradigm: An Interview

ReVision Journal: Of various authorities in the transpersonal field, you seem to be one of a very few who have expressed strong reservations about the so-called holographic theories. I wonder if you could tell us why.

Wilber: Well, it's very difficult in a short discussion to explain the various lines of critique. The holographic paradigm is immensely exciting at first glance, I think, but the more you go into it, the more it begins to lose its appeal. You simply have to take all sorts of strands—epistemological, methodological, ontological—and follow them up.

RV: Then you agree with certain theorists, such as Peter Swartz of The Stanford Research Institute, that the holographic paradigm is a nice metaphor but a bad model of reality?

Wilber: It is a bad model, but I'm not sure it's even a good metaphor. The holographic paradigm is a good metaphor for pantheism, but not for the reality described by the perennial philosophy.

RV: How do you mean that?

Wilber: Well, the perennial philosophy—the term was made famous by Huxley but coined by Leibniz—the transcendental essence of the great religions—has as its core the notion of *advaita* or *ad-vaya*—"nonduality," which means that reality is neither one nor many, neither permanent nor dynamic, neither separate nor unified, neither pluralistic nor holistic. It is entirely and radically above and prior to *any* form of conceptual elaboration. It is strictly unqualifiable. If it is to be discussed at all, then, as Stace so carefully pointed out, it must involve paradoxical statements. So, it is true that reality is one, but equally true that it is many; it is transcendent, but also immanent; it is prior to this world, but it is not other to this world—and so on. Sri Ramana Maharshi had a perfect summary of the paradox of the ultimate: "The world is illusory; Brahman alone is real; Brahman is the world."

RV: So if you leave out any of those paradoxical aspects, you end up advocating one side of a subtle dualism?

Wilber: Yes. The transcendentalists, and also the monists, agree that "the world is illusory and Brahman alone is real," but they overlook the equally true but paradoxical fact "Brahman is the world." On the other hand, pantheism is the reverse, and perhaps worse—it agrees that "Brahman is the world," or the sum total of the universe, but it overlooks the equally important fact that Brahman is radically prior to the universe.

RV: Why is that "worse"?

Wilber: Because pantheism is a way to think about spirit without having to actually transform yourself. If God is merely the sum total of the empirical universe, you don't need to fundamentally enlighten yourself to see that god, because *that* god is already clunking around in your visual field. Pantheism is the favorite god of the empiricists—the "nothing morists," as Plato would say—those who believe in "nothing more" than can be grasped with the hands.

RV: And the perennial philosophy maintains that the absolute is immanent in the world but also is completely transcendent to it?

Wilber: Yes. Plato's cave is still an excellent analogy, as long as we remember its paradoxical nature. There are the manifest shadows in the cave; there is an absolute Light of reality beyond the cave; and ultimately they are not-two . . .

RV: The shadows and the Light . . .

Wilber: Yes. But none of those three points can be overlooked, as Ramana said. Now the problem with pantheism is that it mistakes the totality of the universe with that which is radically prior to or beyond the universe. That is, pantheism confuses the sum total of all the shadows *in* the cave with the Light beyond the cave. And the danger of that philosophy is that, if one thinks Godhead is merely the sum of things and events in the universe, the sum of shadows in the cave, then one ceases to try to get *out* of the cave. One merely contemplates one's own level of adaptation, and tries to add up the parts.

RV: What's the danger with its opposite world view, that of extreme transcendentalism?

Wilber: A hatred of the shadows. It shows up in violent asceticism, in antimaterialism, and especially in antisexual ethic and life repression. The idea is that the world itself is somehow evil, whereas all that is evil is the world perceived apart from, or other to, God. When God is seen to be in the world, as the world, the world is radically divine. Grace, as St. Thomas said, is supposed to perfect nature, not obliterate it.

RV: So you were saying the hologram is a good metaphor for pantheism.

Wilber: Yes, in my opinion, because it basically deals only with the totality of parts, the holographic blur, and its relation to individual parts. In the hologram, the sum total of the parts is contained in each part, and that sum-of-the-parts-being-in-each-part is supposed to reflect the transcendental oneness underlying the manifold separateness. But the only way you can say that the hologram is a metaphor for Brahman or Tao is by reducing Brahman to that sum of the parts, which is then present in each part. But that by itself is exactly pantheism.

RV: You mean the whole is not the same as Brahman, or the absolute?

Wilber: No, of course not. Brahman is *in* the world *as* the *whole world,* it is true, but the whole world in and by itself is not exclusively Brahman, because you could theoretically destroy the whole world but that wouldn't destroy Brahman or Buddha Nature or Tao. Anyway, pantheism makes the mistake of confusing the whole world with Brahman, and the hologram is a good metaphor for the whole/part relation.

RV: And you're not saying that is totally wrong, just partial.

Wilber: Yes, it covers the immanent but not the transcendent aspects of the absolute.

RV: What about the notion that the holographic paradigm posits a frequency realm or implicate order under the explicate order of events. Isn't that analogous to the unmanifest, or the Light beyond the cave?

Wilber: Well, again, I think that is initially the obvious thing to say, and a lot of people have agreed with it. I'm not sure it holds up, however. To begin with, Bohm's implicate order is directly related to something like a vast sea of quantum potential energy, out of which there crystallizes, so to speak, concrete matter events. These events are related not by field forces, Einsteinian or Newtonian, but by their degree of implication, or how far out of the matter-energy sea they have emerged.

RV: That implicate sea has been compared by many to the unmanifest and infinite source of the mystics.

Wilber: Yes, I know, but the problem is that the quantum potential is merely tremendously huge in size or dimensions; it is not radically dimensionless, or infinite in the metaphysical sense. And you simply cannot equate huge in size, potential or actual, with that which is without size, or prior to any dimensions, high or low, subtle or gross, implicate or explicate.

RV: So the implicate sea, potential or actual, is really quite different from the infinite ground of mysticism.

Wilber: In my opinion, that's exactly right. They merely sound similar if described in superficial language, but the actual difference is profound. But see, David Bohm is perfectly aware of that. That's why he speaks of the "source" as being beyond both the explicate and implicate spheres. Somehow, people seem to ignore that part of what he says.

RV: OK, and Pribram's holographic brain?

Wilber: If you take a tape recorder and record various sounds, the tape will store those sounds or "memorize" them. So will storage systems based on optical holography. The noises come in all dynamic and flowing—or temporal—but they get translated into a "frozen" or "timeless" state in the tape. But just because the information is stored in a "timeless" fashion doesn't mean that the tape recorder is in a transcendental or eternal state. The human brain also stores information, perhaps holographically; in the process it naturally translates it from a dynamic or moving state into a "timeless" or stored condition, and when you call up that information you read it out from this frozen state. But this "timeless" or frozen condition has little to do with a metaphysical or mystical eternity. For one thing, break the tape recorder—destroy it—and there goes your eternity. An eternity dependent for its existence on a temporal structure, tape or brain, is a strange eternity.

RV: But what about the frequency realm?

Wilber: Yes, the brain is said to read out information by analyzing frequencies, or by plugging into a realm where "there is no space, no time, only events (or frequencies)." Now I am not questioning that theory; I'm sure the brain does analyze spatial and/or temporal frequencies. I just don't see that that has anything to do with a transcendental ground which is eternal and infinite. First of all, frequency means cycles per second or space per time. The same is true of "event densities." The fact is, the so-called frequency realm is simply a realm with space-time structures different from those of the linear or historical mind, and the mind has to impose its structures upon the less structured frequency realm. But in any event, or in any way you wish to interpret it, the frequency realm still has *some sort of structure,* whether that structure be blurred, vibratory, frozen, or whatever. And structure cannot be confused with that which is radically without structure, or perfectly dimensionless, transcendent, and infinite. If you do mistake that frequency realm for some sort of eternal ground, instead of seeing that it is simply less structured noise, then it appears that you're dealing with some sort of mystical theory, whereas you're actually dealing with the simple mechanics of sensorimotor perception.

RV: But that theory is frequently coupled with Bohm's ideas.

Wilber: Yes, that is initially the obvious thing to do. If you equate the frequency realm with the implicate order, and then equate the unfolded or read-out information with the explicate realm, it naturally appears that you have a paradigm which covers the emergence of manifest thought and things from an unmanifest and timeless ground.

RV: But since both the implicate order and the frequency realm have some sort of form . . .

Wilber: Yes, it's not a good metaphor for the perennial philosophy. At best, it's a decent metaphor for pantheism.

RV: In your original critique of the holographic theories [see chapter 5], you used the concept of hierarchy quite often. Do you still feel it is important?

Wilber: Yes, absolutely. If we return to Plato's analogy, there are the objects in the cave and there is the Light beyond—but the point is that some objects are closer to the opening of the cave. That is, there is a gradation in ontology—as Huston Smith summarized the essence of the world's great mystical traditions, "Existence is graded, and with it, cognition." That is, there are levels of being and levels of knowing, leading, as it were, from the very back of the cave up to and through the opening.

RV: And the absolute is the highest level of this gradation?

Wilber: Not exactly, because that would be dualistic. It is paradoxical, again. The absolute is both the highest level of reality *and* the condition or real nature of every level of reality. It is the highest rung on the ladder, *and* it is the wood out of which the ladder is made. The rungs in that ladder are both the stages of evolution at large and the stages of human growth and development. That was Hegel's and Aurobindo's and Teilhard de Chardin's message; evolution is moving through the links in the Great Chain of Being— starting with the lowest, or matter, and moving to biological structures, then to mind, then to subtle and causal realms, and finally to supermind or spirit. It's not that the absolute or supermind only comes into existence at that last stage—it existed all along, but could only be *realized* when consciousness itself evolved to its highest estate. Once we get out of the cave we see there is and always has been *only* Light. Prior to that final and highest stage, there seems to be nothing but shadows, but we don't realize they are shadows, having no point of comparison. So, anyway, the absolute is both the highest stage or goal of evolution and the ever-present ground of evolution; your real and present condition and your future potential or realization. Anything less than that paradox is dualistic.

RV: Where does hierarchy fit in?

Wilber: Well, the stage-levels of evolution and ontology *are* the hierarchy. But hierarchy only covers one half of the paradox—it covers the fact that certain levels are closer to the Light than others.

The other half of the paradox is, of course, that all things are already and fully Buddha, just as they are. All things are already One, or always already One, and all things are trying to evolve toward the One, or omega point.

RV: That's why you are Buddha but still have to practice.

Wilber: Yes, if Buddha were not omnipresent, it would not be Buddha, but if it were only omnipresent, you would be enlightened right now. Dogen Zenji has made all that very clear. But if you leave out any side of that you get into theoretical trouble. You could paraphrase Orwell: "All things are God, but some things are more God than others." The first part of that is God's omnipresence; the second part is God's hierarchy. The stage-levels of evolution show increasing structural organization, increasing complexity and integration and unity, increasing awareness and consciousness. There is even a sense in saying, as Smith and Schuon and the traditionalists do, that each higher level is more real, or has more reality, because it is more saturated with Being. In any event, evolution is hierarchical—rocks are at one end of that scale, God the Omega is at the other, and plants, reptiles, mammals, humans, and *bodhisattvas* fill up the middle, in that order. *And,* God is the very stuff, the actual essence, of *each* stage-level—God is not the highest level, nor a different level itself, but the reality of all levels.

RV: I think you are right that most or all of that has been overlooked by the holographic theories, but is all of that really necessary for a basic paradigm? Aren't you being picky?

Wilber: I know what you mean—why not take the paradigm and run? Don't spoil a good thing; physicists are talking mysticism! [Laughing] I can see the headlines now: "Scientists at M.I.T. today announced they discovered God. That's right, God. Asked whether God was compassionate, merciful, all-pervading, radiant, all-powerful and divine, a senior researcher was heard to say, 'Gee, we're not sure; we think it's a photon.'"

Look, it was some of the proponents of the holographic theories that claimed they had a paradigm that could explain the fundamentals of mystical religion. So we go to the authorities on mystical religion, or the perennial philosophy in general, and see what they say. According to Huston Smith, for example, four levels of being are the absolute minimum you can use to explain the world's great mystical religions. Those are physical-body, symbol-mind, subtle-soul, and causal-spirit. No major religion recognizes less than that. Many, however, give a more detailed cartography, frequently involving seven levels—the seven *chakras,* for instance, of kundalini yoga, which is probably the most archetypal paradigm of existence ever devised. The seven generally are: (1) physical or material, (2) emotional-sexual (*prana* or bioenergy), (3) mental, (4) higher mental or psychic, (5) subtle or archetypal, (6) causal or unmanifest, and (7) ultimate or unqualified.

Finally, you can, if you are very careful, group these levels into three broad categories, for convenience, say. Since most people have evolved to the mental level(s), it's useful to speak of those levels below the mind—the material and biosensory realms—as premental or submental, and those above it—soul and spirit—as transmental. That gives us three general realms, known variously as matter, mind, and spirit; or subconscious, self-conscious, and superconscious; or instinct, reason, and intuition, and so on. Those three realms, for instance, have been explicitly mentioned by Hegel, Berdyaev, and Aurobindo.

RV: All of which has been overlooked . . .

Wilber: All of which has been overlooked. The problem with the popular holographic theories, as well as the general "new physics and Eastern mysticism" stuff, is that they collapse the hierarchy. They go from saying "All shadows are ultimately illusory" to saying "All shadows are equally illusory." That is, they latch on to such phrases as "All things are One" or "Separate entities don't exist" or "Isolated things are merely shadows" and then overlook the distinctions between the shadows themselves. They collapse the shadows; they collapse the hierarchy.

RV: Now you said "popular" theories. Do the more academic versions escape this problem?

Wilber: The theories don't, but I think many of the theorists do. Most of the people who either introduced the physics/mysticism thing or at least used it for effect have increasingly refined and sophisticated their views. David Bohm has clearly moved toward a more articulated and hierarchical view, even if he objects to the word hierarchy. And Fritjof Capra never said that physics and mysticism were the same, although he did try to draw so many parallels that the public thinks he did. Anyway, he has moved quite beyond his introductory statements in *Tao of Physics*. I'm just afraid the public never will. They have latched onto physics equals mysticism with such passion that Capra's new and more sophisticated—and necessarily complicated—ideas will never reverse the tide. Anyway, it's not so much those scholars, or ones like Renée Weber who are trying to interpret their findings for us, that I have in mind when I criticize the pop mysticism and the new physics or holographic craze. But definitely the holographic paradigm, in and by itself, falls into that pop mysticism, and I simply think that is a real problem.

RV: Now that hierarchy collapse which occurs in the holographic paradigm—that's related to the error of pantheism, correct?

Wilber: Yes. Almost identical. It mistakes the sum of illusions for reality. You take the phenomena, the shadows, claim they are "all one," and then confuse that sum total of shadows with the Light beyond. As Schuon put it in a blistering attack, pantheism denies distinctions on precisely the plane that they are real. It confuses an essential with a substantial identity. That's also exactly what the holographic paradigm does.

RV: The implications of that collapse would be what? Or, well, what does a theory lose when it loses those various dimensions?

Wilber: It loses all the differences in methodologies, epistemologies, and cognitive interests. All of those crumble.

RV: Could you back up?

Wilber: First off, each higher level cannot be fully explained in terms of a lower level. Each higher level has capacities and characteristics not found in lower levels. This fact appears in evolution as the phenomena of creative emergence. It's also behind synergy. But failing to recognize that elemental fact—that the higher cannot be derived from the lower—results in the fallacy of reductionism. Biology cannot be explained only in terms of physics, psychology cannot be explained only in terms of biology, and so on. Each senior stage includes its junior stages as components but also transcends them by adding its own defining attributes.

RV: Which generates hierarchy . . .

Wilber: Yes. All of the lower is in the higher but not all the higher is in the lower. A three-dimensional cube contains two-dimensional squares, but not vice versa. And it is that "not vice versa" that creates hierarchy. Plants include minerals but not vice versa; the human neo-cortex has a reptile stem but not vice versa, and so on. Every stage of evolution transcends but includes its predecessor—as Hegel said, to supersede is at once to negate and to preserve.

RV: But that doesn't apply to Godhead or the absolute, does it?

Wilber: It applies to the paradoxical aspect of God that is the highest of all levels of being. God contains all things but all things do not exclusively contain God—that would be pantheism.

RV: The other side of the paradox is that what every person or thing is, whether enlightened or not, is still only God.

Wilber: Yes. Anyway, each stage-level of the hierarchy is, as Huston Smith pointed out, a more or less unified totality that can stand on its own, so to speak. Likewise, all of the elements of each level are said to be mutually interdependent and interrelated. Each level of hierarchy, in other words, is a type of holography.

RV: So the elements of *a given level* are mutually interacting. But what about elements from *different* levels? How do they interact, or do they?

Wilber: They interact, but *not* in a mutual or absolutely equivalent fashion, and for the simple reason that they aren't equivalent. If the higher levels contain attributes not found on the lower levels, you simply can't have bilateral equivalence between them. My dog and I can interact on the level of sensorimotor perception, but not on the level of symbolic mind—I mean, we don't discuss Shakespeare.

RV: But don't the Eastern traditions say that all things are perfectly, mutually interpenetrating?

Wilber: No, that's pure pop mysticism. The actual traditions are much more sophisticated than that. But I suppose you are referring to Hua Yen Buddhism, or Kegon—the school associated with the *Avatamsaka Sutra.*

RV: That seems to be the most often quoted or referred to.

Wilber: According to Hua Yen, there are four fundamental principles of existence, none of which can be dismissed. One is *shih,* which means "separate thing or event." Two is called *li,* which means "transcending principle or pattern." Three is called *shih li wu ai,* which means "between principle and thing there is no obstruction," or perhaps "between noumenon and phenomena there is no boundary." And four is called *shih shih wu ai,* which means "between phenomenon and phenomenon there is no obstruction." Now the last item has been seized, isolated from its context, and made the basis of pop holistic philosophy. It's very misleading.

Anyway, the point is that the world is indeed an interrelated and interpenetrating series of thing-events, but not in the merely one-dimensional fashion of pop mysticism. All things interact through karmic association and karmic inheritance, but those of greater structural organization do not act absolutely equivalently with their junior dimensions, nor can junior dimensions embrace senior ones.

RV: OK, but now we come to the crux of the matter. What about the absolute? Isn't it equally at every point?

Wilber: It is, as I said, paradoxical. All of the absolute is equally at every point, *and* some points are closer to the absolute than others. The hierarchy deals with the manifest universe, where there are levels of increasing reality (or decreasing illusion) leading up to the absolutely real. And those levels are not one-dimensionally and equivalently interacting. I don't know of a single authority on the perennial philosophy—Smith, Schuon, Guénon, Coomaraswamy, Pallis—who would make that type of statement, or who would deny relative hierarchy.

RV: But couldn't physics have discovered the other side of the paradox—the absolute oneness or infinite whole underlying the manifest world?

Wilber: Follow it through. We already saw that what physics has found is actually a unified interaction of material shadows; it discovered that various physical particulars are interrelated processes—but interrelated shadows aren't the Light. As for the implicate order, we saw it was actually a huge energy dimension; it wasn't radically dimensionless or metaphysically infinite. And if you mean that physics could actually have evidence, concrete evidence, for the absolute . . . Well, the absolute itself, being all-pervading and all-inclusive, is not other to any phenomenon and therefore could not be detected by any sort of instrument or show up in any sort of equation. That which can be functionally useful in an equation must be a variable *different* from other variables, but the absolute is different from, or set apart from, absolutely nothing.

RV: I see; so there is no way it could even enter an equation or make any difference in terms of theoretical information?

Wilber: None whatsoever, or else it would be itself merely more information, which would make it perfectly relative, or nonabsolute.

RV: Then what is it that the new physics *has* discovered? I mean, if it's not the Tao, what is it?

Wilber: In my opinion, it is simply the holography of level–1, or the fact of material or physical energy interrelation. The biologists discovered the holography of their level—level–2—about thirty years ago; it's called ecology. Every living thing influences, however indirectly, every other living thing. The sociopsychologists discovered the holography of the mental level—the fact that the mind is actually an intersubjective process of communicative exchange, and no such thing as a separate or radically isolated mind exists. Modern physics—well, it's what, almost a century old now?—simply discovered the analogous holography on its own level, that of physical-energetic processes. I don't see any other way to read the actual data.

RV: OK, but now why couldn't that physical holography actually be the *same* oneness underlying the biological and psychological and other levels? Why couldn't all of these approaches—physics, biology, psychology, and so on—simply be approaching the same underlying holistic reality from different angles?

Wilber: Start by explaining what you mean by "different angles," and you will find you are necessarily reintroducing the very differences you wished to overcome by saying "one reality." That is, you have merely moved the problem back one step. *If* there are these fundamentally different approaches to one reality, then tell me first *why* the approaches *are* different. Tell me why the study of physics is different from the study of literature, for instance. As you pursue that question very carefully, you will find that those differences are not merely arbitrary. They are not simply interchangeable or equivalent approaches, because they take as their subject matter various classes of events that *are* different because they display different dimensions of structural organization and evolutionary advance and developmental logic. The approach to studying hydrogen is fundamentally different from the approach to studying, say, the meaning of *Hamlet,* if for no other reason than that the one is submental and the other is mental. Now those are *not* two different approaches to the same reality, they involve two different levels of reality. Further, that reality—the absolute as absolute—is disclosed in its entirety or essence only on the highest or ultimate level of being. And then only to the soul that has itself evolved perfectly to that estate.

RV: I understand. So there's only one more possibility—can't you say that since all things are ultimately made of subatomic particles, physics *has* shown us an ultimate oneness?

Wilber: All things are not ultimately made of subatomic particles; all things, including subatomic particles, are ultimately made of God. But you mention the most popular position, which is really an extreme form of reductionism. It's popular, I guess, because it fits the hierarchy collapse.

RV: Reduce all things to material particles, then discover the particles are holographic, then claim that that holography is the Tao.

Wilber: Yes, that's right. There's a strange appeal in the simplicity of the reductionism. Part of the problem is simply that the physicists are so used to working with the material world, they tend to call it "*the* world" or "*the* universe," and so they say things like "Physics has proven all things in the world are one," when of course it has done no such thing. It has not explained or even touched bio-ecological unity, let alone sociopsychological community, and so on. Physics deals with four major forces—strong and weak nuclear, electromagnetic and gravitational. But it can't tell you anything about the force of emotional-sexuality, which comes into existence on level–2. It can't tell you about what constitutes good literature, or how economics works, or why children have Oedipal complexes, or the meaning of a dream, or why people commit suicide, and so on. All of those are mental symbolic events that begin on level–3. Physics doesn't deal with "*the*" world, you see? As I say, the whole thing has been very misleading.

RV: But there are important parallels, is that right?

Wilber: You mean parallels between the various levels, laws of the various levels?

RV: Yes. I mean, can't the laws of physics tell us something, anything, about the higher levels?

Wilber: Yes, I think they can, but we have to be very careful here. The lower will display its version of an analog law first—the lower emerges first in any developmental sequence, and so it is extremely tempting to say that the lower stands in a causal relation to the higher analog law. That's why I went to such pains in *Up from Eden* to point out that the higher comes *through* the lower, then *rests on* the lower, but doesn't come *from* the lower.

RV: It comes from, or gains its reality from, its senior dimension, not its junior dimension, correct?

Wilber: Yes, via the process of involution.

RV: Maybe we can come back to that point. For now, what is an "analog law"?

Wilber: The idea is simply that every event and principle on a lower level is merely a reduced version or a reflection downward or a lesser degree of those events and principles found on higher levels.

RV: Could you give some examples?

Wilber: This is not a novel idea; it's extremely well developed in the traditional philosophies. According to Hinduism, for example, the absolute bliss of Brahman goes through a series of stepped-down versions, or dilutions, until it appears as the sexual thrill of orgasm. In Christian mysticism, you find such ideas as that natural law is simply a partial version of mental rationality, which itself is merely a reduced reflection of the Divine Logos. The Buddhist *vijnana* psychology holds that there are four classes of consciousness, each being a stepped-down version of Universal Mind. This is correlated with the idea of the four bodies of Buddha; which is almost identical to the Vedanta notion of four bodies and four major states of awareness—gross, subtle, causal, and ultimate or *turiya*. The point, with reference to bodies, is that the body or substance of a physical entity, such as a simple rock, is actually a reflection downward of the freedom and vitality of the subtle body associated with mind, and the subtle body itself is merely a trickle of the causal body—and *that* is just a contraction in the face of eternity or *turiya*.

RV: The idea also exists in the West?

Wilber: Oh yes; I assure you you can give just as many examples, from the neo-Platonists to the Victorine mystics. Interestingly, it forms the crux of one of the most influential of modern Western philosophers—Whitehead.

RV: Was he influenced by the traditionalists?

Wilber: He must have been aware of them, but I think he came to the notion more or less on his own. You know, the truth will out and all. I'd like to think the obviousness of the truth simply couldn't escape one such as Whitehead. Anyway, he took the notion of junior dimensions being essentially reduced versions of senior ones, and completely turned the typical approach to reality on its head. He said that if you want to know the general principles of existence, you must start at the top and use the highest occasions to illumine the lowest, not the other way around, which of course is the common reductionist reflex. So he said you could learn more about the world from biology than you could from physics; and so he introduced the organismic viewpoint which has revolutionized philosophy. And he said you could learn more from social psychology than from biology, and then introduced the notion of things being a society of occasions—the notion of compound individuality. Naturally, he held that the apex of exemplary pattern was God, and it was in God, the ultimate compound individual, that you would ground any laws or patterns found reflected in reduced versions in the lower dimensions of psychology, then biology, then physics. The idea, which was brilliant in its statement, was that you first look to the higher levels for the general principles of existence, and then, *by subtraction,* you see how far down the hierarchy they extend. You don't start at the bottom and try to move up by addition of the lower parts, because some of the higher parts simply don't show up very well, or at all, on the lower rungs. Perhaps his favorite examples were creativity and love—God, for Whitehead, was especially love and creativity. But in the lower dimensions, the creativity gets reduced, appearing in humans as a modicum of free will but being almost entirely lost by the time you get to atomic particles. Maybe we could say that the Heisenberg uncertainty principle represents all that is left of God's radical freedom on the physical plane. But the point is that if you try to understand the cosmos in the reverse direction, from atoms up, you are stuck trying to account for free will, for creativity, for choice, for anything other than a largely deterministic cosmos. The fact is, even with its little bit of Heisenberg indeterminacy, the physical universe is much more deterministic than even level–2, biological beings. Any good physicist can tell you where Jupiter will be located a decade from now, barring disaster, but no biologist can tell you where a dog will move two minutes from now. So Whitehead, by looking to illuminate the lower by the higher, and not vice versa, could make creativity the general principle, and then understand determinism as a partial restriction or reduction of primary creativity. If, on the other hand, you start at the bottom, then you have to figure out a way to get free will and creativity out of rocks, and it just won't work. That it is reductionistic is the nicest thing you can say about such approaches.

RV: That's extraordinary, because I've seen so many attempts by new age thinkers to derive human free will from electron indeterminacy, or to say that human volition is free *because of* the indeterminate wave nature of its subcellular components, or some such.

Wilber: Yes, it appears the thing to do. It's a reflex thing to do—finally, after decades of saying the physical universe is deterministic and therefore human choice is an illusion, you find a little indeterminacy in the physical realm and you go nuts. It's only natural you then try to explain human freedom and even God's freedom as a blowup of the lowest level. You get so excited you forget you have just pulled the reductionist feat of the century; God is that big electron in the sky. The intentions are so good, but the philosophy is so detrimental. And imagine this: there are plenty of physicists who feel that the physical realm really is purely deterministic—Einstein, for one—and that future research may disclose subatomic variables that *are* purely causal. I'm not saying that will or will not happen, but theoretically, what if it does? Does poor God then lose Its creative power? The day the determinate variables are found, does human will evaporate? You see the problem?

RV: Yet so many new age thinkers are using physics and neurophysiology to establish their claims of higher transcendence or mysticism or just human free will.

Wilber: Yes, and in a way that even orthodox philosophers find horrifyingly reductionistic. Let me read you a quote from a recent president of the American Philosophical Association: "The body can be free, no matter what may be true according to quantum laws; and moreover, it could not be free by virtue of the latter alone. For if its freedom is merely that of electrons, then, as has been well said, it is freedom of the electrons but not of the body. This objection to some recent attempts to treat human freedom as simply derivative from quantum mechanics and nerve structure is, I believe, quite valid." The point, of course, applies even more so to the Tao, and yet new agers seem to be applying it even less.

RV: I think all that is very clear. But now on a popular level, a general level, is there anything wrong with such books as *The Dancing Wu Li Masters* or *The Tao of Physics* or any of the other new age, new paradigm books?

Wilber: I'm simply saying that you have to be very careful about the statements you make if you want to extend them from popular hyperbole into a real and enduring paradigm. Statements like "The universe is a harmonious, interrelated whole" or "All things are One" or "The universe is dynamic and patterned, not static and fixed" are superb introductory material; we've all used them to get our points across in a general way. But beyond that, they are very misleading.

RV: How, specifically?

Wilber: Well, if you take two columns and in column *A* you write words like fixed, static, isolated, manyness, discrete, and in column *B* you write fluid, dynamic, pattern, holistic, oneness; then I would guess the vast majority of new age thinkers imagine that the mystical view is column *B*. But in fact mysticism is concerned with transcending *both* column *A* and *B*. Column *B* is just as dualistic as column *A,* for the simple reason that the two columns are opposites or mirror images and thus both are partial. Reality is *not* holistic; it is not dynamic, not interrelated, not one and not unified—*all* of those are mere concepts about reality. As Chuang Tzu said in "Three in the Morning," to say all things are one is just as dualistic as to say all things are many. That's why Zen says reality is "Not-two! Not-one!" That is not some sort of very subtle or terribly sophisticated mystical doctrine. It is the simplest and most fundamental of all mystical doctrines. Murti's classic, *The Central Philosophy of Buddhism,* has made that very clear, certainly for Mahayana, as have writers from Schuon to Guénon to Coomaraswamy for the other traditions. That is simple, bottom-line mysticism.

RV: The absolute cannot be qualified in any sense?

Wilber: Correct, including the sense you just gave it. The absolute—and here we have to speak somewhat poetically—cannot be characterized or qualified because it is not set apart or different from any thing and therefore could not be described as one thing or event among others. It is *nirguna,* without attributes, or *shunya,* void of characterization. Since there is no place outside the absolute, there is no place you could take up a stance so as to describe it. If you could get outside it, it would cease to be the absolute.

RV: And so . . .

Wilber: Well, here's a crude analogy. Say the entire universe consists of only three objects—a square one, a round one, and a triangular one. God is not the sum of those objects, whether they are considered things or events. . . .

RV: As pantheism maintains. . . .

Wilber: Yes; God is not the sum of those objects because you could destroy those objects and God would still exist. Therefore neither can you describe God as being any of the attributes of each thing—God is not a circular square triangle. And most important, God is not another object in addition to the three objects. God is not One Thing set apart from the many. God is not a dynamic thing, a holistic thing, or a patterned thing.

RV: Staying with your analogy, can you say anything about what God would be?

Wilber: As long as you remember it is a metaphoric and not descriptive statement. God is not one thing among many things, or the sum of many things, or the dynamic interaction of many things— God is the condition, the nature, the suchness, or the reality of each thing or event or process. It is not set apart *from* any of them, yet neither is it in any way confined *to* them. It is identical *with* the world, but not identical *to* it.

RV: Is that why you earlier said the absolute is prior to the world but not other to the world?

Wilber: Yes. That is the doctrine of *tathata,* or suchness—Eckhart called it the *isness* of each thing-event; the Taoists call it *tzu jan,* the so-ness of every object; it is also very close to the meaning of both *dharma,* for Buddhism, and *sahaj,* for Vedanta. Anyway, the doctrine of suchness, combined with the doctrines of *advaita* or nonduality and *shunyata* or unqualifiability, form the most fundamental and elemental starting point for all mystical traditions, although the terminology is, of course, different.

RV: And it's those basics that seem to get left out of so many new age accounts of science and mysticism?

Wilber: I think so, yes. Apparently the author wants to say that modern science has discovered that certain objects are actually processes and not static things, or triangles and not circles, and so the Tao is triangular, just as good ole physics says. But, in fact, the Tao contains things and it contains events, but it can be characterized by neither. It is not different from them, but neither is it defined by them.

RV: And you could also say that because the frequency realm is actually a different realm from the read-out realm, these are merely two *different* realms, and so the one could not be the mystical suchness of the other?

Wilber: Yes, that would be another important point. The frequency realm is simply one realm among others, not one without a second. I hadn't thought of it that way before, but that's true. Please let me say again that I think the frequency realm does exist, but that I honestly think it just doesn't have anything to do with mystical events or with a truly transcendent-immanent ground, and you've simply given another and very fundamental reason why.

RV: I wonder if we could now move on to the notion of epistemology, because you said earlier that the evolutionary hierarchy is also a hierarchy of knowledge. Could you elaborate?

Wilber: Each level of the Great Chain is a level of prehension, as Whitehead might say. Each level prehends, or somehow touches or cognizes, its environment. As we said earlier, each level is a stepped-down version of absolute consciousness. Anyway, if we use our simple three-level hierarchy of body, mind, and spirit, then the three corresponding modes of knowing are sensory, symbolic, and intuitive. The Christian mystics refer to them as the eye of flesh, the eye of reason, and the eye of contemplation. Even Aristotle was perfectly aware of these realms—he referred to them as *techne, praxis* (or *phronesis), and theoria.*

RV: And they are hierarchic?

Wilber: Yes. Just as the eye of reason transcends but includes the eye of flesh, the eye of contemplation transcends but includes the eye of reason.

RV: Can science as we know it be extended to cover all three realms? Can we have a higher science of being?

Wilber: Yes, I think we can speak of these higher realms and their knowledge as being scientific, but we have to be extremely careful by what we mean. Look at it this way; we have at least these three modes of knowing—sensory, symbolic, and contemplative. These modes correspond to the physical body, the mind, and the spirit. That is simple enough, but it becomes a little more complicated when you realize that the mind, for instance, can look not only at its own level but at the other two levels as well, and in each case you could get a fundamentally different type of knowledge. Here, I could draw it like this:

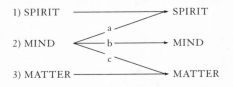

1) SPIRIT ──────────→ SPIRIT

        a

2) MIND ⟵──b────→ MIND

        c

3) MATTER ──────→ MATTER

RV: So we have three basic modes and realms of knowledge: the physical-sensory, the mental, and the spiritual. (These are numbered 1, 2, and 3.) And then, within the mental mode itself, we have, what, three subsets?

Wilber: Subsets is fine. . . . (These are lettered a, b, and c.)

RV: Depending upon which of the three realms the mental mode takes as its object?

Wilber: Yes. Following my favorite orthodox philosopher, Jürgen Habermas, we can characterize the three mental subsets like this. When the mind confines itself to sensory knowledge, the mode is called empirical-analytic, and its interest is technical. When the mind works with other minds, the mode is hermeneutic, phenomenological, rational, or historic, and its interest is practical or moral. We now add the mystic view, which Habermas doesn't directly cover, and we say that when the mind attempts to cognize the spiritual realm, its mode is paradoxical or radically dialectical, and its interest is soteriological. Here, I'll put it on the diagram.

           ↗ SPIRIT — PARADOXICAL-MANDALIC / SOTERIOLOGICAL

MIND ⟨──→ MIND — HERMENEUTIC-PHENOMENOLOGICAL / MORAL

           ↘ MATTER — EMPIRICAL-ANALYTIC / TECHNICAL

RV: What exactly is hermeneutics?

Wilber: The study of interpretation and symbolic meaning. In the hands of such sophisticated philosophers as Gadamer or Ricoeur, it really comes to mean mentality in general, or symbolic intentionality and meaning and value. See, the reason that empirical-analytic studies are so limited—limited, in fact, to the sensory realm—is that they can't even disclose the nature or meaning of mental productions. There is no empirical test, for instance, which will disclose the meaning of *Macbeth,* or the meaning of value, the meaning of your life, and so on. Meaning is a mental production and can be determined only by interpretation, or what Heidegger called the hermeneutic circle.

RV: Most people understand what you mean by empirical-analytic. Could you comment on the third subset, the paradoxical?

Wilber: The idea is simply that when the mind attempts to reason about the absolute, it will necessarily generate paradoxes, for exactly the reasons we have been discussing. When reason operates in this mode, we call it paradoxical. I have also heard the word "mandalic reason" used, and I like that. Either one is fine.

RV: Now you are saying that mandalic reason is not contemplation, but it does have its uses, correct?

Wilber: Yes, exactly. Both of those points should be emphasized. The first is that paradoxical or mandalic reason—which is what results when you try to think or write about the Tao or Spirit or Buddha Nature—is not itself spirit, nor does it disclose spirit per se. Here, let me just number all five modes like this:

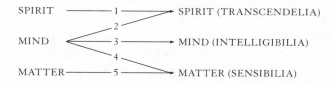

Number 5 is simple sensory-material or sensorimotor perception. Number 4 is empirical-analytic mental knowledge, or mind's ideas about the sensorimotor world. Number 3 is hermeneutic and introspective and phenomenological knowledge, or mind's knowledge about mind. Number 2 is paradoxical or mandalic reason, or mind's attempt to think about spirit. Number 1 is spirit's direct knowledge *of* spirit, which is nonmediated or nonsymbolic knowledge, intuitive and contemplative.

RV: And your first point is that #2 should not be confused with #1.

Wilber: Yes, and that is an extremely elemental point. There is no way to directly understand spirit except by radical spiritual transformation, or the direct opening of the eye of contemplation in your own case. You can read, think, and write about the Tao all day, and none of that is the Tao. No mental theory is even close to Brahman.

RV: And since, if you do reason about Tao, you will only generate paradoxes, there is no way to state one position over another. I mean, you can't say the Tao is dynamic flux, because that's half of a dualism in the paradox.

Wilber: That's true. You can't say it without contradicting yourself, as both Nagarjuna and Kant clearly pointed out.

RV: I'm not sure I follow that point.

Wilber: Well, suppose you say the Tao is constantly changing, that nothing is permanent, everything changes. That's a self-contradiction, because you are claiming everything changes except, apparently, the fact that everything changes, which must therefore be a *permanent* fact. It won't work. Same thing happens if you claim reality is relative, dynamic, one, and so on.

RV: So the Tao is permanent and impermanent?

Wilber: Or neither, or even neither-neither, as Nagarjuna would have it. But you see the point—reason generates paradoxical statements when it tries to grasp the absolute.

RV: But your second point was that that type of reason has certain uses?

Wilber: Definitely so, as long as we don't confuse mandalic reason (#2) with actual intuition-contemplation (#1). One of its uses is to try to hint to other minds what God might be like. Hegel used such dialectical reason with great force, although he always came too close to confusing it with spiritual intuition. Another purpose, which was used with extraordinary skill by Nagarjuna, is to use the dialectic to demolish reason itself and thus pave the way for actual contemplation, or prajna.

RV: How, exactly?

Wilber: Nagarjuna would be faced by an opponent who wished to characterize the absolute—the Brahmins claimed God was absolute being, certain nihilist Buddhists claimed it was extinction, others claimed it was pattern, others said it was monistic or unitary, and so on.

RV: All of which are partial and dualistic?

Wilber: Yes, and Nagarjuna would demonstrate that point by turning the opponent's logic back on itself, at which point it would contradict itself. See, if you try to make a statement about reality as a whole, then your statement is part of that reality, at which point it becomes like a hand trying to grasp itself or a tongue trying to taste itself. You end up either in an infinite regress or in a blatant contradiction. Nagarjuna would use this inherent limitation in reason to exhaust reason's attempts to grasp spirit, at which point, if the thing is done carefully, you become more open to actual contemplative insight—the mind just shuts up, and in the gap between those thoughts, prajna is born, or at least can be. But as far as reality goes, it is neither being nor nonbeing, nor both nor neither—those were Nagarjuna's four categories, and they were based on the Buddha's original "inexpressibles." Whatever reality is, it can only, only be "seen" upon satori, or via actual contemplative insight (mode #1).

RV: And if you try to state what is "seen" you will only generate paradox. . . .

Wilber: Yes, but those paradoxes, used skillfully, as *upaya,* constitute mandalic reason (mode #2)—and that is one of its uses.

RV: We were talking about science, about a higher science.

Wilber: Well, as I said, we have to be very careful here. If by science you mean consensual and experimental knowledge, then all realms, including the higher, can be scientific. [See chapter 2.] But they cannot be merely empirical; nor are all of them directly involved in forming *theories.*

RV: Because a theory is a mental production?

Wilber: Yes. The sensory mode—#5—does not itself form theories because it is presymbolic. And the spiritual mode—#1—does not itself form theories because it is transsymbolic; its actual operation is immediate and nonconceptual insight.

RV: So that limits theoretic activity to the three mental subsets.

Wilber: The activity itself, yes. It is only the mental modes that form theories, although the theories themselves can try to take account of the other realms, realms which themselves do not directly form theories. Of course, classical science was theory directed toward the biomaterial realm. That is, it was empirical-analytic theory or mode #4. The mind creates a theory-map of the objective biomaterial world, looks carefully at that world, usually by altering that world in controlled ways, and then fits the map to it. A good map becomes a model, and a model that is never disproven becomes a law.

RV: What about theory in mode #3?

Wilber: That is phenomenological philosophy, introspective psychology, intersubjective communication, interpretation, value systems, and so on. This mode does form theories or maps of what the subjective and intersubjective world is like.

RV: But those theories are not checked by empirical-analytic means, because they aren't sensory referents?

Wilber: That's right; they are checked by hermeneutical procedures, by interpretation, by communities of like-minded interpreters, by direct phenomenological apprehension, and so on.

RV: Could you give an example?

Wilber: What you and I are doing right now. We are exchanging meaning, symbolic meaning, and arriving at interpretive understanding. "What do you *mean* by that?"—meaning, you know. That is not an empirically reducible event, and it cannot be explained by physics, chemistry, or biology. *Hamlet* is not made of electrons; it is constructed of symbolic units of meaning which, if reduced to the paper on which they are written, are simply destroyed. But I suppose a classic example is Freud. Despite his rampant attempts at sociobiological reductionism—and it was absolutely rampant—his methodology was almost entirely hermeneutic and phenomenological, which is why I think he still has much to tell us, and why so many structuralists are returning to him for insight. Lacan is now said to be the foremost psychological thinker in Europe, and Lacan is two things: a structuralist in the line of Lévi-Strauss and a brilliant Freudian. Anyway, Freud's methodology was basically to watch the client's production of words and symbols and then try to figure out what those symbols might really mean. His assumption was that a dream, for instance, must occur on two levels, because the client is actually the author of the dream—it's her or his dream—but the client either professes not to understand its meaning or suffers the dream as a passive witness. The dream, in other words, is composed of two texts, a manifest text and a latent or hidden text. And it's the hidden text that is causing the problems. So part of the analyst's job is to find this hidden text, decipher it, and interpret it to the client. It's like finding an Egyptian hieroglyphic, and no merely sensory evidence will help here, because what you are dealing with is how trains of subjective symbols slide over each other to create a world of meaning, intention, value, desire, and so on. It's exactly like a Rorschach blot—the empirical blot is fixed and given; it's composed of so much ink arranged in just one way. But the symbolic meanings that can ride on that blot are numerous, and they can't be determined by empiricism at all. So Freud's technique was to use linguistic dialogue in order to disclose hidden texts, then translate or interpret those texts so as to make the meaning of hidden symptoms more transparent to the client. It was that transparency, where before there had been opaqueness, that helped effect the cure. The interpretation, in other words, leads to insight or understanding. Through repeated observations and interpretations, Freud was able to create various maps or theories of the psychological sphere, theories that could not be tested empirically, like mere behaviorism, but which *could* be tested by those who were willing to take up the discipline of introspective interpretation. That Freud's reductionism crippled many of his maps and theories is sad, but that is not the fault of his methodology. It was a pure case of in garbage, out garbage.

RV: So mode #3 can be theoretic in that it also forms and uses maps and models of its own level.

Wilber: Yes, but its verification test is hermeneutic, not empiric. Or rational-phenomenological, not sensory. Or linguistic, not physical. If you wish, call it phenomenological science [dialogic science; see chapter 2].

RV: And mode #2. That's paradoxical—can that be theoretic?

Wilber: I think so, but theory in a looser sense. As I said, paradoxical reason has its uses, as long as we are careful. Theory in this sense would involve creating maps or cartographies of the higher and transcendental spheres, for the aid of those who have not yet seen them, and also for general knowledge purposes. Mandalic maps, as it were, and mandalic science [chapter 2].

RV: Could you check those maps?

Wilber: Yes, but only by actually transforming to the spiritual realm, or by awakening mode #1. You absolutely could not verify them using empiric or hermeneutic procedures.

RV: But would those maps also be paradoxical?

Wilber: Yes, definitely. It sometimes doesn't appear that way because each system, merely for consistency, usually works with only one side of the paradox. Thus the Buddhists will call the highest level Void, Hindus will call it Being, the Taoists will claim it is ever-changing, and the Christians will say it is everlasting. All are right—or wrong; it makes no difference. It's paradoxical. You see, paradox is simply the way nonduality looks to the mental level. Spirit itself is not paradoxical; it is not characterizable at all. But when the mind tries to think about it, then nonduality shows up as two contradictory opposites, both of which can be shown to be equally plausible because neither is complete by itself. The best you can do therefore is affirm *both* sides of the duality, or deny them both. The former gives you paradox; the latter, double negative. I use mandalic reason to cover both, although it applies better to paradox. But my point is that neither of them should be confused with mode #1 or actual contemplation—true contemplative or transmental and transtheoretical science: the science of Spirit *as* Spirit, not merely as symbolized by mind. So all these various modes can be called "scientific," as long as we are careful in each case to explain exactly what we mean. My only worry has been that advocates of a "new and higher" science all too often have in mind one of these modes, usually the empiric, and they want to expand that mode over all the others. That results in reductionism, which leads to hierarchy collapse, which involves the fallacy of equivalent shadows, which gives pantheism. . . . So use "science" any way you wish, but first please say what you mean by the term, give its methodology, distinguish it from other modes and disciplines, and then we'll see what you've got.

RV: On the notion of the applicability—or inapplicability—of empirical science to higher realms, such as the mental-subjective or the transcendental-spiritual; doesn't research in brain physiology—which is empirical—tell us something about mind and its operations?

Wilber: Yes, of course. Brain research is extremely exciting and important, but I think it is also extremely limited.

RV: In what sense?

Wilber: Well, take Freud's thoughts on the matter. In his last book he stated pretty clearly that even *if* we could figure out every connection between the brain and consciousness, then—and these are his own words—"it would at most afford an exact localization of the processes of consciousness and would give us no help toward understanding them." As I said—and as almost everybody has recently discovered—Freud was primarily interested in hermeneutics—in interpretation and meaning and symbolic discourse.

RV: His first major book was *The Interpretation of Dreams.*

Wilber: Yes. Even if we can localize the dream—say, in the right hemisphere—and even if we can describe its chemical components, we still don't know its *meaning.* That meaning is discoverable only in the hermeneutic circle, only in my life's history and its intentions.

RV: Mode #3 and not #4.

Wilber: Yes. And this insight is now producing an entire renaissance in nonempirical, nonreductionistic, nonbiological psychology. You have the interpersonal or object-relations theorists—Sullivan, Guntrip, Fairbairn, Jacobson, Erik Erikson. You have the linguists and structuralists—Lacan, Piaget, Kohlberg, Roy Schafer, Ricoeur. The information theorists—Bateson being the most famous. All of these are related to symbolic transfer or hermeneutics, and it's revolutionizing psychology.

RV: Can you give a short example, say in terms of pathology?

Wilber: Sure. Originally symptoms were conceived in energetic or biophysical terms: The id pushes here, the ego pushes back, the compromise is a substitute gratification in the form of a symptom. The shadow, or personal unconscious, was a product of forces. Very thermodynamic. Now without denying that bioenergetics are also involved, the new understanding simply points out that the self is not so much a present biophysical event as it is a story or a history. The self, the mental self anyway, is a linguistic structure, a creation of history and a creator of history. It lives via communication or dialogue, it is constructed of units of meaning or symbols, and it lives out a course in time or history. It is a story; it is a *text.* And the only way you understand *War and Peace,* for instance, is by good interpretation. What does it really *mean,* see? What does my life mean? Where is it going? Why am I doing this? What value does this have for me? And that's hermeneutics.

RV: And pathology?

Wilber: Pathology is related to bad interpretation or maybe mis-interpretation. And the shadow is no longer the seat of unconscious forces, it's the seat of misinterpretation. In a sense, the shadow is a hidden text or subtext, and so it produces scripts whose *meanings* baffle you—bad hermeneutics, or poor hermeneutics, as when the person says, "I don't know why I did that, wonder what it means?" The shadow is a text you secretly write, a text whose authorship you refuse to admit.

RV: And so therapy?

Wilber: Is a process of assuming or reassuming the authorship or responsibility for your own life text, your own self.

RV: And none of that can be easily explained in empirical or physiological terms?

Wilber: The hermeneutics? No. But I would like to add that the system I'm working with utilizes both the bioenergetics of the body's prana, or emotional-sexual distributions, and the mental units of meaning that transcend but include the simpler bioenergetic feelings. Both are important, but the hermeneutics more so. In the seven-level scheme I gave earlier, diet and exercise deal basically with level–1; bioenergetics and emotional-sexual cathexis deals with level–2; and hermeneutics and symbolic interpretation deals with level–3 and part of level–4. None of those can be tossed out. The problem with pure hermeneutics is that it tries to say the id is just language, which is silly. A dog has sexual impulses and no language. Humans have both. Trying to reduce one to the other is just not useful. They both slot in the hierarchy.

RV: And so, is empirical physiology without any fundamental use for the understanding of mental hermeneutics?

Wilber: No, no, that's reverse reductionism, I didn't say that. Hermeneutics transcends but includes the effects of physiology, as I have said for each level of the hierarchy. So the effects of physiology can be best understood in terms of degeneracy theory, I think.

RV: Which is?

Wilber: If you look at every stage in evolution, what you find is that—this has been pointed out often—each higher stage is synergistic to its junior components; it includes them but is more than them.

RV: That's "transcends but includes."

Wilber: Yes, same idea; synergy is the same idea. Bring lifeless matter together in certain complex ways, and you generate something that is more than the sum of its parts. You generate life or prana. Life is synergistic in reference to matter and cannot be reduced to, or fully explained by, matter. Likewise, bring prana together in certain complex ways, and symbols begin to emerge. But symbols—or psychology—cannot be explained by life—or biology—just as biology cannot be explained by rocks. Each is synergistic in reference to its predecessors. Now the opposite of synergy is degeneracy. If *A* is degenerate to *B,* then two or more states of *B* can be sustained on top of a single state of *A.* For example, if you make a telephone call, then a certain amount of electrical energy is passing along the lines. But information is also passing along the lines, and you cannot tell how much information, what type of information, or the quality of information that is being transmitted on the mere basis of the amount of energy supporting it. For example, with the same amount of energy—say, 100 kilowatts or whatever—you could say "Hello, how are you" or "zizzy lollop thud." The former carries information; the latter, mere noise. Several *different* states of information transfer can be sustained on the *same* state of energy exchange. In this case, energy is degenerate with regard to information.

RV: And that occurs at all stages of evolution?

Wilber: Yes, at every level of the hierarchy. Really, it's a simple notion; it's just the opposite of synergy.

RV: And you see that relationship in the brain and mind?

Wilber: I think that is certainly a possible explanation. The brain is basically the biophysical substrate for the mental processes. We would also expect spiritual processes to leave their footprints in the biophysical substrate, either directly or via the mind. But in no case could mind or spirit be reduced to brain or explained entirely or merely by brain physiology. The Rorschach blot is still a good analogy: There is one physical substrate, the actual ink blot, but it supports several different mental interpretations, and you can't say the interpretations are just ink. I think it's the same with brain and mind.

RV: The brain is degenerate with regard to mind?

Wilber: Yes. That would mean that the changes in brain physiology would not be correspondingly as significant as the changes in mind values. For instance, I can be in the beta brain-wave state, and have two successive thoughts of wildly different truth-values, say, "$2 + 2 = 4$" and "$2 + 2 = 5$." The difference in EEG between those thoughts is extremely small, but the difference in truth-value is tremendous. So there *are* physiological correlates, but they are degenerate with regard to mind. The differences in physiology are not as significant as the differences in the truth-values of the propositions. Incidentally, notice that you cannot establish the truth or falsity of the propositions by any amount of physiological studies. You have to go outside the brain's physiology, into the intersubjective circle of logic and communication, in order to verify mental truths, because, as we've said, mind transcends but includes physiology, and the truths of the former cannot be entirely contained in the truths of the latter. No amount of EEG sophistication could help you prove or disprove Keynes's theory of macroeconomics, for instance.

RV: But that would still give brain physiology an important effect on mind but not a causal effect, correct?

Wilber: Yes. This theory still gives us a definite brain-mind connection and interaction, but it doesn't postulate wild dualism on the one hand or simple monism or identity on the other. Further, it suggests that the brain is as complex as it is because nothing less complicated could serve as the biophysical substrate for logical and symbolic processes, but it avoids the reductionism of saying, for example, that literature is fancy electrons.

RV: So theoretically, if we understood brain physiology in depth, we could produce general states and moods and improve the substrate, like memory capacity and so on, but we could not produce specific thoughts or ideas in the mind.

Wilber: Yes. Changing physiological states would be like changing Rorschach blots. You would get a whole new series of moods and responses, but you couldn't control all the specific mental interpretations or actual contents. So brain would still have a significant effect on mind but not a determinant or causal effect on mind. This also fits very well, I think, with such researchers as Elmer and Alyce Green, who maintain that "all of brain is in the mind but not all of the mind is in the brain."

RV: That's hierarchy and degeneracy.

Wilber: Absolutely. But this still leaves us with the important tasks of mapping out the degenerate relationships between mind and brain, and also between spirit and brain. Correlations of brain waves with dreaming, for example.

RV: And because of degeneracy, you can tell from physiological changes *that* a person is dreaming but not exactly what he or she is dreaming?

Wilber: Yes, that's exactly degeneracy.

RV: This is slightly off the topic, but what *would* determine the dream content?

Wilber: Well, a quick answer would be that the past history of the text-self is now getting a reading, especially its hidden subtexts. The shadow is on stage. And the content of the shadow is not determined by present physiology as much as it is by past history, the actual past events that constitute the story and the history that this person recognizes as a self. That's why Habermas calls this mode the hermeneutic-*historic*. And finally, that's why Freud was drawn to the idea of trying to trace the *historical* genesis of symptoms. He wanted to use a historical reconstruction method to help the person see when he or she began to write hidden or secret or guilty texts and stories, to see how the person repressed the shadow by creating a secret author. The secret author shows up in dreams and symptoms, and the job of the therapist is to help the person *interpret* the meaning of the symptoms—you know, "your anxiety is really masked or hidden rage"—until the person can re-own them, re-authorize them, re-author them. So even if physiology can't tell us what the shadow says or means, it can tell us when it is on stage—and that's tremendously important. I think the same thing will hold true of any psychospiritual correlates we can find in the biophysical substrate. So these correlations, even though they are degenerate, are very important.

RV: And this theory allows us to look for correlations of the higher in the lower without having to reduce the higher to the lower?

Wilber: That's my opinion, yes.

RV: In a related vein, what do you think of Prigogine's work? Doesn't it offer an empirical basis of higher transformations?

Wilber: In my opinion it doesn't, because I agree literally with Marilyn Ferguson that Prigogine's work—I'll read this—"bridges the critical gap between living systems and the apparently lifeless universe in which they arose."

RV: In other words, it applies basically to the gap between level–1 and level–2 in the seven-level hierarchy?

Wilber: I think so. It describes the complexities of material perturbations that allow life or prana to emerge through—but not from—matter. They are really exciting equations, but they don't easily or clearly cover the higher levels, levels 3 through 7.

RV: Why not? Surely it has some general applicability?

Wilber: Well, it is definitely true that there are analog laws on all levels of the hierarchy, as we earlier said. The question is not whether transformation occurs on all levels, because it does; the question is which level of structural organization do these equations actually describe? I think it is fairly well agreed that these equations deal primarily with thermodynamic energies and entropy, not with symbolic information and not with transphysical and transmental insight. Dissipative thermodynamic structures seem best representative of biomaterial transforms, or levels 1 and 2. They are *examples* of general transformations, therefore, but not paradigmatic among them. They are a subset of evolutionary transformations, and not the sole or exemplary type. As we earlier put it, they are downward reflections, or reduced versions, of the transformations that occur on the higher levels, and so naturally they all have certain similarities, just as the electron and human will are "indeterminant." But trying to use the lower-level manifestation of the general principle to explain the higher-level prototype of that very principle is what we want to try to avoid. So I think Prigogine's work is very important, not because I can then say he has proven the laws of psychological or spiritual transformation, but because he has demonstrated that the transformation process itself extends all the way down the hierarchy to the lowest levels. It shows up in an extremely reduced form, as we would expect, but there it is.

RV: So thermodynamic dissipative structures would be degenerate with regard to higher transformations?

Wilber: Yes. With respect to the brain-mind interface, if dissipative structures apply to levels 1 and 2, it follows they would apply to the brain or biophysical substrate of the mind, and thus assume the importance, limited but definite, that we discussed earlier.

RV: But are there ways to explore and verify any of the higher modes themselves, since they aren't empiric?

Wilber: Yes, of course. There is phenomenological investigation and its verification in a community of intersubjective interpreters—just as you and I are doing now. There is contemplative practice and its verification by a community of transsubjective meditators—as happens, say, between Zen Master and student [see chapter 2].

RV: But using phenomenology and hermeneutics as an example, wouldn't mere interpretation make truth a wildly subjective affair?

Wilber: It depends upon the caliber of the community of interpreters. Real philosophy, psychology, and phenomenology—not behaviorism and not positivism, those are empiric and not rational affairs—depend in large measure upon the quality of the community of interpreters. Good interpreters, good thinkers, ground good phenomenology. They discover those truths that apply to the subjective realm, and in that sense the truths are subjective truths. But that doesn't mean mere individual whim. First of all, a bad interpretation will simply not mesh with general subjective consensus. It is rebuffed by a reality that is subjective but very real and very lawful, just as a bad empiric fact is rebuffed by other facts. Second, a phenomenological truth, in order to be recognized as truth, must be *tested* in a community of like-minded interpreters, just as an empiric fact, to be so, must be tested against the community of other facts. It's no mere wishful thinking and subjective license. The hermeneutic test is just as stringent and demanding as the empiric test, but of course the empiric test is easier because it is performed by a subject on an object, whereas phenomenology is performed by a subject on or with other subjects. Much more difficult.

RV: Isn't that what has helped reductionism so much? Everybody wants the methodological elegance of physics?

Wilber: I think so. We are lured into thinking physics has *the* method, instead of seeing that physics is working with the simplest level of structural organization and thus produces relatively simple and easily reproducible truths.

RV: But aren't you pulling a type of reverse reductionism yourself? I mean, when we look into the subatomic world it's every bit as complex as the biological world or the human symbolic world.

Wilber: Well, it's complex, but not as complex as higher levels, for the simple reason that a human being contains electrons but electrons don't contain human beings. Thus all the complexities of the electron are contained in humans, but humans also contain other complexities found only in humans—guilt, anxiety, despair, desire.

RV: Yes, I see. So we should give equal or greater emphasis to rational-phenomenology and hermeneutics and so on?

Wilber: Yes, certainly, but hermeneutics alone is not the ultimate answer. See, just as empiricism wants to reduce symbol to sensation, hermeneutics wants to reduce spirit to symbol. It wants to claim God is a mere idea, or only an idea, in the community of intersubjective interpreters. It refuses to include in its methodology the practice of contemplation—mode #1—and thus it fails to see that God can be verified as a transcendental reality by a community of trans-subjective mediators.

RV: Even though, on the mental plane, various communities of meditators would interpret spirit differently. Mind is degenerate to Spirit.

Wilber: Exactly. When the mind speaks of spirit, it generates paradox or contradictory interpretations. That's as it should be. But what is verified in meditation itself is not a particular interpretation of spirit, but a direct and immediate identity with and as spirit, and that occasion is not subject to interpretation because it is not a symbolic or mediated event. On the mental level, however, there are only interpretations of the event, most paradoxical, and that is inescapable. "They call Him many who is really one."

RV: Aren't there a lot of paradoxes in modern physics—what have been called "quantum koans"—and couldn't that suggest that physics is somehow involved in fundamental reality, in mandalic logic?

Wilber: Yes, that point has been raised a lot. But first off, just because the absolute always generates paradox doesn't mean that paradox always indicates the absolute, OK? But beyond that, I personally think there are very few genuine paradoxes in any branch of science. A real paradox, remember, means that two mutually contradictory occasions are known to occur simultaneously and equally. For instance, if at this very moment it is raining and not raining on my house, that would be a real paradox.

RV: What about wavicles—a particle acting as a wave in one situation, and a particle in another?

Wilber: Well, that's the point; it is a wave in one situation and a particle in another. In any given experiment, it never acts equally and absolutely as a perfect wave and a perfect particle simultaneously. It oscillates, or alternates, its mutually exclusive truths, and that is a complementarity, not a real paradox.

RV: Are there no genuine paradoxes in science or philosophy?

Wilber: I wouldn't put it that strongly, but I think it is safe to say that most apparent paradoxes turn out to be ordinary contradictions, which simply means you have made a confused step somewhere. In empiric research, contradictions usually indicate that a series of experiments have been run incorrectly. It is usually cleared up by more refined research. In rational-conceptual inquiry, what seems to be a paradox usually results, as Russell and Whitehead demonstrated in *Principia Mathematica,* from violating the theory of logical types. Even though Spencer Brown has suggested ways to reformulate the types theory, it is still extremely useful. Bateson almost made an entire career out of it.

RV: To put it bluntly, what is it?

Wilber: It simply states that a class cannot be a member of itself. It came up in trying to define number as the class of all classes similar to a given class. But the idea is very simple: The class of all chairs is not itself a chair, the class of all apples is not itself an apple, the alphabet is not itself a letter, and so on. Anyway, if you violate the logical typing of your symbols, then you generate a pseudoparadox. It's not a real paradox because it's just based on bad semantics. For instance, if you take one word-symbol, say, "chair," and then give it two meanings, each of a different logical type, then create a sentence using that word, you can generate a pseudoparadox. You might say, "That chair is not a chair." It is a particular chair but is not a universal chair, not the class of all chairs. When semanticists say—Korzybski's famous utterance—"Whatever you say a thing is, it isn't!"—that's not a real paradox. What they mean is that "whatever you say a thing is"—that is, the name you give it, the symbol you use to describe it—is not to be confused with the particular thing itself. The former is the class; the latter, the member, and the class is not a member of itself—that is a direct application of logical typing, and it is behind much of modern semantics and the map/territory theories. And it says that wherever you generate what looks like paradox, you've confused your logical types.

RV: I remember that theory now. Isn't it the way Russell solved the famous paradox about the Cretan who said, "Everything a Cretan says is a lie." Since a Cretan said it, was he telling the truth or lying?

Wilber: Yes, the idea was that the Cretan was making a statement about statements, and that is of a logical type different from statements in general, and so he wasn't contradicting himself. You judge the statement and the meta-statement on their own terms, decide in each case whether it is true or false, and there goes the paradox. See, the theory of logical types is really just a way to group classes and sets into a hierarchy of increasing comprehensiveness. Each level in the Great Chain, for example, is of a higher logical type, even though not all of the levels themselves are actually made of logic. And in that larger sense, the theory of logical types—which says don't confuse types—says "don't collapse the hierarchy."

RV: Didn't the types theory also lead to the double-bind theory of schizophrenia?

Wilber: It really was the heart of most of Bateson's work. What happens in schizophrenia, according to Bateson, is that two messages of different logical types contradict each other, and the person, who takes both to be equally true, oscillates between them, until he shakes himself to pieces, so to speak. Because he cannot easily differentiate logical types, he takes both messages, which are merely contradictory, as being equally true or paradoxical. Then he can neither reach a compromise with them nor throw one of them out, because they are now equal but opposite.

RV: He's in a double bind.

Wilber: He's in a double bind. He violated logical typing, which generated a pseudoparadox which shakes him apart. It happens in any sort of information feedback system. If you take a machine that is supposed to turn itself "on" at a given lower limit and "off" at a given upper limit, and then you start moving those limits together, the machine will turn off and on in increasingly shorter intervals. If you then collapse the difference between the limits, the machine will tell itself to turn off at the same time it tells itself to turn on. It's caught in a "paradox" and right there in front of your eyes it will shake wildly until it breaks down. Anyway, I am saying that just as in such schizophrenic thinking, and unless you are explicitly using mandalic reason, then paradox usually means there is actually just a contradiction somewhere—it indicates sloppy thinking, not transcendental reason. In empirical-analytic theory and research as well as in phenomenological-rational theory and research, what appears to be a paradox is usually an indication of pathology in your system—something went wrong somewhere. Instead of saying I'm working with the Tao, I'd go back and retrace my tracks.

RV: You earlier mentioned Whitehead and how, in your opinion, he didn't exactly agree with the holographic theories. I think what you said then was clear enough, but the more I think about it the more confusing it is.

Wilber: How so?

RV: It is generally thought that Whitehead's philosophy fits the holographic theories in at least two ways. One, he said everything in the cosmos interacts with everything else. And two, doesn't his philosophy fit with the notion, made famous by the Heisenberg uncertainty principle, that the subject affects the object when it perceives it? Or do you disagree with Whitehead there?

Wilber: Well, no, I generally agree with Whitehead, but Whitehead disagreed with both those ideas.

RV: Didn't Whitehead say that everything prehends everything else in the cosmos?

Wilber: What he said was that a thing prehends everything in its actual universe, and its actual universe consists only of its ancestors, not its contemporaries and not its descendents.

RV: I don't follow.

Wilber: Whitehead maintained that the universe consists of a series of occasions which come into existence for a few seconds or so and which then fade into cosmic memory, so to speak—very like the Hinayana Buddhist notion of momentary *dharma*-events. Anyway, each entity or occasion, as it comes into existence, is regarded as a subject, and this subject prehends, or is somehow aware of, its immediate predecessors or those occasions that helped to form it. So those predecessors, or ancestors, are objects to the present event, the subject. As that subject passes, it becomes object for its descendents, and so on. So each subject prehends all of its ancestors, to some degree, however minimal—but notice that no event can prehend its descendents, and no event can prehend its contemporaries.

RV: Why not?

Wilber: Because events just coming into existence don't have time, so to speak, to get to know each other. Two truly simultaneous events are without mutual influence at the precise time of their simultaneity. They haven't had the chance to enter the causal or karmic stream. The influence they do have will be on the occasion that immediately succeeds it—that influence is causality in Whitehead's system. If two subjects are in the same vicinity, the odds are high that they both may become object for the same eventual subject. But otherwise, no interaction. And an entity cannot prehend its descendents any more than Christopher Columbus could be aware of you or me.

RV: So an entity prehends all its ancestors, but not its contemporaries and not its descendents?

Wilber: That is Whitehead's view, yes.

RV: And you agree with that?

Wilber: Yes.

RV: But what about precognition. Isn't that an example of a present occasion prehending a future one, or a descendent?

Wilber: Look, if precognition is absolutely real and absolutely possible, then all events are already absolutely determined for all time. There is then no such thing as free will, no such thing as actual creativity or true free emergence, there isn't even such a thing as Heisenberg's uncertainty principle. The universe is, through all times and on all levels, absolutely a deterministic machine. I don't buy it, myself.

RV: OK, what about the second point, the idea that physics has supposedly proven that the subject in many ways creates its object.

Wilber: Are you asking whether I agree or whether Whitehead does?

RV: Start with Whitehead.

Wilber: He disagrees absolutely. And remember Whitehead was perfectly aware of modern quantum mechanics.

RV: He denied quantum mechanics?

Wilber: No, he denied, or at least refused to embrace, some of the terribly unsophisticated philosophical interpretations of QM, such as that the object is created or even altered when prehended by a subject.

RV: What was his idea?

Wilber: As each occasion comes to be, as it becomes subject, it prehends its ancestors or causal objects and is thus changed by the objects, or formed by its immediate past. But the object is not changed, and indeed could not be changed, by its subject or by being prehended, because the object now only exists in or as the past, and you can't alter the past by merely thinking about it or prehending it. Again, it's like saying that what Columbus did could affect you, but what you do now does not affect Columbus. Whitehead's point was that, since all events are coming to be and ceasing to be in a stream of flux, change, or time, then essentially the same thing applies during the milliseconds involved.

RV: You agree?

Wilber: Yes, definitely. That is simply another way of saying that the subject contains the object but the object doesn't contain the subject, and *that* is simply another way to say that there are indeed nonmutual or nonequivalent relationships. Hierarchy is, of course, the strong version of that fact.

RV: So you don't agree with the new age theories that say the human brain as subject creates the objective world it perceives?

Wilber: It might indeed create order in its world of perception, or in the material world of noises, but it doesn't create that world itself.

RV: If it did there would be an infinite regress?

Wilber: Yes. But the point can be established more easily—the human brain didn't evolve until 6 million years ago, but the cosmos is 13 billion years old. There were lots of things around before brains existed. As for the so-called participant-observer in physics, or the necessity for the object to be perceived by mind in order to collapse its state vector, the vast majority of physicists—including David Bohm's classic 1975 paper that perfectly shredded Jack Sarfatti's wild claims on the subject—find the idea either unnecessary or downright ridiculous. But many new age theorists think they must believe in the idea because they confuse the events occurring on the merely physical level with the entire Tao; they think that because Buddha Nature or God is one with all things in the act of perceiving-creating them, that the human mind itself must try to do the same thing for electrons.

RV: What about such related topics as the Whorf-Sapir hypothesis, the idea that language, or the mind, creates the world, and that different languages in fact create different worlds. There seems to be a lot of support for that notion.

Wilber: There is a partial truth there, but it is very confused, because again we have failed to say what we mean by the phrase, "the world." Do we mean the physical world, the biological world, the sociological world, what? Because, you see, I believe that the Whorf-Sapir hypothesis is perfectly wrong in reference to the physical, biological, and submental spheres in general. I do not believe that the linguistic mind creates rocks and trees, although obviously it creates the words with which we represent those entities. A diamond will cut a piece of glass no matter what words we use for "diamond," "cut," and "glass."

RV: So if there were no human minds, there would still be physical and biological entities in existence.

Wilber: Yes. Again I remind you of the obvious fact that those levels antedated the human brain or mind by billions of years.

RV: So where is the Whorf-Sapir hypothesis correct?

Wilber: Symbols do not create the material or biological spheres—levels 1 and 2—but they do create, literally, the mental spheres—level–3 and parts of level–4. But it's not just that there are these higher mental levels and that symbols reflect them. The higher mental levels *are* symbols. They are *made* of symbols the way a tree is made of wood. So notice we have these two general realms under discussion—the mental and the submental—and that symbols play a different role with regard to each. They basically *reflect* the submental world but they help to *create* the mental world. In the first case they basically *represent;* in the second, they also *present.* For example, the symbol "rock" represents an independently existing rock. Take away the symbol, and the rock, or whatever it is, is still there. Language does not create that world. But entities such as envy, pride, poetry, justice, compassion, goals, values, virtues exist only in and as a stream of symbols. Take away the symbols and those entities are gone. Alter the symbols, and you shift the sense of those entities. Different languages do exactly that, and that is where the Whorfian concepts find some applicability.

RV: Now isn't the difference between the symbols that *represent* the submental realms and the symbols that *create* the mental realms the same as the difference between empirical-analytic modes and hermeneutic-historic modes?

Wilber: Definitely—same thing. And that's why the methodologies, the interests, the structures, and the verification processes are so different in the two modes. See, if you are working with the empirical-analytic mode, then you are basically working with the "mirror" model of truth—the model made famous by the positivists, such as Wittgenstein's early work. Propositions are true if they reflect the facts correctly—that type of thing. An empiric proposition is true if it more or less accurately mirrors or pictures or represents the sensory world. That is all as it should be. That model is fine for empirical truth [see chapter 2 for details]. But when it comes to the purely mental or phenomenological world, the simple mirror or only reflective model no longer works. In a sense you are still doing reflective work—you know, you are still proposing theoretic maps and models, as we earlier discussed; but you are no longer using symbols to represent nonsymbolic occasions. You are using symbols to look at other symbols, a process which *creates* new worlds with new possibilities and new truths, and those truths are not empirical or merely sensory, and so a simple mirror model no longer works. Or we could put the analogy like this: With empiric propositions you are trying to mirror the lower realms in symbols so as to better comprehend them. But in the mental world, where symbols look at symbols, it's like using one mirror to reflect another mirror which reflects the reflection, and so on in a circle of meaning that you and I co-create whenever we talk. That is the hermeneutic circle. The self is aware of itself only by taking the role of other—but the same is equally true of the other. So here we are, two mirrors in discourse, co-creating each other in communicative exchange. And the way you find your way around in that world, that hermeneutic circle, is radically different from dropping rocks and seeing if they fall at the same speed in a vacuum, right? In empiricism, the symbols you use to represent the world simply represent the world, more or less. But in the mental and linguistic world, the symbols you use to represent that world are also involved in creating that world, and there is the great difference.

RV: What happens if you ignore that difference?

Wilber: The phenomenologists try to make all empirical truths into mere subjective co-creations. You know, the human mind helps co-create dirt, and so on. Similar to the overextended version of the Whorf-Sapir hypothesis. The empiricists, on the other hand, try to reduce the hermeneutic circle to mere sensory transactions. Since they can't find any sensory referents, however, they proclaim mind to be a black box. They refuse to try to map out the hermeneutic circle and instead content themselves with monitoring muscle twitches, as Tolman put it. Philosophy degenerates into only positivism, and psychology degenerates into only behaviorism.

RV: So an overall paradigm . . .

Wilber: An overall paradigm, in my opinion, would have to include all of the modes of knowing we have discussed, and all the correlative methodologies. It would include sensory investigations and empirical-analytic hypotheses and tests. It would include hermeneutic-historic investigations and interpretations, conceptual analyses and syntheses. It would include mandalic cartographies of the higher realms, however paradoxical at spots, and it would include an actual summons to contemplative practice. Further, the overall paradigm, its simple existence, would demand a social evolutionary stance, a social policy geared to help human beings evolve through the stage-levels of existence. This would involve both attempts to help vertical transformation to higher levels and also attempts to clear up the distortions and oppressions that have occurred horizontally on the levels already in existence. The vertical is connected with soteriological interests; the horizontal is the normative or emancipatory interests, as Habermas uses the term.

RV: Couldn't that lead to "we-know-best-for-you" social engineering?

Wilber: No, because in this paradigm transcendence cannot be forced. There are only *participants* in emancipation. You can only force slavery; you can't force a person to be free.

RV: It seems to me that your major concern over the holographic or new age paradigms in general is that most of these issues in methodology and epistemology are overlooked or ignored. The hierarchy, as you say, has collapsed.

Wilber: What happens is that when the hierarchy is collapsed, you lose all these relative distinctions. The different methodologies—sensory, empirical-analytic, mental, and so on—collapse. And the different interests of human inquirers—technological, moral, emancipatory, soteriological—all collapse. And all sorts of other problems start up. That was the problem with the original holographic paradigm. Since they had only two levels, then the frequency realm had to be the same as the implicate realm, and the read-out information had to be the explicate realm. And dissipative structures had to be the link between the frequency realm and the fold-out information—and so on. But then Bohm stated that the implicate level wasn't ultimate; there was a realm "beyond both." That gives three realms. Recently, he has spoken of several levels of the implicate realm. That gives us maybe six levels in all. Now that's much closer to the perennial philosophy. My own feeling is that as soon as he starts describing these realms in a little more detail, he's going to end up describing the traditional Great Chain. He's already speaking of "relatively independent subtotalities"—pretty much Huston Smith's definition of realm or level for the perennial philosophy.

RV: In the last interview in *ReVision,* he tended to include matter and thought as one realm.

Wilber: Well, I think that is part of the problem he might have inherited from Krishnamurti. Because Krishnamurti is so interested in the Light, he almost refuses to even discuss the shadows. Hence, he tends to commit hierarchy collapse and lump things like matter and symbol together.

RV: Because all shadows are ultimately illusory he thinks they are equally illusory.

Wilber: Yes, that's hierarchy collapse. I think Bohm stepped into this rather loose philosophy, and so he tended to include matter, prana, and mind as more or less equivalent parts of the explicate sphere. He then had to look at the implicate sphere as something that existed more or less equally alongside or under material things and mental thoughts. He thus veered off from the traditional view, which would say that what is implicate to matter is simply élan vital, prana, the life force.

RV: So prana is the implicate order in which matter is embedded?

Wilber: I think that would be correct, traditionally. But that doesn't preclude the possibility that matter rises from a physical energy sea. This seems to me the original meaning of Bohm's physical implicateness or, at least, quantum potential. My point is that both matter and the physical energy sea crystallize out of prana. In that sense, prana is implicate to matter.

RV: And prana is what? Or mind relates to prana how?

Wilber: Prana is implicate to matter but explicate to mind; mind is implicate to prana but explicate to soul; soul is implicate to mind but explicate to spirit; and spirit is the source and suchness of the entire sequence. (You have to be very careful with terminology here—you can almost reverse the sequence of wording, depending upon your definition of "implicate." If by implicate you mean enfolded as in "enveloped," then prana envelops or implicates matter, or contains it. This might seem trivial but I have seen many writers use Bohm's concept in what are really diametrically opposed senses. I am using implicate to mean the larger ground out of which the explicate emerges.) Anyway, in my opinion, because Bohm originally didn't distinguish systematically between matter, prana, and mind, he started looking horizontally for hidden dimensions of implicateness, failing to see that those three realms are already vertical dimensions of implicateness with regard to each other. But I think he's looking carefully at his scheme, but we'll have to wait and see.

RV: One last question. Anybody who knows you knows that you'd much rather work on your own writing than critique the works of others. What jarred you away from your own work?

Wilber: Well, the notion was rapidly spreading that all you have to do to be a mystic is learn a new mental world view. If you actually think you can include the absolute Tao in a new paradigm—and get anything other than a mass of contradictions and paradoxes— then you foster the idea that by merely learning the new paradigm, whatever it may be, you are actually transcending—really transcending. I have actually heard that claim made. That is a disaster.

So naturally you're moved to put your two cents in. But the fact that spiritual transformation takes years of meditative or contemplative practice, that it takes moral and physical purification, that it takes, or is helped by, direct contact with a living adept in divine realization, that it takes a direct opening of the eye of contemplation and has nothing to do with merely learning another mental paradigm—all of that was being left out. You know, we went through all this with Alan Watts. God knows nobody did more for mystical studies, especially Zen, than Alan, and I don't know a single person of my generation interested in transcendence who wasn't touched deeply by the man. Nobody could write like Watts, nobody. But it was just that—words. It was only at the end of his life that he rather surreptitiously began to admit that the core of Zen is, in fact, zazen. But by then, most of the people who began with Alan were now with Suzuki Roshi or Sazaki or Soen or Katagiri—that is, they were actually practicing, actually working on spiritual transformation. That is not Square Zen, as Alan finally admitted. Thus, the only good function of a book on Zen should be to persuade the reader to engage in zazen and to encourage those already practicing to continue and deepen their efforts. In the same way, the only major purpose of a book on mysticism should be to persuade the reader to engage in mystical practice. It is precisely like a cookbook: You give recipes and invite the reader to go out and perform the recipe, actually do it, and then taste the results. You are not supposed merely to learn the recipes, memorize the recipes, and then claim you're a cook. But that is exactly what many—not all—of the proponents of the new paradigm have in mind. Like Watts himself would say, it's like eating the menu instead of the meal. The new paradigm is just a new menu, but nobody's talking about the meal anymore, and that bothers me.

I just wanted my voice added because sometimes these themes simply don't get emphasized enough, so anxious are we to forge a new mental picture of that which is really transmental. And the only way you actually know the transmental is to actually transform. You cook the meal and eat it, you don't emboss the menu. So that's what we're trying to say.

7

The Pre/Trans Fallacy

W E HAVE SEEN that one of the greatest obstacles to the emergence of a truly comprehensive or integral paradigm is the attempt to base it on only one of the several modes of knowing available to the soul—an attempt known as category error. For it now seems certain that until the full spectrum of knowing is acknowledged, the full spectrum of being—the comprehensive world view—will likewise remain hidden, obscured, elusive.

But there is another obstacle to the emergence of a comprehensive world view, and by all accounts this obstacle is the most fascinating of all. In its various forms, this obstacle, this fallacy, has infected psychologists from Freud to Jung, philosophers from Bergson to Nietzsche, sociologists from Lévy-Bruhl to Auguste Comte; it lurks as equally behind the mythological and romantic world views as behind the rational and scientific; it exists to this day in both the attempts to champion mysticism and the attempts to deny it. Until this obstacle is overcome, until this major fallacy is exposed, a truly comprehensive world view will, I believe, most definitely continue to evade us. This obstacle we call the "pre/trans fallacy"; this chapter is an attempt to unravel it.

The essence of the pre/trans fallacy is easy enough to state. We begin by simply *assuming* that human beings do in fact have access

198

to three general realms of being and knowing—the sensory, the mental, and the spiritual. Those three realms can be stated in any number of different ways: subconscious, self-conscious, and super-conscious; or prerational, rational, and transrational; or prepersonal, personal, and transpersonal. The point is simply that, for example, since *pre*rational and *trans*rational are both, in their own ways, *non*-rational, then they appear quite similar or even identical to the untu-tored eye. Once this confusion occurs—the confusion of "pre" and "trans"—then one of two things inevitably happens: the transratio-nal realms are *reduced* to prepersonal status, or the prerational realms are *elevated* to transrational glory. Either way a complete and overall world view is broken in half and folded in the middle, with one half of the real world (the "pre" or the "trans") being thus profoundly mistreated and misunderstood. And it is *that* misunder-standing which will concern us in this chapter.

THE GENERAL NATURE OF THE PRE/TRANS FALLACY

The concept of the pre/trans fallacy—and let us call it "ptf" for short—stems from both developmental philosophy, which is repre-sented most effectively by Hegel in the West and Aurobindo in the East, and developmental psychology, which is epitomized by Bald-win and Piaget in the West and kundalini yoga in the East. This general developmental-evolutionary view holds that *in the world of maya* all things exist in time; since the world of time is the world of flux, all things in this world are in constant change; change implies some sort of difference from state to state, that is, some sort of *devel-opment;* thus all things in this world can only be conceived as ones that have developed. In essence, *all phenomena develop,* and thus true phenomenology is always evolutionary, dynamic, or develop-mental—this was, for example, the burden of Hegel's *Phenomenol-ogy of Spirit.*

According to this viewpoint, then, any given phenomenon exists in and as a stream of development, and one of the best ways to grasp the phenomenon's nature is to attempt to reconstruct its develop-ment—trace its history, map out its evolution, discover its *context* not just in space but also in time. That point is crucial in itself, and we shall return to it again and again. But for the moment, let us go straight to the next point: if one attempts to look at the world-at-large in such developmental terms, the world itself appears to be evolving in a definite direction, namely, toward higher levels of structural organization, toward greater holism, integration, awareness, consciousness, and so on. Indeed, a brief glance at the evolutionary record to date—matter to plant to lower animal to mammal to human—shows a pronounced growth toward increasing complexity and awareness.

Many philosophers and psychologists, looking at this evolutionary course, have concluded that not only can phenomena be best understood as ones that have developed, but that development itself is heading toward noumenon. We are all familiar with Teilhard de Chardin's evolutionary conception of the omega point and with Aurobindo's evolutionary drive toward the supermind, but the same concept was held in the West by such philosophers as Aristotle and Hegel. Hegel, for example, maintained that "The Absolute is Spirit [in] the process of its own becoming, the circle which presupposes its end as its purpose and has its end as its beginning. It becomes concrete or actual only by its development. . . ."³¹ The "end" of which Hegel speaks is similar to supermind and omega—it is a state of "absolute knowledge" where "Spirit knows itself in the form of Spirit."

Thus history (evolution) was, for Hegel as for the perennial philosophy in general, the process of the self-actualization of Spirit. Significantly, Hegel maintained that this developmental process occurs in three major stages. It begins with nature, the lowest realm—the realm of matter and of simple bodily sensations and perceptions. This realm we shall be calling the *prepersonal* or the *subconscient*. Hegel often speaks of subconscient nature (i.e., the prepersonal realm) as a "fall" (*Abfall*)—but it is not that nature is set against Spirit or divorced from Spirit. Rather nature is simply "slumbering Spirit," or "God in His otherness." More specifically, nature is "self-alienated Spirit," or the *lowest* form *of* Spirit in its return *to* Spirit.

In the second phase of the return of Spirit to Spirit, or of the overcoming of self-alienation, development moves from (prepersonal) nature to what Hegel calls the self-conscious stage. This is the stage of typical egoic or mental awareness—the realm we shall be calling personal, mental, and self-conscious.

Finally, according to Hegel, development culminates in the Absolute, or Spirit's discovery of Spirit as Spirit, a stage/level we shall be calling transpersonal or superconscious.

Note, then, the overall sequence of development: from nature to humanity to divinity, from subconscious to self-conscious to superconscious, from prepersonal to personal to transpersonal. This is

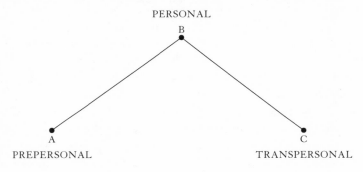

FIGURE 1

represented in Fig. 1. Precisely the same three major stages can be found in Berdyaev and Aurobindo, and Baldwin comes very close to it with his notion of prelogical, logical, and hyperlogical. In any case, the conception has an extremely broad grounding.

We need only one last theoretical tool. If the movement from the lower to the higher is evolution, then the reverse, the movement

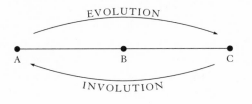

FIGURE 2

from the higher to the lower, is *involution*. (See Fig. 2.) Nature became a "fall" or "slumbering God" or "self-alienated Spirit" through the prior process of involution, or the descent and "loss" of the higher in the lower. Call it the Big Bang, when matter—the lowest realm—was flung into existence out of the Void (*shunyata*). Evolution is the subsequent reversal of the Abfall, the return of

Spirit to Spirit via development. Aurobindo has written extensively on this subject, and I shall do no more than recommend his works. It should be said, however, that one may take involution symbolically and metaphorically, or one may take it literally and metaphysically, but in no case should involution be confused with any movement or sequence of movements in *evolution*. That would be like confusing growing up with being conceived. In any event, even if we totally reject Hegel's or Aurobindo's cosmological notions of involution, we can nevertheless certainly speak of involution in the general sense of moving from higher to lower—in this sense, it is simply the phenomenon of regression. Either of these interpretations will suffice for this chapter.

But now we return to the overall process of *evolution,* or growth and development in general, and here is where the ptf comes in (I'll give its simplified form first, and we can refine it as we go along):

Since development moves from prepersonal to personal to transpersonal, and *since* both prepersonal and transpersonal are, in their own ways, nonpersonal, *then* prepersonal and transpersonal tend to appear similar, even identical, to the untutored eye. In other words, people tend to confuse prepersonal and transpersonal dimensions—and there is the heart of the ptf.

This fallacy has two major forms: the reduction of the transpersonal to the prepersonal, which we call ptf-1, and the elevation of the prepersonal to the transpersonal, or ptf-2. With reference to Fig. 1, the point is that if the subtle but drastic differences between *A* and *C* are not understood, then the two ends of one's developmental map are collapsed into each other. In ptf-1, *C* is collapsed or *reduced* to *A* (and thus ceases to exist *as C*)—Fig. 3. In ptf-2, *A* is *elevated* to *C* (and thus ceases to exist *as A*)—Fig. 4. Instead of two legs of development, we get a single axis.

This collapse instantly creates two opposed world views. Since the real world still contains *A, B,* and *C,* then ptf-1 and ptf-2 will still run into the whole spectrum of existence, but both will necessarily interpret the world in light of their respective deficiencies. Thus, correlative with the two forms of ptf, there are generated two major world views—reductionism and elevationism—precisely as shown in Figs. 3 and 4.

Now both of these world views recognize the personal realm,

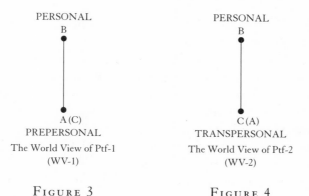

PERSONAL B	PERSONAL B
A (C) PREPERSONAL	C (A) TRANSPERSONAL
The World View of Ptf-1 (WV-1)	The World View of Ptf-2 (WV-2)
FIGURE 3	FIGURE 4

and, moreover, in both views development is thought to have *culminated* in the personal realm (this is because the personal realm is the pivot point *B,* the only point the two views have in common). Beyond that, the two world views diverge dramatically, but their characteristics can be read with frightening accuracy from Figs. 3 and 4, respectively.

World view one (WV-1) sees development moving from a prepersonal source in nature, through a series of intermediate advances, to a culmination in the "high point" of evolution, that of human rationality. It recognizes no higher source or goal of development, and it vehemently denies the necessity of even mentioning such supposedly "higher" levels. Man is a rational being, and rationality is all that is necessary to comprehend and order the cosmos. It looks very much like orthodox science.

WV-2, on the other hand, sees development moving *from* a spiritual source ("in heaven") to a culmination in a "low point" of alienation, that of a sinful humanity or of the individual and personal ego. History is thus the history of a falling down, not a moving up, and mankind (or personal ego) is at the *end* of the fall, just as depicted in Fig. 4. It looks a lot like orthodox religion.

Now the difficult and intricate part is that while the pre/trans fallacy itself is simply an error, the two world views generated by the two ptfs are half true and half fallacious—and *that* is what has made it so hard to decide on their relative merits. They are true when dealing with the half of development that they have not exalted or reduced, and fallacious when dealing with the half they have so mistreated. To be more specific:

We can look basically at overall development in terms of both (1) its nature, or its components—which involve prepersonal, personal, and transpersonal aspects, and (2) its directionality—which entails some sort of understanding (implicit or explicit) of evolution and involution. We would then expect each of these two major but partial world views to say something true and false about both the nature and directionality of development. That is, each of these world views contains *two* important truths and *two* major errors. Specifically, and with regard in each case to nature and direction: WV-1 is correct in maintaining that (1) we possess a prepersonal, irrational, and subconscious component, which did indeed precede the rational and personal in evolution, and (2) the direction of actual or historical evolution is indeed from the lower to the higher. It is wrong when it (1) denies the existence of a transpersonal component and thus (2) denies that there can be a real moving down or descent from Spirit, an involutionary Abfall from union with and as Godhead.

WV-2 is correct in maintaining that (1) there is a transpersonal component to the cosmos, and (2) there is some sense in which we are all "in sin," or living alienated and separated from a supreme identity with Spirit. It is wrong, however, in maintaining that (1) the individual ego, or rational thinking personhood, is the height of alienation from Spirit, and wrong in thus maintaining that (2) a true Eden *preceded* the ego in *evolution*.

The last two points perhaps require clarification. WV-2 maintains, as one block view, that the rational ego is the high point of alienation from Spirit and that, therefore, *evolution* prior to the ego was a Garden of Eden free from original sin. Correlatively, then, the rise of ego (Adam) is, of practical purpose, synonymous with the rise of original sin.

But that is simply the world view of ptf-2. In fact, as both Hegel and Aurobindo demonstrated, *original alienation,* or the high point of alienation, starts with material nature. Nature, or the prepersonal world, is *already* self-alienated Spirit, without any help whatsoever from the ego; and further, nature is the *greatest* point of alienation from Spirit. WV-2 misses the crucial point because it sees clearly only the movement from *C* to *B,* and thus misviews the existence of the leg *B* to *A,* which constitutes the actual extreme of spiritual separation. The ego (*B*) is merely the first structure developed enough to self-consciously *recognize* that the world is *already* fallen from Spirit. What happened in the historical Garden of Eden (some hundreds of thousands of years ago) was not the instigation of original sin (or original separation from Spirit) but the original apprehension of an already original separation. The fact that the ego can now *choose* to act toward Spirit, or choose to deny it, merely adds to the illusion that the ego's existence alone is the instigator of all alienation in the cosmos.

In other words, WV-2 confuses the real Fall that occurs in involution with a supposed fall that occurred in evolution. And it is forced to do so simply because it only recognizes clearly the axis between *B* and *C,* and therefore fails to take accurate account of the *prior* fall to low-point *A.* It then appears that with the evolutionary rise of ego, Spirit reaches its zenith of alienation, whereas in fact, with the rise of ego, Spirit is halfway back home: It has gone from the pre-personal subconsciousness of nature to the personal self-consciousness of Spirit. The fact that the ego, as a halfway house back to Spirit, is the first structure intelligent enough *to be aware of* the already fallen state of existence, makes it appear incorrectly that the ego caused the disease itself, when in fact it is halfway through the cure.

To be sure, the ego is certainly *part* of the fallen or alienated world, and as the first recognizer of this alienation, it suffers doubly. This new suffering makes the ego think that since it did not suffer yesteryear, yesteryear must have been a transpersonal bliss, whereas it was merely a prepersonal ignorance. Nature is asleep in sin, and God is awake without sin—but human beings are caught in the middle: awake *with* sin. Or: Nature is unconscious imperfection, God is conscious perfection, but poor humanity is conscious imperfection. Now human beings can indeed act "sinfully," by choosing against Spirit, or they can act "morally," by choosing Spirit, but that choice, however crucial, still rests upon a sea of already prior alienation. It is not that by choosing wrongly men and women introduce alienation; it is that by choosing correctly they are helping to overcome it.

But failing to grasp that point not only devalues the place of ego, it elevates and romanticizes nature. Nature, instead of being seen as unconscious imperfection, is viewed as unconscious perfection, as if there could be perfection outside of Self-realization. But it then appears that the previous stages of evolution—the prepersonal, subhuman, subconscious stages—constituted some sort of transpersonal heaven, whereas they really added up to nothing but physical forces and animal impulse.

Thus arose the universal Eden myths, which unfortunately were not taken as an allegory of a prior Abfall constituting involution but as a literal story of what happened in earth's recent *evolution*. Naturally the scientists, who did happen to be correct on the *A*-to-*B* leg of the evolutionary record, proceeded with glee to point out that what preceded human beings was not angels but apes, whereupon most orthodox religions began a long series of undignified retreats and ridiculous apologetics, trying to make as a matter of absolute faith the acceptance of the *wrong* half of their otherwise acceptable world view.

Now that is a simple and general introduction to the ptf and its two basic forms of world views. What we will do in the rest of this chapter is examine these two forms of ptf as they have appeared, and are still appearing, in psychological, anthropological, and sociological theories. But I must make very clear what the following discussion attempts to do and what it does not attempt to do. Because this is an introductory presentation, I shall usually only give one (occasionally two) *general* examples of each ptf we shall discuss, avoiding technical details where possible. This does not mean these are the only examples, or necessarily even the most significant ones, but only that they more readily lend themselves to our discussion. The fact that a particular theorist is explicitly mentioned as following a ptf in one instance does not necessarily mean she or he commits the fallacy in all other instances. Also, I do not mean to imply that various theories always fall cleanly into one or the other of these two ptf world views (although that happens quite often)—there are several minor variations on this fallacy, with some occasional combinations and mixtures between its two forms. Finally, many important theorists completely, or at least largely, avoid ptf collapse. Besides Aurobindo, Baldwin, Hegel, and Berdyaev, whom we have already mentioned, I would like to include Maslow and Assagioli among the many transpersonalists who, in my opinion, do not commit significant pre/trans fallacies. My overall goal is simply to use several different examples to suggest how the pre/trans fallacy might be lurking behind various theories, personal and transpersonal, and how we might begin to redress the respective imbalances.

EXAMPLES OF PTF IN PSYCHOLOGICAL THEORIES

In the *The Atman Project,* I took a dozen or so variables and described how human psychological development moves through the three general realms with regard to each variable. These variables included time, space, abstract logic, ego, self-control, socialization, conventional morality, subject/object differentiation, the notion of union or wholeness, verbal mentality, perceptual clarity, angst-guilt, and death-terror. The point, in general, was that development tends to move from, for example, prelogical to logical to translogical modes (cf. Baldwin); from preconventional to conventional to postconventional morality (cf. Kohlberg); from presubject/object differentiation to subject/object differentiation to transsubject/object differentiation; from prepersonal id to personal ego to transpersonal spirit; and so on with each of the variables.

The conclusion was that unless it is clearly understood how pretemporality differs from transtemporality, how pre-egoic impulsiveness differs from transegoic spontaneity, how prepersonal ignorance differs from transpersonal emptiness, how preverbal impulse differs from transverbal insight, how prepersonal fusion differs from transpersonal union, and so on through almost every conceivable variable, then the ptf swings into action in either of its two notorious forms.

With regard to human psychological development, the two major examples of ptf-1 and ptf-2 are, respectively, Freud and Jung (although, as we will see, they do not exhaust the field). Freud correctly recognized the prepersonal id (*A*) and the personal ego (*B*), but he reduced all spiritual and transpersonal experiences (*C*) to the prepersonal level; transtemporal insights are explained as pretemporal id-impulses; transsubject/object *samadhi* is claimed to be a throwback to presubject/object narcissism; transpersonal union is interpreted as prepersonal fusion. In every respect, Freud follows WV-1 (Fig. 3). WV-1, of course, is not confined to Freud. It is standard, orthodox, unquestioned Western orthodoxy—Piaget to Sullivan to Adler to Arieti.

In my opinion, Jung errs consistently to the opposite side. He correctly and very explicitly recognizes the transpersonal or numinous dimension, but he often fuses or confuses it with prepersonal structures. For Jung there are only two major realms: the personal and the collective—and as Assagioli himself pointed out, Jung thus tends to obscure the vast and profound differences between the *lower* collective unconscious and the *higher* collective unconscious; that is, the prepersonal collective and the transpersonal collective realms. Thus, not only does Jung occasionally end up glorifying certain infantile mythic forms of thought, he also frequently gives a regressive treatment of Spirit. In any event, he and his followers thus tend to recognize only two major realms—ego and Self—and human development is therefore viewed as occurring along an ego-Self axis, which is actually drawn precisely as in Fig. 4, with Self at bottom and ego at top. This is pure WV-2, and, as we shall see, it is generally accepted by many transpersonal psychologists, even those who disavow Jung.

Incidentally, the Jungians do recognize that development occurs in two major phases: the development and then the transcendence of the ego. So far, so good. However, since they are working more or less with only one *actual* leg of development (*B-C*), they are forced into making that single axis do double duty. Instead of seeing development as going from *A* to *B* to *C*, they see it as going from *C* to *B* and then *back* to *C*. Not unconscious prepersonal to personal to transpersonal, but unconscious transpersonal to personal to transpersonal. Not pre-ego to ego to transego Self, but Self to ego back to Self. Instead of Fig. 1, they have in mind Fig. 5, which, for convenience, they depict precisely as in Fig. 4. (The fact that Fig. 5 has two legs should not conceal its ptf-2 essence.)

In these types of theories, the prepersonal realm *qua* prepersonal realm seems to get left out. However, what actually happens, behind the theoretical scenes, is simply that the prepersonal realm gets ele-

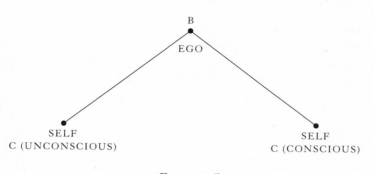

FIGURE 5

vated to quasi-transpersonal status. Among numerous other results (which we will investigate below), it might subsequently appear as a type of infantile psychological Garden of Eden. And while we can agree that infancy is free of certain conceptual anxieties, that "freedom" is not due, in my opinion, to transpersonal protection but prepersonal ignorance, a point on which Maslow was equally insistent.

Such theories, in effect, posit a type of U-turn right in the middle of development—a simple and predictable result of ptf-2 collapse. But this U-turn also seems bolstered by a related misunderstanding. Instead of seeing that involution goes from *C* to *B* to *A*, and evolution goes from *A* to *B* to *C*, it views *A-to-B* as involution (or the movement of "greatest" alienation—called "alienation from Self" in Jungian theory) and *B-to-C* as the "sole" movement of evolution. It consequently overlooks or denies that *A-to-B* is the *first* part of evolution, and that, as far as involution or alienation goes, it is *A*, not *B*, that stands farthest from Self (or Spirit). Thus the ego-mind, in true WV-2 form, mistakenly appears as the high point of alienation, instead of the high point of self-conscious recognition of already alienation and the halfway point of *return* to Self, or the overcoming of already alienation.

In my opinion, besides Jung and his followers, this ptf-2 and its world view is found, although in different outer forms and to different degrees, in a large (but certainly not total) number of transpersonal psychologists, in the immensely influential works of Norman O. Brown, in Matte Blanco's *The Unconscious as Infinite Sets*, in my own early works, *Spectrum of Consciousness* and (to a lesser degree)

No Boundary, in Welwood, Alan Watts, aspects of Bergson, Wordsworth, and virtually all romantic psychologists and philosophers. Since it is understood that Spirit is beyond ego, but since the non-egoic realms are not clearly differentiated into pre-egoic and trans-egoic, the result is a pervasive devaluation of ego and/or elevation of pre-ego. It might be necessary, then, to remind ourselves, as Meher Baba put it:

> Human consciousness would be no more than a repository of the accumulated imprints of varied experiences did it not also contain the principle of *ego-centered integration.* The process [that is ego] implies capacity to hold different experiences together as parts of a unity and the capacity to evaluate them by mutual relation. The integration of the opposites of experience is a condition of emancipating consciousness from the thraldom of [prepersonal] compulsions and repulsions which tend to dominate consciousness: and the *early attempts in securing such integration are through the formation of the ego.*
>
> The part played by the ego in human life may be compared with the function of the ballast in a ship. The ballast keeps the ship from too much oscillation; without it, the ship is likely to be too light and unsteady and in danger of being overturned. The psychic energy would be caught up in the mazes of dual experience and would be frittered away were there no provisional nucleus to bind together the active tendencies born of the relatively independent instincts inherited from [prepersonal] animal-consciousness. The formation of the ego serves the purpose of giving a certain amount of stability to conscious processes, and secures a working equilibrium which makes for organized life.[69]

Thus, concludes Baba, "it would be a mistake to imagine that, as the ego arises only to vanish, it fulfills no need in the long journey of the soul. Though the ego is not meant to be permanent since it can be transcended and outgrown through spiritual endeavor [leg *B* to *C*], the phase of ego-formation [*A* to *B*] must nevertheless be looked upon as necessary for the time being."[69]

The ptf-2 misunderstanding, which devalues ego and elevates pre-ego, takes on ominous proportions when it comes to some (but certainly not all) forms of "avant-garde" or "human potential" or "humanistic/transpersonal" psychotherapies. Put simply, the problem is that many, perhaps most, people who seek or need therapy are suffering in large part from *prepersonal* fixations, dissociations, and obsessions, and haven't the ego-strength to transcend those subhuman angers, impulses, and drives which therefore threaten to overwhelm their very existence. Introduced to a purely WV-2 therapist, they are invited to "let-go" of the very structure—that of egoic conceptualization and integration—that they are in such desperate need to create and strengthen. Such WV-2 therapists overlook the elemental fact that, in devaluing ego and elevating pre-ego realms— realms such as body, feeling, impulse, sensation, experiential immediacy, *chakras* 1–3—they are actually championing realms which are *more* self-centric and narcissistic than the ego, and realms which therefore (if not transcended) actually constitute much of the very problem that they seek to overcome.

There is a marvelous passage in Salinger's *Franny and Zooey* that keys this whole issue. Franny, becoming deeply drawn to contemplative (transpersonal and mystical) practices, decides that all misery in the world is, in essence, the fault of ego, and that the ego consequently must go. As someone sarcastically but accurately explains her views, "everything's ego, ego, ego, and the only intelligent thing for a girl to do is lie around . . . and beg God for a little mystical experience that'll make her nice and happy." Finally Zooey reacts: "You keep talking about *ego*. My God, it would take Christ himself to decide what's ego and what isn't. . . . But don't go screaming about egos in general. In my opinion, if you really want to know, half the nastiness in the world is stirred up by people who aren't using their true egos. Take your Professor Tupper. From what you say about him, anyway, I'd lay almost any odds that this thing he's using, the thing you think is his ego, isn't his ego at all but some other, much dirtier, much less *basic* faculty."

Baldwin, who skillfully avoided ptf, elegantly pointed out that in the highest stage of growth (*B* to *C*), "Consciousness achieves a freeing *from* logic as before [*A* to *B*] she worked to secure the freeing *of* logic." The point, of course, is that one can indeed be freed *from* ego-logic, but if and only if one frees, liberates, and establishes ego-logic *in the first place*. The majority, the vast majority, of common pathological problems derive from a miscarriage of development that prevents the conscious movement *from* self-centric, infantile, and prepersonal modes *to* rational, integrative, and conscientious ego-structures. Most neurotics suffer not because of lack of ego-transcendence, but from the prior lack of ego-esteem, and therapy must be, first and foremost, the *facilitator of strong ego-esteem* and then— but only then—the facilitator of ego-transcendence.

In my opinion, Jungian psychology manages to avoid such therapeutic, if not theoretic, WV-2 problems, simply because it so highly emphasizes that one must first strengthen ego, *then* transcend it. And yet that is the crucial insight missing from so many human-potential therapies, those which, caught in the notion that the ego is the height of alienation-pathology, end up strengthening the very modes that are actually the source of the problem, while denigrating the only structure capable of solving it.

PTF IN SOCIOLOGY AND ANTHROPOLOGY

In *Up from Eden,* I extended and clarified the discussion of ptf (in ways we shall soon examine) and also tried to point out some of the ways both its forms seem to have infected anthropological and sociological theories.

We have already mentioned briefly the two forms as displayed in anthropological theories. WV-1 forms the basis of general Darwinian evolutionary theory, which correctly sees evolution as moving from lower to higher, and reminds us, as Darwin said, that "man still bears in his bodily frame the indelible stamp of his lowly origin." But the strict theory of natural selection, a true WV-1, suffers from not acknowledging the role played by Spirit in evolution. It consequently attempts to derive the higher *from* the lower instead of from Spirit, and further refuses to see any *higher* stages of evolution. WV-1 is, of course, standard, orthodox, Western anthropology.

It has as its opposite or mirror image the Eden corpus—Eden interpreted as literal evolution instead of as prior involution. From this WV-2 angle, Eden is seen, not as a state of prepersonal ignorance and immersion in self-alienated nature, but as some sort of actual, transpersonal heaven on earth. The necessary rise of self-conscious ego is then misinterpreted as a fall from a heavenly and spiritual estate, whereas it is simply an anxious halfway point on the way back from the lowest reach of self-alienation and subconsciousness to a real superconscious heaven in actualized Spirit. This WV-2 theory is not confined to a religious myth; there is a whole and vastly influential school of anthropology that takes it as just so. They consequently imbue what are often primitive and barbaric rites of pre-egoic stages with all sorts of transegoic symbolism, and read deeply mystical insights into crude rites of ritual butchery. They damn the rise of modern intelligence and slander the use of logic, and make it all appear believable by elevating every inarticulate slobber of the savage to a transcendental status, so that the poor mental-ego, by comparison, appears the devil incarnate. From its more dilute and secular forms, such as the romantic anthropology of Rousseau (the idea of the "noble savage"), to its more religious forms, which see the sacrifice mythology of the Bronze Age as the Golden Age of Transcendence, to its outright decadence theories, such as those of Klagess, that see the rise of reason as a fundamental error in the cosmos, this whole WV-2 anthropology—which places the present mental-ego at the end of a long slide downhill, a slide whose results outweigh any corresponding advances—has been immensely influential in its various guises.

Incidentally, Max Schlerer, as Berdyaev notes, "has established four types of anthropological theory: (1) The Jewish-Christian—the creation of human beings by God and the Fall; (2) the ancient Greek conception of men and women as the bearers of reason; (3) the natural science view of men and women as the products of evolution . . . ; (4) the decadence theory which regards the birth of consciousness and reason as biological retrogression, a weakening of life [and creation of angst]."[9] The overall theory we are presenting here attempts, by taking out what are suggested to be ptf elements in *each* view, to make possible a general synthesis of *all* of them. We have already examined what, in my opinion, constitute both the true and false halves of the first three theories. I simply add here that we even make room for the decadence theory, *if* it is understood that humanity's early evolution (*A* to *B*) does indeed involve an increase in guilt, anxiety, and angst-sickness, *not* because human beings are becoming fundamentally weaker in nature but because they are becoming more complex, with increasing responsibilities in consciousness (as was carefully explained in *Up from Eden*). With those ptf corrections in mind, not only do I agree with each of those theories, I absolutely endorse them.

We come now to sociological theories, specifically those addressing the "new age." On the one hand, there are those who, like Christopher Lasch and Peter Marin, clearly show that much of the so-called new age is actually infected with, if not based on, narcissistic regression and self-centric fixation. I personally happen to agree with the great bulk of their analyses, and consequently I think that we transpersonalists are going to have to get very straight, very fast, and evidence the most rigorous of intellectual discrimination and conceptual clarity, if we are to avoid theoretical oblivion.

Unfortunately, like most subscribers to WV-1, Lasch and others throw out the baby with the bathwater. After tracing the prepersonal rampage of the new age narcissism, they are forced (explicitly or implicitly) to include in the pathological heap all transpersonal experiences as well, simply because they have no way to tell the difference between prepersonal regression and transpersonal progression. They thus assume that every time there arises a consciousness not exclusively bound to history, ego, time, or logic, the person involved must be regressing into presocial and pre-egoic worlds, overlooking the fact that the person might, just might, be contacting transtemporal and transegoic truths. These critics would be forced, by their very reasoning, to the conclusion that Christ must have been hallucinating, Lao Tzu was psychotic, Buddha was schizophrenic, and so with Plato and Hegel, Aurobindo and all.

The new age enthusiasts, such as Roszak—or any of those who have suggested that we are or will soon be experiencing the greening of America, the new cultural revolution, a great transpersonal wave—often seem to err in the opposite direction (ptf-2). In their understandable haste to move beyond ego, they frequently fail to specify clearly in which direction that movement is or should be occurring. Two things then tend to happen: They either elevate pre-egoic license to the status of transegoic freedom (as the "*dharma* bums" did), or they simply denigrate the role of mind, ego, secondary process and logic, and in its place they argue for a mode that is called simply "nonegoic," "nonrole bound," "nonlogical," and so on. In such cases, this "nonegoism" usually conceals a mixture and confusion of pre-egoic fantasy with transegoic vision, of preconceptual feelings with transconceptual insight, of prepersonal desires with transpersonal growth, of pre-egoic whoopee with trans-egoic liberation. Jack Crittenden, in a long and thoughtful review of this whole stance, concluded, "It seems that Roszak, along with many other chroniclers of the Aquarian Age, misconstrues ego license for ego transcendence."[32]

Perhaps the problem is that such chroniclers correctly see that future evolution involves a conscious resurrection of Spirit, but they muddle that realization with the thought that almost any mode that isn't mental-egoic must be transcendent. And so, as they look around at the present social and world situation and see the widespread disintegration of logic, they tend to conclude that imminent spiritual transformation is at hand, overlooking the extraordinarily ominous indicators that what is at hand might be prepersonal holocaust, not transpersonal enlightenment. Their writings then tend to see every social disintegration as "creative" and every pathology as cause for jubilation. We repeat that the true half, the true aspects, of their writings are extremely important; but, taken at face value, they fail to discriminate ego transcendence from ego annihilation. Thus, aside from misreading present-day sociological trends, they often end up recommending a course of action that is actually a mixture of up and down: They inadvertently advocate now progression, now regression, now New Age, now Dark Age, now breakthrough, now breakdown.

Whenever a Lasch-type gets together with a Roszak-type, sparks fly. The new agers deny that their movement is narcissistically tinged just as vehemently as Lasch and others deny that they have an antispiritual bias. Each tends to claim simply that the other is fundamentally prejudiced in his or her world view, or that the other is a victim of old paradigms. I am trying to suggest that both may be partially right (and partially wrong), and that both need to be untangled from any ptfs they conceal and then integrated in a sane fashion. This is all the more urgent, given the present-day social turmoils. Granted that standard mental-egoic translations are beginning to fail, and that society at large is undergoing some kinds of significant transformations. But in which directions? Transegoic or pre-egoic or some exotic mixture of both? Unless we spot the nature of the disease, we had better be very careful about the cures we advertise.

Transcendence, Repression, and Regression

The course of development is defined at every stage by increasing differentiation, integration, and transcendence. It is not that transcendence per se occurs only in the highest realms—although it certainly occurs there royally—but that each stage of growth, no matter how lowly, *transcends its predecessor* to some degree by definition and by fact. Thus, for example, the mind transcends and animates the body just as Spirit transcends and inspires mind.

But this places a burden on each successive stage of development, for not only must it cleanly transcend or differentiate from its lower predecessor, it must *integrate* and *include* that lower level in its own higher wholeness and greater structural organization. As Hegel said, "To supersede is at once to negate and to preserve"—that is, to transcend and to include; to transcend and thus negate the partiality and lopsidedness of the lower level but to include and thus preserve its essential structures and functions. For example, to transcend mind in Spirit is not to lose mind or destroy mind but merely to include mind in the higher-order wholeness of the superconscient. What is negated is the exclusivity of mind; what is preserved is the capacity of the mind.

One of the main themes of *The Atman Project* is that if development miscarries at any point, then instead of differentiation there is dissociation, instead of transcendence, repression. The higher stage does not transcend and include the lower, it dissociates and represses it (or aspects of it). The dissociated component—now cut off from the conscious sweep of ongoing development and structuralization—sends up its disturbing derivatives in the form of pathological symptoms and symbols. In these instances, as Freud demonstrated, therapy involves in some sense, a reintegration of the dissociated aspects, a re-membering of components previously dismembered.

This becomes especially obvious if we look at the general transition(s) from the prepersonal to the personal realm, which was Freud's speciality. Freud's essential message was that the personal realm—mind, ego, logic—can and too often does repress the prepersonal realm—id, emotion, sex, nature. The famous Oedipus complex—a rebellion against father (law and culture) and incestuous return to mother (sexuality and nature)—simply represents a failure to transform from prepersonal to personal, with consequent fixation, dissociation, and pathology.

As this general understanding began to reach the public at large, it actually seemed to bolster antirationality and romantic regression, due to a simple misunderstanding. Individuals at large mistakenly thought that abstinence from (or discipline of) emotional-sexuality was the same as the repression of emotional-sexuality. Thus common wisdom began to recommend as "healthy" the general indulgence and overindulgence of emotional-sexual release. In the span of a few decades, large blocks of Western culture traded repression of sex for fixation to and obsession with sex. The *same* dissociation of mind and body was at work, but individuals were now exploiting the body side of the split, where previously they had at least the virtue, however misplaced, of hanging to the mental side. *Repressive* culture was replaced by *regressive* culture, and the cult of narcissus was everywhere upon us.

In the hands of such intellectuals as Wilhelm Reich, the regression from mind to body was given alibi. Reich started with the extremely important idea that mental-egoic character structure was responsible for large-scale libido-body (or orgone) repression. The fundamental problem, said Reich, was to heal the split between mind and body, thus resurrecting a total psychophysical organism. So far, so good. The problem, however, was that Reich increasingly began to "heal" the body-mind split by championing *only* the body and its orgone energies. He went from saying that body unrepressed by mind is higher than body repressed by mind, to saying that body is higher than mind, period. This is really a modern psychological version of the Eden myths: blame the repression of the lower, not on something the higher may or may not do, but on the *very existence* of the higher—then throw out the higher; that is, cure the repression by regression.

But Reich, and especially his modern followers, in effect covered their tracks by renaming the body level. They called it the "body-mind." Now in my opinion there is indeed a bodymind level, because there is a developmental progression from the body to the mind with a further and consequent possibility of integrating mind and body into a higher-order wholeness of bodymind union (the centaur). That is, the developmental progression is body to mind to bodymind. However, the neo-Reichians (among numerous others) frequently collapse the body and the bodymind levels and refer ambiguously to "*the* bodymind." Instead of body and mind and bodymind, they have only mind and bodymind. The body *qua* body seems to get left out, *except* that, in neo-Reichian style, what they mean by "bodymind" usually turns out to be the preverbal body all by itself, and therefore what is really getting left out is the actual union of verbal-mind and feeling-body—the true bodymind (centauric) union. Further, since what they call "bodymind" is said to be a "higher reality" than the mind, all they have done is put the mind back on the lowest rung of the ladder by elevating the preverbal body to exalted status, and by giving that body a newspeak name that makes the whole affair sound holistic.

This miniature pre/trans fallacy (and the reason that it is a ptf will be explained shortly) can be found even in the works of such sensitive psychologists as Carl Rogers. According to Rogers, there are two major realms of awareness, the conceptual self and the experiential self. The experiential realm is variously called organismic sensing, organismic experiencing, or ongoing psychophysiological flow. The implication is that the psychophysical realm is in fact a bodymind (centauric) integration. But Rogers frequently uses the term to mean what we would recognize only as the body, or feeling-experience and emotional-valuing. Thus, he states that traditionally his theory of the psychophysiological flow was indeed "stressing primarily the emotional-experiential component of being." His theory was thus widely viewed as similar to sensory awareness, felt meaning, experiential therapy, body-based awareness, and so on. But of late he has begun to emphasize that the experiential flow or organismic feeling is really "more than heightened sensory awareness of internal bodily states and of limbic system activities. It is the integration of this [body] awareness with awareness of those functions represented by the neocortex [mind]."[101]

My point is that one cannot have it both ways. One cannot use a psychophysical or bodymind-union concept to refer to "the inherent wisdom of the body," and then claim it is also and really a total integration of logic-mind and body-feeling. And if by the concept one really means just integrating capacity in general, then there is every reason to assign that function more to the mind than to the subhuman body, as Meher Baba said.

Rogers is very careful to try to avoid such ambiguities, and more often than not he succeeds. But in the hands of less capable psychologists, his theory tends frequently to support and encourage the elevation of the body past the mind to bodymind status. Instead of body-sensing, mental-insight, and bodymind integration, there is only "bodymind experiencing" versus mental-logic—and there is the mini-ptf that has tended to denigrate linguistic communication and devalue the very structures that allow men and women to transcend body-bound and narcissistic impulse.

(It should be said that I am a staunch supporter of body-oriented therapies and recommend them, along with diet and exercise, as the first step of any overall therapy [especially Yoga, Rolfing, focusing, Alexander]. We all seem generally out of touch with the body and must begin by rebuilding the base. It is one thing, however, to re-contact the body so as to reintegrate it, quite another to recontact the body and stay there. Unless the released body-feelings are taken up and made a part of the higher stream of *communicative exchange* and *intersubjective sharing,* they merely reinforce an isolated I-ness. For it is *only* the mind, via symbol-exchange in communicative discourse, that reaches intersubjective and interpersonal bonding. The body as body is merely self-referential; it cannot take the role of other and thus cannot enter community. It merely senses and emotes over its own separate self-existence. The body is merely subjective; the mind is intersubjective; spirit is transsubjective—and the lower you go on that ladder, the more narcissistic and self-centric you become. In therapy, it is necessary to reverse this trend, and so we start at the bottom with body-therapies. But we certainly don't stay there, and we don't elevate muscle twitches above mental insight.)

But my point in bringing all this up is merely to suggest what historically happened when a genuine *transpersonal* orientation was introduced to this prevailing humanistic notion that distinguished and recognized basically only a "bodymind" and a mind, with mind on the lowest or at least lower rung. Since mind was pictured as the lowest or most alienated level, and since "bodymind" (read body) was thought to be higher, then supermind or big mind was imagined to lie in and through the direction of the "bodymind." Here was the scheme:

mind
"bodymind"
supermind

My suggestion is that the scheme should have been:

body
mind
bodymind
supermind

And, in fact, since by "bodymind" most writers actually (if unwittingly) meant body, their scheme amounted actually (if unwittingly) to confusing supermind or Spirit with the very *end limit of a sequence of regression* from the mind to the body (an end limit we will soon describe as the primary matrix). The point is that the neo-Reichian legacy often played straight into ptf-2 and its world view: the personal, logical, conceptual mind is a devalued structure, and almost any other mode, from bodily feelings to emotional sensing, is theoretically viewed or actively pursued as part of the higher consciousness. And although this did not solely cause, it certainly did not stem, the subsequent theoretical disaster.

The Primary Matrix

Beginning with Freud's initial speculations and culminating with such research-theorists as Hartmann, Klein, Jacobson, Spitz, and Mahler, it was becoming increasingly obvious that the earliest stages of infant development were ones of narcissistic fusion: the infant does not clearly differentiate self from other, subject from object, inside from outside but, rather, lives in a primary matrix where such distinctions are as yet largely absent (the pleroma).

The metapsychological problem arises: How to interpret the primary matrix? What meaning could it have? What role might it play in subsequent development?

In a sense, the Jungians gave the first real metatheory: The primary matrix represents the original, primal, all-encompassing unity of ego and Self. In fact, they suggested, the primary matrix *is* the primary Self (or, technically, an unconscious identity with Self), the total-unified wholeness at the start, prior to separate ego development. Now we said that Freud's own speculations were leading toward this type of original primary-matrix self, and so it is not surprising that modern Jungian thought has already joined in part with many neo-Freudian schools, especially the British Kleinians and the American object-relationists and certain ego-psychologists. In essence, their central point of agreement is stated popularly by Brown as follows: "Freud says not only that the human ego-feeling once embraced the whole world [the primary-matrix self], but also that Eros drives the ego to recover that feeling. In primal narcissism [original matrix] the self is *at one with a world of love and pleasure;* hence the ultimate aim of the human ego is to reinstate what Freud calls 'limitless narcissism' and find itself once more at one with the whole world in love and pleasure."[26]

Already we are handed a problem, because the phrase "at one with the *whole world*" gives the primary matrix a connotation of almost universal wholeness. But surely the infant could not be one with the *whole* world. The infant is not one with the mental world, the social world, the personal world, the subtle world, the symbolic world, the linguistic world, the communicative world—because, in fact, none of those yet exist or have yet emerged. Infants are not one with those levels, they are perfectly ignorant of them. One might as well claim a dog is one with the United Nations because it does not display conflict toward it. Rather, what infants are basically one with, or fused with, is just the material environment and the biological mother—they cannot distinguish their physical body from the physical environment—no levels higher than that enter this primitive (pleromatic) fusion state. It is prepersonal, not personal *or* transpersonal.

Thus, it is a grand ambiguity to refer to this early fusion state as a "oneness with the whole world," if by "whole world" we mean anything other than primitive bio-material fusion. And further, that primitive fusion-matrix simply cannot be equated, in my opinion, with the Self or with Self-identity. But there exactly was the prob-

lem with the Jungian (and neo-Jungian) view, which maintained
that this early state was an identification with Self, an *identification
that is subsequently lost in development and then regained in enlightenment* (precisely as depicted in Fig. 5, and here our argument joins
up with our preliminary discussion of this WV-2 theory). For the
Self is the totality of psychological structures, not the lowest psychological structure; the totality has not yet manifested itself in the infant, and it is impossible to be actually one with only a potential,
just as you cannot actually eat a potential apple. *Or,* if you do take
that view metaphorically and say that the Self is always present even
if unrealized (or unconscious), then you must also admit that *all*
levels, prior to enlightenment, are one with Self in an unconscious
fashion, but then it makes no sense whatsoever to say that that state
is *lost* in subsequent development. Either way, the view is fallacious.

Now what *is* lost in subsequent development is the relatively
blissful ignorance of the subconscious, prepersonal, bio-material fusion. That is, the infant does break an identity, not with Self, but
with the prepersonal matrix (the pleroma). And further, it is precisely the personal ego that has the consciousness, strength, and
power to break and transcend that primitive fusion, and thus move,
not away from Self, but halfway back to Self.

What role, then, if any, does the Self play in development? We
can begin by agreeing with Vedanta that *all* levels and stages are one
with Self, but prior to enlightenment, this oneness is unconscious (or
unrealized). The prepersonal state—as with Aurobindo's subconscient and Hegel's nature—is also in essence one with Self, but since
it is the state of "God in His otherness," then ignorance (*avidya*) or
unconsciousness is at its extreme limit, and thus awareness is poorly
developed or absent altogether (this is the primary matrix). With
the next major stage, the personal ego rises above the prepersonal
sphere and shakes off some measure of unconsciousness, and thus
awakens as a self-conscious, self-reflexive entity. The ego is also essentially one with Self in a still unrealized fashion, but it at least
begins to consciously awaken to the Self in a half-measure (contrasted with the prepersonal stage, which consciously realized no
measure).

The ego, then, is no longer protected by ignorance but not yet
saved by Self, and *therefore* it, alone of all the stages, experiences

guilt, angst, and despair. But that angst, as it appears in evolution, is not, to repeat, a sign of alienation from or deintegration of Self, but the symptom that a cure for the disease of Self-alienation is half in progress. In evolution, the loss of the prepersonal ignorance does indeed introduce angst, but that angst is not a symptom of a just-broken ego-Self unity but of a just-transcended ego-animal slumber. Most WV-2 theorists, since they conflate pre-ego and transego, tend to take the rise of ego and angst as indicators of a fall down from Self, whereas in evolution it actually signals a rise up from subconsciousness. It's not *real* decadence, it just feels like it. And while I attach much significance to, and make abundant theoretical room for, the developmentally emergent feelings of angst and decadence and regret and guilt, I do not interpret them along the lines of ptf-2.

At any rate, in the final major stage, individual consciousness returns itself to its Self, now in a fully conscious and realized form, so that Spirit knows itself as Spirit in Spirit, with a subsequent and final overcoming of angst and alienation.

Since the Self was both the *ground* of every stage of development and the *goal* of every stage of development, it is perfectly acceptable to say that the Self was present all along, "guiding," "pulling," and "directing" development, so that *every* stage of development is drawn closer and closer to Self-realization (as when Jantsch characterized evolution as "self-realization through self-transcendence"). What seems objectionable is confusing the transpersonal with the prepersonal leg, and then assigning to the prepersonal matrix an exalted status of Self-identity *which is simultaneously denied* to the higher structure of the mental-ego, and *then* covering the obfuscation by saying the first Self-identity is unconscious anyway, and *then* denying even *that* status to the mental-ego. This is nothing but a vicious and denigrating attack on the ego, fueled by ptf-2.

But our theoretical problems with the primary matrix are not over, because we still have to examine ptf-1. To begin with, right where the Jungians place the unconscious Self, the orthodox Freudians place the unconscious id. In that regard anyway, the Freudians seem correct (development goes id to ego to Self), but then we already expect the Freudians to have the more accurate view of the prepersonal to personal leg. In my opinion, there *is* a transpersonal

Self (Jung), but the primary matrix is prepersonal (Freud). The problem comes when Freudians are faced with a truly transpersonal and actually mystical event, for then they are forced to explain it as regression to the primary matrix, or regression/fixation to primary narcissism and omnipotent valuation (cf. Ferenczi). Now I believe there is most definitely such a regression, in both is useful forms—called regression in service of ego, wherein the ego can occasionally relax its upward growth by slipping back to lower levels, gathering strength and moving forward again—and in its pathological forms—mild regression/fixations in neurotic symptoms and full-scale regression/fixation in psychotic reactions. But the transpersonal Self—and true mystic union—lies in *precisely* the opposite direction. As *The Atman Project* tried to suggest, mysticism is not regression in service of ego, but evolution in transcendence of ego.

But—and without letting the Freudians off the hook—the immediate problem was that, to make it all worse, many transpersonalists, spearheaded by various Jungians, countered this wrong half of the Freudian WV-1 with nothing but the wrong half of their WV-2. Instead of working to the other and high end of the spectrum, they began fighting with the Freudians for control of the same low territory—the primary matrix. The problem was (and still is) that many transpersonalists see the primary matrix and want to use it as a base of operations for the *unio mystica,* or transcendent oneness (overlooking the fact that the primary matrix is presubject/object, not transsubject/object, and prepersonal fusion, not transpersonal union). They have therefore been perfectly willing and even eager to use the *Freudian* notion of regression in service of ego in order to explain and even validate mystical experience. Prince and Savage did precisely that, and Deikman's classic paper on mysticism explains it as a deautomatization—"a shift to a structure *lower in the hierarchy,*"[84] a move downward "towards dedifferentiation," a shift "in the direction of primitive thought"—that is, regression. And he rests the whole argument on a confusion of transpersonal union with prepersonal fusion. But notice that his explanation is not meant to denigrate mysticism; it is an attempt to validate it, to ground it, to explain it in "real" terms—and it is now widely accepted by transpersonalists as *the* explanation of mystical union.

We can see the same "primary matrix" difficulties running

through various anthropological and sociological theories, because modern anthropological research (from Lévy-Bruhl to Gebser to Cassirer) has established as highly likely the fact that primitive men and women lived in a type of *participation mystique,* a vague indissociation of self and group, self and nature, self and animals (hence totemism, the clan-self, kinship ritual, etc.). Participation mystique can, of course, sound very transcendent, holistic, holographic, or whatnot, until you carefully examine the evidence. It soon becomes obvious that such primitives did not transcend subject and object, they simply couldn't differentiate them in the first place. Participation mystique is not a capacity; it is an incapacity. Participation mystique, in fact, is an almost exact phylogenetic parallel of the ontogenetic primary matrix—it is a prepersonal and prerational fusion state, out of which subsequent men and women, in the form of mental-ego, eventually managed to evolve.

But already you can guess what theoretical uses have been made of this concept. On the one side, WV-1 theorists—who are correct in picturing participation mystique as a primitive incapacity and primitive fusion—take any state of *actual* transcendence and claim it is a throwback to the primitive fusion of our ancestors. These "critiques" can be put with terrifying assurances of what will happen to someone in "transpersonal states," simply because what *did* occur in the *prepersonal* realms of participation mystique was in fact quite often horrifying—human sacrifice, blood feasts, cannibalistic orgy, and mass suicide/regicide.

Jonestown, for instance, is probably a perfect example of group regression to participation mystique, or egoic dissolution and self-clan fusion, with subsequent, will-less obedience to totem "master," with emotional-sexual obsessions, sadistic rituals, and mass human sacrifice. WV-1 anthropologists and sociologists are quite right in pointing that out. Problem is, they are forced to apply similar analyses to transpersonal communities headed by actual spiritual masters. Since they cannot theoretically tell the difference between a transpersonal community or *sangha* and a prepersonal clan or cult, such theorists are convinced that all contemplative master-student communities are always on the edge of Jonestown.

Just to make sure, they consult a psychiatrist—who, as a likely subscriber to WV-1, cannot distinguish prepersonal helplessness and dependence on a father figure from transpersonal surrender and submission to a spiritual master—and the psychiatrist assures the sociologist that all such devotees are indeed mass hysterics with borderline personalities and dangerously low self-esteem. In their understandable and perhaps justifiable attempts to save us from Jim Jones and the Reverend Sun Myung Moon, such theorists come very close to saving us from Socrates, Christ, and Buddha.

To return to the other side of the anthropological fallacy: WV-2 theorists agree that there is (or was) a participation mystique among primitives, but they use it to bolster their Eden view of yesteryear. We needn't go into the specifics, since we have already discussed WV-2 anthropology. Suffice it to say that these anthropologists elevate participation mystique to a quasi-transcendental status, and embue the horrifying rituals often accompanying it with mystical significance—ritually murdering a sacrificial victim is "really" a form of "transcending self" ("that takes care of *that* ego"). In pure WV-2 form, participation mystique, like the primary matrix, is elevated from prepersonal fusion to transpersonal union (or unconscious transpersonal union, in the more sophisticated versions of Fig. 5).

Translate this whole discussion into the realm of pathology, and it is no surprise that where the WV-2 psychologists see the supreme Self, the WV-1 psychologists see the supreme pathology. The former therefore tend to see all psychotics as half-saints, while the latter see all saints as half-psychotic. (Examples, respectively: Norman O. Brown, *Love's Body,* and Group for the Advancement of Psychiatry, *Mysticism: Spiritual Quest or Psychic Disorder?*) It seems that until both sides cease fighting each other with the incorrect half of their ptf world views, both real saints and real psychotics will continue to be misrepresented and therefore victimized.

One final note: not only is there a difference between "pre" and "trans," there is a difference between "pre" and "de"; that is, depersonal is not to be confused with prepersonal or transpersonal. For example, in saying that the actual psychotic is regressing to a prepersonal stage, which I agree is in part what happens, it does not follow that the prepersonal stage is a schizophrenic disease. As Bleuler pointed out long ago, the schizophrenic in some ways regresses to child-level, say age three, but the three-year-old child is not a little schizophrenic. Age three is not a disease. The lower levels are pre-personal, but the schizophrenic is *de*personal—and there the vast difference. On top of the regressive movement itself, the depersonal crash carries with it the cascading fragments of higher structures that have ruinously disintegrated. In every way it is a nightmare of destructuring and devolving. And if depersonal cannot be confused with prepersonal, even less can it be called on to explain transpersonal. But when ptf occurs, just that confusion is made, in either of the two basic directions: depersonal psychotics are called saints, and transpersonal saints are called psychotic.

Summary: Our more refined developmental map can be pre-

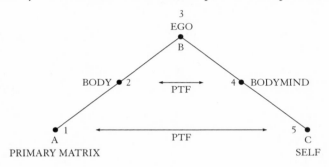

FIGURE 6

sented as in Fig. 6, and we can then summarize our discussion very quickly. In my opinion, Freud is more or less correct in his articulation of 1, 2, and 3, but he denies the existence of 4 and collapses 5 into 1—and that gives perfectly the WV-1 of Fig. 3.

On the other side: Jung clearly believes in, and often eloquently elucidates, 5, but he frequently elevates or confuses 1 with it, thus generating the WV-2 of Fig. 4. And this WV-2 was strengthened by the humanistic mini-ptf: they articulate well the existential, integrated, bodymind union, 4, but, under the neo-Reichian conflation, they often elevate or confuse 2 with it. On this side, the neo-Reichian conflation has joined with the Jungian primary matrix conflation to present an almost invincible WV-2 theory, while on the other, the early Freudian research has today culminated in, and joined with, the extremely influential and widespread school of orthodox ego psychology, to generate a perfect and perfectly entrenched WV-1.

FREUD, EROS, AND THANATOS

Just as numerous theorists—both pro and con—have eagerly used the Freudian notion of regression in service of ego to explain (or explain away) the *nature* of mysticism, so several theorists—again both pro and con—have been drawn to Freud's concept of thanatos (or something similar to it) as a possible explanation for the *dynamic* of mysticism. The starting point is that, as is well known, mystical experience involves "ego-transcendence" or "ego-death"—that is, apparently some sort of thanatos-like elements. From this point, the theorists line up on opposing sides of the same concept: if you are for transcendence, then you interpret thanatos as a drive to surrender ego and find unity in Spirit; if you are against transcendence, then you interpret thanatos as a drive to abdicate ego and regress to morbid id. Norman O. Brown, Charles Garfield, Ronald Laing, and perhaps the majority of transpersonal psychologists would line up on the first side; Freud, Ferenczi, Ernest Becker, and orthodoxy, on the second.

By now you might expect that I shall claim both sides are half-right and half-wrong, and that is true enough. But in this case the discussion becomes extremely intricate, for not only do we have to tease out possible ptf elements from these concepts, we have to wade through a swamp of semantic confusion, primarily about the word "death," but also and consequently about the word "life," for both of these terms have been used to mean something very, very good and something very, very bad. At the very least, then, we are faced with distinguishing between (1) death in the bad sense (premature and useless destruction, or simple degeneration) and (2) death in the good sense (connected with "ego-death" in transcendence); and consequently the difference between (3) life in the good sense (promoting unity and vitality) and (4) life in the bad sense (refusing to give up the "life" of the old so as to make room for the new). As we shall see, all four of these meanings have been used indiscriminately by modern theorists, with resultant and almost total confusion.

Perhaps we can best begin to sort things out by describing some of the actual dynamic factors of structural development without specifying their possible life-death connotations. Once that is done, we can then assign various shades of life-death meaning to them—in both what we are calling "good" and "bad" senses—and use this assignment to analyze the various death-transcendence theories.

To begin with, we have already seen that there are two major "directions" of consciousness movement: The first is ascending, progressive, evolutionary; the second is descending, regressive, involutionary. The evolutionary movement is marked by a series of structures that display ever-increasing holism, transcendence, integration, and unity. The involutionary movement is simply a shift in the opposite direction—it is a move *down* the hierarchy and thus is marked by increasing alienation, fragmentation, lack of unity, and disintegration. Where the aim of evolution is the resurrection of the ultimate Unity in only Spirit, the aim of involution is the return to the lowest unity of all—simple matter, physical insentience, dust.

Now, not only are individuals moved vertically to *change* levels (i.e., evolve or involve), they are moved horizontally *within* levels. The former we call *transformation,* the latter, *translation.* Although it is acceptable to view translation or horizontal movements as tangential derivatives of transformative factors (i.e., as compromises of evolutionary and involutionary drives), it would be helpful if we could also specify the translative forces in their own terms; that is, what, in general, drives horizontal translation?

Without excluding other and more complex elements, we can for simplicity's sake mention two major dialectical forces of translation. For, with regard to any given structure, an individual basically has two drive-choices: to *preserve* the structure or to *alter* it. The first, the preservation factor, seeks to consolidate, close, and fortify the elements of the present structure or level of consciousness. This is similar to Piaget's notion of assimilation and the analytic concept of alloplastic regulation—the structure remains essentially unchanged and the environment is fitted to it.

Against this preservation factor there looms the possibility of the altering, rearranging, or changing of the present structure itself. This is similar to Piaget's accommodation and the analytic autoplastic regulation—the structure must change in order to fit the environment. We may, in the most general sense, refer to it as the release factor, since some present configuration is being released and subsequently altered, or even abandoned altogether. The overall point is that *within* a given level, the individual's actions are a dialectic of preserving, acting, and holding that structure on the one hand, and an altering, rearranging, or releasing that structure on the other. We can display our two translative (horizontal) forces and the two transformative (vertical) forces as follows:

With that display as background, we can now reexamine the various theories of life-death-transcendence, starting with Freud. In *An Outline of Psychoanalysis*,[46] Freud gives a classic (and final) statement of his drive theory. "After long hesitancies and vacillations," he begins, "we have decided to assume the existence of only two basic instincts, *Eros* and *the destructive instinct*. . . . The aim of the first of these basic instincts is to establish ever greater unities . . . —in short, to bind together." We shall qualify this in a moment, but so far that instinct is what we have called the ascent factor—the evolution to ever higher unities and totalities, drive #1.

Freud continues: "The aim of the second is, on the contrary, to undo connections and so to destroy things. In the case of the destructive instinct we may suppose that its final aim is to lead what is living into an inorganic state. For this reason we also call it the *death instinct*." Freud, of course, was severely criticized by everybody, including his own followers, for proposing the death instinct (thanatos), but clearly it is exactly what we have in mind with the descent factor (#2), or the involutionary drive. It is simply the impulse to move to a lower level in the hierarchy, and its final aim, as we said earlier, is therefore insentient matter. In that sense, it is a death instinct, a death drive, a primal masochism. Not a fear of death, but a drive toward it.

Now I do not agree with everything Freud said about this instinct (or its counterpart), nor do his statements exhaust the theoretical dynamics of death, but so far, and within only the definitions I have given, I agree completely with Freud's assessments of both eros and the death instinct.

It should be said, however, that I reject entirely the notion that eros is generated only in the soma and consequently displaced to mind. In my opinion, *each* level is defined by its own unitive tendencies in the arc of evolution, and, as a matter of fact, the higher levels (such as mind) possess more holism and holistic drive—more eros—than the lower ones (such as libido). For example, biological or body-sex eros can only form a union with two bodies at a time, whereas mental eros can unite whole peoples in a community of discourse, and spiritual eros can unite the entire manifest universe in radical oneness. I share none of Freud's biological, sexual, libidinous reductionism. Not only can spirit-transcendence not be reduced to id, neither can ego-mind.

Notice, too, that because Freud is working within WV-1, he correctly sees that the aim of involution is the return to the lowest level of all (inanimate matter), but he refuses to see that the aim of evolution is the resurrection of ultimate unity in Spirit. "If we assume," he says, "that living things came later than inanimate ones and arose from them, then the death instinct fits in with the formula we have proposed to the effect that instincts tend towards a return to an earlier state. In the case of Eros (or the love instinct) we cannot apply this formula. To do so would presuppose that living substance was once a unity which had later been torn apart and was now striving towards re-union."[46] Of course, for the perennial philosophy, that is *exactly* what happened—all things were "torn apart" from Spirit-unity during prior *involution,* and evolution, driven by love (#1), is now reuniting and re-membering all elements in a climb *back* to unity-Spirit. That, for example, was precisely Plato's view ("This becoming one instead of two [is] the very expression of humanity's need. And the reason is that human nature was originally One and we were a whole, and the desire and pursuit of the whole is called love"). Incidentally, Plato's *Symposium* was exactly what Freud was trying to deny with this passage. Needless to say, I side with Plato.

At any rate, this overall discussion gives us the meaning of death in the bad sense—a driving toward less unity via contraction and fragmentation—and life in the good sense—ascending to higher unities via love and expansion. These are factors #1 and #2 in our display.

What we need now is the sense in which death may be good and life bad. For we have seen, first off, that what has sparked so much interest in Freud's thanatos or death instinct is that transcendence seems to involve some sort of ego-death, and this death must be "good" in some sense. What sort of death is good?

To begin with, the ego-death is actual transcendence has absolutely nothing to do with Freud's thanatos. Rather, actual transcendence demands the death of the present structure in the sense that the structure must be *released* or let-go of in order to make room for the higher-order unity of the next structure. The *release factor* in this case is indeed a type of *death;* it is a real dying to an exclusive identity with a lower structure in order to awaken, via love-expansion or transcendence, to a higher-order life and unity. In this sense, such death-and-transcendence occurs at every stage of growth, matter to body to mind to bodymind to spirit. One accepts the death and release (#4) of the lower stage in order to find the life and unity of the next higher stage, and so on until either growth arrests and preservation (#3) alone sets in, or actual Spirit is resurrected in the Great Death of final transcendence and ultimate unity.

That is death in the "good" sense—the release factor (#4) allowing subsequent ascent. The reverse of that is simply the refusal to release and transcend, and that is the preservation factor (#3) gone rigid, sterile, and overbearing. One quits all transformation and seeks merely to preserve one's present structure of consciousness. And while preservation has its important functions, in this case it serves merely stagnation and life gone rigid—and there, finally, is our last factor, life in the "bad" sense. This is the factor the Buddhists have in mind when they speak of attachment, clinging, permanence, fixation, and unyieldingness.

Since we have established two major but different meanings of both life and death, let us distinguish them with uppercase initial letters, thus:

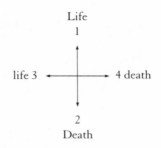

Now we are in a position to easily untangle the various life-death-transcendence theories. To begin with, the "good" factors, those promoting growth, unity, and transcendence, are Life and death. The "bad" factors, those preventing growth and transcendence and even urging the reverse, are life and Death. Already you can see the semantic problems, for these various meanings simply are not differentiated in most modern theories, and the semantic confusions have insinuated themselves deeply into present-day theories to produce several contradictions. I shall give only two major examples.

1. We already mentioned that Buddhism maintains that grasping, clinging, and a desire for permanence (*trishna/svabha*) are the root problems of suffering, simply because those factors prevent growth, and it is only growth leading to Spirit (*dharmakaya*) that can remove suffering (*dukhka*). It therefore recommends life denial and an embrace of self-death (*anatta*). This has led to all sorts of charges that Buddhism is, on the one hand, antilife, antilove, antipurpose, and, on the other, death-obsessed, nihilistic, and necromaniacal.

But, of course, when Buddhists say that the cause of suffering is life-desire, they are repudiating not Life but life. They disavow not love, openness, growth, and transcendence, but status-quo clinging, attachment, fixation, and fear of change (*anicca*). Conversely, the self-death recommended is not Death but death, not regression but release, not involution but accommodation.

Perhaps this confusion started with Schopenhauer, who nobly tried to interpret the Upanishads and *Prajnaparamita Sutras* for the West, but who, in trying to argue for death always sounded like Death, and in denying life always sounded as if he hated Life. In any case, it is a confusion as deep-seated as it is unfair.

2. We come now to the modern death and transcendence theories, notably those of such theorists as Brown, Laing, Garfield. For,

amidst the extremely significant conceptualizations that these researchers are putting forward, there seems to lie a ptf in the form of a persistent ambiguity about the nature of ego-death itself. Put simply, *they do not always or clearly distinguish between ego-death leading to transcendence and ego-death leading to regression.* The ego *dies* in each case, but how different the deaths! And these theorists rarely distinguish them—they confuse or conflate death and Death, factors #4 and #2.

Garfield, for example, suggests that if "the drive to intentionally alter consciousness possesses a thanatomimetic element, as suggested by Robert Kastenbaum and Ruth Aisenberg, then it may well be that this hypothesized drive to thanatomimesis (and its experiential core, ego-loss or ego-death experience) is also innate."[52] Because this does not distinguish between ego-death leading to transcendence and ego-death leading to regressive dissolution (i.e., #4 and #2), Garfield then falls straight into the course of adopting Freud's thanatos (#2)—the drive to material Death—in an attempt to explain the drive to transcendent Life: "In fact," he says, "Freud's description of the operation of Thanatos, the death instinct, approximates, if not duplicates, phenomenological accounts of the Eastern notion of the highest state of consciousness, i.e., satori, nirvana, etc."[52] That is incorrect on both Freud's side and the Eastern side.

Yet this fallacy—or at least theoretical ambiguity—has gained widespread acceptance among transpersonalists, largely, I suppose, because it fits so well with that other widely adopted WV-2 belief, namely, that the primary matrix—that primitive and prepersonal fusion state—is some sort of transpersonal union. Since Freud's thanatos does indeed have as its aim the primary matrix of prepersonal de-struction, and since this matrix is mis-taken to be Self, then it appears that Freud's thanatos has as its aim ego-death in transcendence, whereas in fact its aim is ego-dissolution in regression.

In my opinion, what these transpersonal theorists mean to say is that the mystic union demands not the Death of the ego, but the death of the ego—the death and transcendence, the death and release (#4), of the ego-mind in order to discover the higher Life and Unity of Spirit. That death is truly experienced *as* a death, *is* in fact a death, and so naturally looks like a death. It just isn't Death. As they stand now, however, lacking this elemental distinction, the present-day theories represent a truly bizarre marriage:

The *wrong* half of WV-1 (its reductionism: "mysticism is really just thanatomimetic regression in service of the ego") has joined up the *correct* half of WV-2 (there *is* a transcendent Self), with the even more bizarre but reverse corollary that the *correct* half of WV-1 (in total regression the ego dissolves back into prepersonal fusion) is being used to explain the *incorrect* half of WV-2 (the oceanic matrix is Self). In short, as the false half of Freudianism was joined to the true half of transpersonalism, the true half of the former was used to explain the false half of the latter.

As an ironic twist on this whole ptf confusion, take one last example: Freud—precisely as described above in the Buddhist example—happened to completely misunderstand nirvana as Life-extinction, instead of life-extinction. Nirvana, for Freud, was complete dissolution, the return to dust. Therefore, Freud explicitly referred to thanatos—which does aim for dust, so to speak—as the *nirvana principle.* Now Garfield (and numerous others), coming from the perfectly opposite angle and trying correctly to explicate nirvana as a truly transcendent state, runs into Freud's concepts. The result is ironic. For, in my opinion, Garfield is right about the existence of a transcendent-nirvana, but wrong about Freud's thanatos; Freud is right about thanatos, but wrong about nirvana. Consequently, however, because of this almost seamless overlap of the two wrongs, they both can use the *same* sentence ("Thanatos gives nirvana") to describe their fundamentally different world views.

As for death-drive, Jung criticized thanatos, saying that humans actually possess phobos, a fear of death, not a drive to death. In my opinion, both are true. Phobos is related to death [#4]—it is the *fear of release,* or the fear of dying to a particular structure, and this phobos remains as long as the life [#3] of the structure is not surrendered in its exclusivity. Both phobos and thanatos are present in the psyche, but phobos definitely plays the more decisive role. But now the crowning confusion—most of the neo-Freudians trying to use Freud's concept of thanatos actually use it to mean phobos. Thus, if you want to use the otherwise important insights of these theorists, you end up using the word thanatos to mean phobos—as occasionally I did in *The Atman Project.* But so goes the promised semantic nightmare. Perhaps, however, if you simply remember the four actual dynamic factors, regardless of their arbitrary names, you will be able to figure out what the various theorists actually mean.

I must end by emphasizing the significance of the true half of the new transpersonal theories, such as those of Brown, Garfield, and Laing. For their collective import is that higher growth is bought only by ego-death, a notion that, almost for the first time in history, gives us a genuine sense of the importance and place of death in the overall scheme of Life. My only point is that we must distinguish between ego-death (#4) leading to transcendence and ego-death (#2) leading to regression. Then we can champion death and release, not Death and regress, and we can urge surrender of life and attachment, not Life and love.

A REFINEMENT

I wish in this last section on the theoretical nature of ptf to outline very briefly the refinements given to it in *Up from Eden*. The essential point is that, although we speak of the ptf as a confusion of "pre" and "trans" around a central pivot, this does not mean that there are *only* three structures involved. To speak of development as moving from pre-ego to ego to transego, for instance, does not mean that there are really and only three stages of growth. In fact, there are a dozen (or more) major structure/stages, and the pre/trans fallacy can be committed with regard to *any* of them. The point is merely that, with reference to any structure *X*, it is easy to confuse a pre-*X* structure with a trans-*X* one (or vice versa). We have already examined the neo-Reichian confusion of the body stage (which precedes mind) with the bodymind stage (which succeeds mind). This is every bit as much ptf as is the confusion of id and God; less conspicuous perhaps, but ptf nonetheless.

In *Up from Eden* I therefore examined eight or so major structures of consciousness in order to discover how they may have been subjected (in the context of both historical development and present-day theories) to either ptf-1 or ptf-2. The structure/stages examined, in order of phylogenetic and ontogenetic development, were:

1. Matter—or material fusion, the lowest stage of structural organization, recapitulated in humans via the primary matrix or pleroma.

2. Body—simple sensorimotor intelligence and emotional-sexual drives.

3. Magic—the first symbolic cognitive mode, the primary process, which confuses inside and outside, whole and part, subject and predicate, image and reality.

4. Mythic—higher representational thought, but still incapable of formal-operational insight; still anthropomorphic; mixture of logic with previous magic.

5. Mental-rational—egoic rationality and formal-operational logic.

6. Bodymind—integration of formal and verbal mind with emotional body; the centaur.

7. Psychic—actual psychic capacity, or the *beginning* of transpersonal modes.

8. Subtle or archetypal—home of archetypes, or exemplary and transindividual patterns of manifestation.

9. Causal—ultimate unity in only Spirit.

My conclusions were that, almost without exception, some lower structure, such as magic, has been and still is confused with some similar-appearing higher structure, such as psychic, and then either the former is elevated to the latter, or the latter reduced to the former. In other words, the pre/trans fallacy. These ptf confusions are summarized in Fig. 7. We have already seen examples of primary matrix-Spirit ptf and of body/bodymind ptf. As for the others, a few brief comments:

Magic, or unrestrained and unrefined belief in action at a dis-

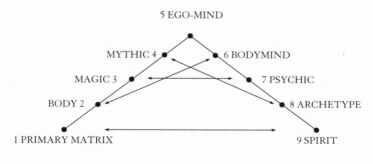

FIGURE 7

tance, characterizes the thinking of two- to four-year-olds, princi-
pally because they cannot yet distinguish image from reality or
symbol from thing, hence believe that to manipulate the one is to
manipulate the other. This mode can sound very holistic and holographic and all that, until you really dig into the actual case details.
Then you realize that magic does not unite subject and object, it
fuses and confuses them; and it does not holographically integrate
whole and part, it simply can't tell them apart in the first place. It's
pure voodoo and hokum. I'm being rhetorical here because I haven't
space to give details, but I am confident that the simplest study of
any good developmental psychologist, Werner to Arieti to Piaget,
will disabuse anybody of the notion that childhood magic is some
sort of heavenly holographic display.

Nonetheless, magic is almost always confused with psychic, or the
actual display of some sort of transcendental vision based *not* on the
fusion of subject and object but on the beginning transcendence of
subject and object. This ptf, of course, goes both ways: Freudians
claim all psychic is really magic, and parapsychologists occasionally
rig up elaborate laboratory experiments in an attempt to prove that
magic is really psychic.

A similar confusion seems to exist with regard to myth and archetype, and here Jung apparently stands most to blame. It's rather
hard to pin Jung down here, because he ended up using the word
"archetype" in several different ways. But his classic definition of an
archetype is a mythic-archaic image or form collectively inherited.
Unfortunately, however, the archaic-mythic level lies on the prepersonal or at least prerational side of the developmental divide. Apparently, the fact that certain archaic-mythic images are *collectively
inherited* was confused by Jung to mean that they are *transpersonally
located,* whereas they are merely part of the lower, prepersonal, collective unconscious. We all collectively inherit ten toes, but that
doesn't mean that if I directly experience my toes I am having a
transpersonal experience. Besides, when Jung explicitly locates the
"archetypes" as the exact counterpart of the biological body instincts,
his position is obvious. Notice, in this regard, that Freud stated explicitly that he agreed with Jung's notion of a phylogenetic heritage,

but that it was in every respect a prerational (*not* transrational) legacy. There, anyway, Freud seems to be in the correct half of his WV-1.

In my opinion, Jung was correctly trying to say that beyond the rational ego there lie important realms of consciousness; unfortunately, as we earlier explained, he failed to clearly distinguish the pre-egoic realms—which contain infantile magic and childish myth—from transegoic realms—which contain actual psychic and real archetypes. Having thus fallen into WV-2, I believe that Jung spent much of his life trying to elevate primitive mythic images to subtle archetypes.

Archetypes, as used by Plato, St. Augustine, and the Buddhist-Hindu systems, refer to the *first* forms of manifestation that emerge from Void Spirit in the course of the creation of the universe. That is, in the course of *involution,* or the emergence of the lower from the higher, the archetypes are the *first created forms,* upon which *all subsequent creation is patterned* (from the Greek *archetypon,* meaning "that which was created as a pattern, mold, or model"). Thus, the archetypes lie, or have their formal location, in the subtle region (level #8 in Fig. 7).

Consequently, archetype has two related but slightly different meanings. One, the archetypes are exemplary and transindividual patterns of existence lying in the upper limits of the spectrum. But two, every structure on every lower level (1 through 7) that can be said to be present collectively, can be said to be archetypal or archetypally determined. The lower structures themselves are not *the* archetypes, but they *are* archetypally or collectively given. Thus, the deep structure of the human body *is* archetypal, as is the deep structure of matter, magic, myth, mind, psyche. But to experience *the* archetypes means to experience level #8, and not, as we said, to experience archetypal toe, and even less to experience some sort of archaic-mythic imagery. I am not denying that, on occasion, some spiritual insight might be expressed in mythic images; I am denying that they are its source. Thus, mythic images are not *the* archetypes; as for being archetypal, so are *all* other deep structures, so there is nothing especially or preeminently archetypal about mythic images—on both counts, Jung's use of the term archetype is incorrect, in my opinion. We can easily agree with him when he more accurately states that the ego and all other major psychological forms are *archetypal,* for indeed they are, but then always in the next breath he's back to claiming that by archetypal he means mythic, and off we go again.

Once Jung confused mythic image with transpersonal archetypes, he could then claim that "the archetypes" were inherited from *actual* past evolution—they live on in us as a reflection of the actual form of yesterday's cognitions. And while it is true that we have inherited the past structures of development, those structures lie on the ape side, not angel side, of the divide. But, for Jung, the archetypes thus came to mean the collective inheritance of the *early* stages of *evolution,* whereas *the* archetypes actually refer to structures at the opposite end of the spectrum. In short, Jung placed the archetypes toward the beginning of evolution, whereas they actually exist at the beginning of involution. Had he avoided that confusion, he could have seen that the *ascent* of consciousness was drawn *toward* the archetypes *by* the archetypes themselves. This would have removed them from the wrong end of the spectrum, where they were forced (unsuccessfully) to do battle with Freud's archaic heritage. It would also have placed Jung firmly in league with Plato, Plotinus, and others. Finally, it would have relieved Jung and his followers from the extremely uncomfortable predicament of having to view the archetypes as both very primitive and very divine. Jungian therapists are forced to alternately worship archetypes and tremble in their presence, simply because their "archetypes"—being in fact a ptf mixture of real archetype and very primitive myth-forms—wobble between transrational glory and prerational chaos. In many ways I consider myself a Jungian, but here, I believe, Jung's theories are in dire need of revision.

Finally, I need hardly mention the reverse fallacy: orthodox analysts and psychologists usually take any truly archetypal material and hold it up as perfect examples of infantile or regressive mythic (or magic) cognition.

CAUTIONS

I would like to end this chapter by pointing out some of the typical mistakes that are often made when one begins to apply ptf to an understanding of various theories. Since the general form of un-winding a ptf is to go from a *bipole* such as

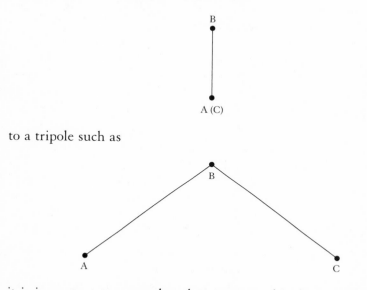

to a tripole such as

it is important to remember that not every bipole conceals a ptf in need of teasing apart. Certain fundamental bipoles, such as yin/yang, heaven/earth, light/dark, left/right, active/passive, rest/motion, one/many, good/evil—whatever else they may be, they are not examples of ptf-bipoles. They are dualities inherent in maya; they are tran-scended not by teasing one of the poles apart, but by uniting, inte-grating, and transcending both, equally, in the Tao. Thus, ego/nonego is a ptf-bipole, yin/yang is not; rational/mystical is a ptf-bipole, active/passive is not.

The problem, however, is that some theorists use real or struc-tural bipoles in order to support and carry their own versions of a ptf-bipole. For example, in the brain the left/right hemisphere is a structural bipole. We don't handle it as a ptf-bipole and then try to introduce *three* "hemispheres." The *L* and *R* hemispheres are real enough. Unfortunately, many researchers such as Ornstein use a ptf-bipole, such as personal/transpersonal or rational/mystical or egoic/nonegoic, then try to cram this false bipole into the structural hemi-spheric bimodes. The result, of course, is that the *L-H* gets logic, ego, time, and language, and the *R-H* gets everything nonlogical, nonegoic, mystical, and so on. This leads Ornstein and others into that disaster of championing nonlogical modes without specifying whether they are prelogical or translogical. Worse, it makes it appear that there is no difference between prelogical, pre-egoic, prepersonal and translogical, transegoic, transpersonal, because there are only two hemispheres and one of them is already taken. Since one hemisphere is definitely logical, the other must just be nonlogical—there's no room for pre and trans. This results precisely because a ptf-bipole is forced into a real bimodal structure.

But what, then, could the L and R hemispheres represent, if not two different modes of knowing termed rational and mystical? We might begin by noting that, in the course of human cognitive development, the individual progresses through, and then has access to, at least a half-dozen major, different, perfectly discrete modes or levels of knowing. For argument's sake, we'll simply use Piaget's four major stages—sensorimotor, concrete representational, concrete operational, formal operational—then add two higher stages— say, the psychic and subtle level—to include transcendent modes. Since we have at least these six major modes of knowing, but only two hemispheres, doesn't it seem obvious that the two hemispheres don't represent two modes of knowing—for in fact there are at least six—but rather represent two different aspects of every mode of knowing, that is, two components present at each of the six structures of knowledge?

I suggest that the L-H simply specializes in the sequential-digital-logical component of any mode of knowing, and the R-H specializes in the pattern-analogic-spatial component. But *every* mode of knowing (with the possible exception of the very lowest and highest, which we will discuss below) contains these two necessary components. As Foulkes's landmark study, *A Grammar of Dreams,* demonstrated, even dreams have a logic, or a sequential unfolding, frame by some sort of frame. There is a dream time (L) just as much as a dream space (R). Conversely, even mathematical logic (L) utilizes images and pattern recognition (R). This also fits perfectly with Piaget's studies, which demonstrated that both the logic (L) and fantasy (R) of cognition follow the *same basic deep structures* of the given level of cognition. Thus both L and R are simply two aspects of each level, not two different levels themselves.

Finally, if you will look at any diagram of the yoga *chakras,* you will see exactly what I am suggesting: There are six major structures (*chakras*) of knowledge-consciousness, *each* of which has a left and right component, or *ida* and *pingala*. These two components exist *equally* at each mode of knowing, from the bodily modes to the mental modes of the psychic and subtle ones. Then, at the forehead and into the crown, they merge into each other and *both* disappear in highest transcendence. It is not that L is egoic-rational and R is nonegoic-mystical. It is that L and R are present at all six stages of knowing, and that the lowest two stages are pre-egoic, the middle two, egoic, and the upper two, transegoic. L and R have, precisely, nothing to do with it.

My final cautionary note is that when we say that, for example, ego/nonego is a ptf-bipole and that there are really two different forms of nonego (pre and trans), we mean that statement only as a semantic convenience. That A and C *appear* similar is never, in my opinion, because they actually and structurally *are* similar, *in anything other than an empty sense*. A has more in common with B than with $C,$ and C has more in common with B than with $A.$

If I may finish with a personal note, I would say that, if I have occasionally appeared harsh in my criticism of those theories that seem to me fallacious, it is in almost every instance due to the fact that I once embraced those fallacies with enthusiasm, especially in their WV-2 form. And, as Husserl observed at the turn of the century, one is most vehement against those errors that one recently held oneself. In my subsequent attempts to take the true half from each major ptf world view, I realize that I run the risk of being disowned by both sides, going down eventually with Shaw's epigram ("He has no enemies but is intensely disliked by all his friends"). Nonetheless, if the true marriage of science and religion—WV-1 and WV-2—is ever to be effected in other than a spurious or empty sense, if we are ever to have a truly comprehensive paradigm, my best judgment is that absolutely no other course is available. We shall take the true from both and discard the false from both, or we shall continue to try to integrate the muddled half truths of each.

8

Legitimacy, Authenticity, and Authority in the New Religions

A Developmental-Structural Approach

O N THE WHOLE, the new religious movements in America are singularly problematic. Perhaps no other phenomenon has caused as much public comment, commotion, or confusion. The Moonies, "brainwashing," Jonestown, cults, Scientology, deprogramming, Jesus Freaks, the Children of God, Hare Krishnas, Synanon—the list itself seems a concatenation of all that might be sinister.

On the one hand, it is certainly true that a great number of the "new religious movements" are—at least in hindsight—disastrous, and Jonestown is paradigmatic. Yet, on the other, some of them seem—at least in theory—genuinely beneficial, even enlightening. The best of Vajrayana, Zen, Taoism, and Vedanta, for example, have graced magnificent civilizations and apparently epitomized the summit of the human idealistic spirit, and there is no reason to suppose that an infusion of such spirit could not resonate with and enrich our own highest wisdoms. Heidegger, for instance, stated that "if I understand Zen scholar Suzuki, this is what I have been trying to say in all my writings,"[6] and we have already seen that the very search for a new and more comprehensive paradigm was generated in large measure by the knowledge claims of transcendental mysticism, predominantly Eastern in form.

It appears that not *all* the "new religions" are merely sophomoric platitudes or mind-numbing cultisms. The great problem, of course, is how to tell the difference. That is, how to devise any sort of *believable* scale or criteria for differentiating the more valid "religious movements" from the less valid or even harmful. This is all the more urgent for those who are striving to present a "new and higher" or comprehensive paradigm, simply because a considerable portion of the transcendental claims of the new paradigm is prompted by or even based on some of the new and specifically mystical religions, and we had better be able to offer believable criteria for differentiating the select "some" (e.g., Zen) from all the rest (e.g., Charles Manson). To Zen scholars, this might seem an outrageously unfair equation, but the simple fact is that the public at large—and many influential scholars—have already simply lumped together, under the single title of "those new religions," all endeavors that are nonorthodox in their religious claims. The burden of "de-lumping" or differentiating these in fact quite different endeavors accordingly falls now, unfairly, on the genuinely transcendental scholars.

In such a terribly complex and problematic field, even a very general and somewhat imprecise scale would be better than none, as long as the scale itself could be externally verified in its general outlines according to the germane criteria of modern psychological and sociological sciences. Acknowledging these broad limitations, I believe several such general scales exist. In fact, throughout this book we have been working with one such (tentative) overview model—a developmental and structural view of the overall "spectrum of consciousness." The lower and intermediate portions of this model are based on the works of Piaget, Werner, Arieti, Kohlberg, Loevinger, Erikson, Freud, and so on; the higher portions are based on the *philosophia perennis*. But the important point is that the existence of each of the stage-levels of this model is open to injunctive inquiry and verification (or rejection). And it is this external verifiability—should it indeed prove sound—that confers upon this type of overview model its *potentially believable* status, and thus allows it, within broad limits, to act as a scale for the *adjudication* of any particular psychosocial engagement, including "religious involvement."

Now by "adjudication" I mean precisely this: We have no difficulty in saying, for instance, that a person at stage-5 moral development (à la Kohlberg) is at a *higher* stage than someone at stage-2. Nor do we have any difficulty in saying that a person at formal-operational (à la Piaget) is at a *higher* stage than someone at preoperational. Nor in saying that conscientious-ego structure is *higher* than conformist-ego structure (Loevinger). Nor so on through a dozen stages openly described by developmentalists as constituting successively *higher* occasions. Just so, with a *general* overview model of psychosocial development on the whole—one that included not only the lower and intermediate stages of Kohlberg, Piaget, Loevinger, and others, but also the upper levels and stages of subtle and causal occasions—we would be better able to judge—adjudicate—the relative *degree of maturity* or *authenticity* of any psychosocial production, moral, cognitive, egoic, or—in this case—religious (and "new religious").

We introduced this general overview model in chapters 3 and 4; we will be looking at it again in the next chapter. For the purposes of this chapter, we will simply work with seven of its major levels. They are:

1. *Archaic.* This includes material body, sensations, perceptions, and emotions. This is roughly equivalent, for instance, to Piaget's sensorimotor intelligence, Maslow's physiological needs, Loevinger's autistic and symbiotic stages, the first and second *chakras,* the *annamayakosha* (physical food) and *pranamayakosha* (élan vital).

2. *Magic.* This includes simple images, symbols, and the first rudimentary concepts, or the first and lower mental productions, which are "magical" in the sense that they display condensation, displacement, "omnipotence of thought," and so on. This is Freud's primary process, Arieti's paleologic, Piaget's preoperational thinking; the third *chakra.* It is *correlated* (as explained in the next chapter) with Kohlberg's preconventional morality, Loevinger's impulsive and self-protective stages, Maslow's safety needs, and so on.

3. *Mythic.* This stage is more advanced than magic, but not yet

capable of clear rationality or hypothetico-deductive reasoning, a stage Gebser explicitly termed "mythic." This is essentially Piaget's concrete operational thinking; the fourth *chakra;* the beginning of *manomayakosha* (Vedanta) and *manovijnana* (Mahayana). It is *correlated* with Loevinger's conformist and conscientious-conformist stages, Maslow's belongingness needs, Kohlberg's conventional stages, and so on.

4. *Rational.* This is Piaget's formal operational thinking, propositional or hypothetico-deductive reasoning; the fifth *chakra;* the culmination of *manomayakosha* and *manovijnana.* It is correlated with Loevinger's conscientious and individualistic stages, Kohlberg's postconventional morality, Maslow's self-esteem needs, and so on.

5. *Psychic.* Here I am including the centaur and the low-subtle as one general level. "Psychic" does not necessarily mean "paranormal," although some texts suggest that certain paranormal events may more likely occur here. Rather, it refers to "psyche" as a higher level of development than the rational mind per se (e.g., Aurobindo, Free John). Its cognitive structure has been called "vision logic," or integrative logic; the sixth *chakra;* the beginning of *manas* (Mahayana) and *vijnanamakosha* (Vedanta). It is correlated with Loevinger's integrated and autonomous stages, Maslow's self-actualization needs, Broughton's integrated stage, and so on.

6. *Subtle.* This is, basically, the archetypal level, the level of the "illumined mind" (Aurobindo); the culmination of *manas* and *vijnanamayakosha;* a truly transrational (not prerational and not antirational) structure; intuition in its highest and most sober sense; not emotionalism or merely bodily felt meaning; home of Platonic forms; *bija-mantra, vasanas;* beginning of seventh *chakra* (and *subchakras*); start of Maslow's self-transcendence needs, and so on.

7. *Causal.* Or the unmanifest ground and suchness of all levels; the limit of growth and development; "Spirit" in the highest sense, not as a Big Person but as the "Ground of Being" (Tillich), "Eternal Substance" (Spinoza), "Geist" (Hegel); at and beyond the seventh *chakra;* the *anandamayakosha* (Vedanta), *alayavijnana* (Mahayana), *Keter* (Kabbalah), and so on.

As we have seen, those seven general structure-stages of development can be further reduced to *three general realms:* the pre-rational (subconscious), the rational (self-conscious), and the transrational (superconscious) (see diagram).

The Pre/Trans Fallacy

In the previous chapter, we saw that one of the great problems with discovering an overall model of development is that, although the rational or self-conscious realms are almost universally agreed upon, the other two realms are almost as universally confused. That is, because the prerational and the transrational realms are, in their own ways, nonrational, they appear similar or even identical to the untutored eye. This confusion generally leads to one of two opposite mistakes: either the transrational is *reduced* to the prerational (e.g., Freud), or the prerational is *elevated* to the transrational (e.g., Jung).

We called any of those confusions the "pre/trans fallacy," and it is the pre/trans fallacy that, in my opinion, rests precisely at the center of the controversy over "the new religions"—*because,* I will suggest, about half of the new religions *are* prerational, and about half are *trans*rational, and *that* is the strange mixture of trick and treat that has made this whole issue so extraordinarily difficult to unravel.

But whatever we decide on that particular point—we will pursue it below—I would like to remind the reader that this general model—which we have simplified as prerational, rational, and transrational, or prepersonal, personal, and transpersonal, or sub-conscious, self-conscious, and superconscious—is based on *develop-*

mental and *structural* criteria that are potentially open to external and experimental verification (as are, e.g., Piaget's or Kohlberg's works). This model is offered hypothetically and experimentally, not dogmatically and conclusively. But *if* it proves sound, then we will be able to draw certain significant conclusions on the nature of the "new religions," not to mention the "old."

LEGITIMACY VERSUS AUTHENTICITY

Recall that the basic defining form of each level is its *deep structure*, whereas a particular element or component of each level is a *surface structure*. A change in deep structure we call *transformation;* a change in surface structure, *translation*. We now introduce a simple notion: Any psychosocial institution that validates or facilitates translation we call *legitimate;* any that validates or facilitates transformation we call *authentic*.

Legitimacy, so defined, is a *horizontal* scale. It is a measure of the degree of integration, organization, meaning, coherence, and stability of or within a given level of structural adaptation or development. One of the greatest needs of individuals—an overarching need—is to find legitimacy at their present level of development, whatever that level may be. For example, persons at the magic-protective level seek legitimacy, or sanctified existence, via the safety or self-protective (preconventional) needs of their animistic and narcissistic world view. Persons at the mythic-membership (conventional) level seek legitimacy through conformist belongingness, trying to be sanctified by the group. Persons at the rational (postconventional) level seek legitimacy via conscientious or self-esteem needs: they can legitimate their existence only by following their own conscience and by interacting with similarly structured social institutions. One of the great tasks of any society is to provide its members with a legitimate and legitimizing world view, one that is capable of validating existence on the average expectable level of structural development reached by its members. (In our society, the average expectable level is approximately mythic-rational.)

Authenticity is a *vertical* scale. It is a measure of the degree of transformation offered by any particular psychosocial institution. Every society has to act as a *pacer* of transformation up to its average expectable level of structural adaptation, and thus it must provide authentic modes of transformation up to and including that level (generally, this task falls to family, educational, and occasionally religious systems). In our society, for example, we attempt to move or develop individuals up to the rational level, or at least the mythic-rational. Those at the archaic level often have to be institutionalized, and those at the magic level are labeled psychotic and subsequently isolated. But somewhere around the mythic-rational stage, our society's force as a pacer of authentic transformation (or vertical growth) drops out, and any higher growth or authenticity has to occur either on one's own or in microcommunities of the higher- and like-minded. In any event, this power and degree of transformation we call authenticity.

Any given religion, like any other psychosocial production, can be judged on the basis of both its legitimacy and its authenticity. That is, does it seek merely to confirm, validate, and sanctify a person at his or her present stage of adaptation, or does it seek to transform a person to genuinely higher levels of growth and development? Not merely help a person *translate* better, but *transform* significantly? Now *both of these scales are important*. Even authentic religions (i.e., ones that explicitly engage transrational, transpersonal, superconscient realms) have to be legitimate on their own levels, and even a legitimate but not very authentic religion (e.g., exoteric Protestantism, civil religion, lay Shintoism) can serve as a stabilizing and organizing force on its own level. It's just that, like prerational and transrational, legitimacy and authenticity are often, even usually, confused (especially by the sociologists of religion). Among other things, this makes it appear that a seeker of higher authenticity is no different than a seeker of sturdier legitimacy. It completely confuses two independent scales, and that—along with the pre/trans fallacy—makes it appear that all the "new religions" are essentially identical in motive. In the recent Graduate Theological Union seminar series (which we will discuss below), Dick Anthony, an influential sociologist of religion, responded to these distinctions, making the following very succinct and important summary:

> This is a theme that has come up over and over again. We need to distinguish between transpersonal criteria, in other words, groups

that are authentically spiritual in some transpersonal sense, versus groups which aren't, and then another dimension, which is groups which are in some sense or other legitimate, such as civil religious sects, or conventional religious groups, or whatever; and groups can deviate in a negative way along either one of those dimensions. And the dimensions interact, so you get a kind of four-cell table. And when we try to make everything fit along some unidimensional criterion of value, then everything falls apart.[55]

The last two sections might be summarized in one sentence: It is these two confusions—pre and trans, and legitimate and authentic—that have so helped to muddle the study of the new religions (as well as the emergence of a new paradigm). I will now attempt to study the new religions without these confusions.

THE CRITERIA

Our methodology is simple: we take the particular socio-religious movement, examine its statements, actions, and belief systems, and subject these to (1) a *developmental-structural analysis* in order to determine its degree of authenticity or vertical maturity; and (2) a *surface-functional analysis* in order to determine its type and degree of legitimacy or horizontal integration and stability.

First, its authenticity. Is it *archaic,* with moments of self-other indissociation, primary narcissism, primitive fusion, oral needs, perhaps even cannibalistic or murderous (homicidal or suicidal) impulses? Or is it *magical,* with "omnipotence-of-thought" rituals (e.g., voodoo, witchcraft), emotional-sexual impulses, magic beliefs, self-clan confusion (totemism)? Or is it *mythical,* with intense conformity needs, a Cosmic Parent world view, authoritarian figure "representative" of the Parent, mythic ritual, emphasis upon in-group (saved) versus out-group (damned), and lack of rational justification? Or does it seem to contain truly transcendental aspirations—aspirations that are defined not by their prerational dogmatism but by their transrational injunctions? Is it psychic, subtle, or even causal—these are characterized by genuine study and discipline aimed at effecting authentic transformation, and in ways that can be impartially determined by strict developmental-structural analysis?

In short, with regard to authenticity, is the group in question prerational (archaic, magic, mythic) or transrational (psychic, subtle, causal)?

Second, we analyze the psychosocial productions of the movement in order to determine their type and degree of legitimacy. That is, we are looking for the degree of integration, meaningful engagement, purpose, and stability offered at the particular level characteristic of the group's degree of authenticity. How and why, within its general level of belief structure, does the group earn its legitimacy? How does it validate its existence? What sanctions are used? How coherent and organized are they? Most importantly, is legitimacy conferred by a whole society or by a tradition or by a single person? That is, within the given level of structural adaptation, who or what has the final power to tell you that you're OK?

Overall, then, once we determine the group's level of authenticity, or its vertical degree of maturity and development, we then try to determine its type and degree of legitimacy, or its horizontal scale of integrative meaning and stability. And it is especially these two scales that can help us tease apart the various strands of the "new religions." But there is one other scale or factor that is also important: the type and degree of *authority* evidenced by the group leader(s).

AUTHORITY

I am going to shorten and simplify this discussion drastically by approaching authority from an angle almost opposite to that usually taken: I am going to discuss not what constitutes "bad" authority—fascist dynamics, authoritarian personalities, group subservience to superego projections, and transference hypnosis—but what constitutes "good" authority; that is, under what circumstances would most people agree that an authority is necessary? What is a benign, useful, nonproblematic authority?

One type of benign authority is the "functional authority," the person who by special training is authorized to perform certain tasks and functions, for example, plumbers, doctors, lawyers. That type of authority is nonproblematic because subjection to it is voluntary. But there are even certain types of *involuntary* subjection to authority that are also generally thought to be nonproblematic—law enforcement, for example. But the best example is probably compulsory education, because its existence is based upon a developmental argument and upon society's need to act as a pacer of development up to at least a certain average-expectable level of adaptation.

The benign authority in this situation is, of course, the teacher. And the teacher has a peculiar form of authority. If, for example, a student says, with regard to a particular task, "But why do I have to do it that way?" the teacher's final authority is, "Because I say so. Once you have learned to do it that way—once you have graduated—you can do it any way you wish. But experience has shown us that that is the best way to learn that task, and that is how you are going to do it in my class if you want to pass."

Now, even though that is a compulsory authority, it is viewed as benign, nonproblematic, and necessary, because (1) it is effecting development, and (2) it is *phase-temporary* or *phase-specific*. That is, the teacher's authority over the pupil is temporary; it effectively evaporates once the pupil's degree of understanding approaches that of the teacher (supposedly symbolized by graduation). At that point, the pupil can become a teacher—and can even disagree with his or her previous teachers.

Phase-specific authority seems inescapable in any process of education (development). Even in higher or noncompulsory education, the gap between the teacher and pupil's understanding of a topic confers on the teacher a phase-specific authority that is only annulled when and if that gap is sufficiently closed. At that point, teacher and pupil become more or less equals; prior to that point, phase-specific authoritarianism seems inescapable.

Now we cannot conclude from those examples that *all* functional and phase-specific authority is benign and nonproblematic. But we can conclude that authority which is *not* functional or phase-specific might very likely be problematic, because then the only major reasons left for its existence are those that tend to fall in the category of "bad" authority—authority that does not serve a necessary (objective) function or a phase-specific (subjective) growth, but rather rests on certain psychological dynamics of "master-slave" (Hegel), "power-over" (Fromm), "superego projection" (Freud), "transference hypnosis" (Ferenczi), "herd mentality" (Hegel/Berdyaev), "emotional plague" (Reich), and so on.

For this presentation I have chosen the shortcut of not attempting to explain the nature of all those various conceptions of "bad" authority; rather, I have simply suggested two major characteristics of "good" authority (functional and/or phase-specific), and then added: if the authority in question displays neither of those "good" characteristics, odds are that that authority is or will be problematic. (And the reader can fill in the nature of the "problem" using whatever theory he or she wishes.)

If we take each of the dimensions or variables we have discussed—authenticity, legitimacy, and authority—and look at their "bad" manifestations, we arrive at a tentative list of *problematic factors,* the more of which any group contains, the more problematic the group probably is (or will become): (1) engagement of a prerational realm, (2) engagement of a "permanent" authority figure, and (3) engagement of a fractured, isolated, and/or single-source legitimacy.

Some Concrete Examples

In a recent Graduate Theological Union seminar series, which capped a year-long research project, some dozen or so "new religious movements" were carefully examined (including in-depth interviews with their proponents). Of those dozen, approximately three out of four were deemed—by orthodox and transpersonal scholars alike—to be problematic, or at least to have degenerated into problematic status. These included such movements as Jonestown, Synanon, an unfortunate twist on Psychosynthesis, and the Unification Church (Moonies).

What emerges from those transcripts is a *general pattern of problematic groups,* and that pattern unmistakably correlates with the three "bad" criteria suggest above. The paradigm for this, of course, was Jonestown. It was (1) prerational (eventually sinking past mythic-belongingness needs to magical-sexual ritual to archaic sacrifice); (2) it was headed by a permanent and not phase-specific authority (the "father" Jim Jones, who was even so addressed); and (3) its legitimacy—the very OKness of every member—rested upon a sole person (isolated legitimacy).

But a similar pattern could be observed in most other problematic groups, even those existing in entirely different circumstances (although few degenerated to the final degree of Jonestown). An unfortunate example is the atypical situation that arose in one particular school of Psychosynthesis. I say "atypical" because Psychosynthesis itself is by and large a rather sophisticated and authentic teaching, and what happened to one of its schools is simply not indicative of its theoretical potential.

This particular group began as a concerned community of individuals—virtually all of whom seemed at or near a rational level of structural adaptation—apparently interested in pursuing an authentic transrational growth and development. Through a series of events that can only be conveyed by the original (and quite terrifying) transcripts, the upward transformation began to go sour. What followed was classic group regression into prerational realms, a regression that almost ended in Jonestown.

We can follow this regression using virtually any of the developmental schemes we have discussed—Piaget, Kohlberg, Loevinger, Maslow, our own overview model. The individuals apparently started out at the self-esteem (conscientious) stages, interested in the higher realms of self-actualization and self-transcendence. As that upward development began to go sour, individuals not only failed their own self-esteem needs, they apparently began to regress to conformist-belongingness modes. Individuality was shunned; the "group ego" began to demand allegiance. In place of rational individuality and logical inquiry there arose mythic-membership and the "wall of terror" that demanded and compelled group allegiance. *Conformity* to the particular world view was now the arbiter of *legitimacy:* to leave the group was "to die." (This is all the more extraordinary because the people so caught up were extremely well-educated—doctors, lawyers, and other professionals.) The move toward and into prerational realms was well under way; nobody was encouraged, or even allowed, to rationally question the teachings. Criterion #1—prerationality—was already in evidence.

Worse, the sole arbiter of "the teaching" soon focused on *one* individual, a situation that represented the abandonment of phase-temporary authority in favor of a for-all-practical-purposes *permanent* authority (criterion #2). This person—call him Smith—was looked upon as the sole and permanent leader of the organization. Eventually Smith began to be perceived (by himself and all others) as the sole and individual bearer of *legitimacy:* Smith, and Smith alone, had the final power to tell you if your actions were or were not OK (criterion #3). So blatant was this power that Smith would spend hours—literally hours—"processing" individuals, either directly or by phone, telling them exactly what to think, feel, and do in order to be OK, to be legitimate, to be validated. And, given the group regression to intense conformity needs, virtually no one objected.

The situation worsened, both on the part of the master and slave. Mythic-belongingness and group conformity soon regressed to the magical stage of primary process cognition and delusional reference systems. Invisible forces—graphically described—were "out to get them"; both master and slave became, literally and clinically, paranoid (as was, e.g., Jim Jones). Had not extraneous circumstances interrupted this pattern, it might indeed have ended in archaic, masochistic, and literal sacrifice: since the world doesn't understand us, in fact, since they are all out to get us, let us get ourselves first, as a heroic statement.

Although not all problematic groups follow exactly that overall pattern, or at least do not follow it to such extremes, I believe the pattern itself is general enough to be considered essentially paradigmatic. I usually refer to this general pattern as the "cult-clan and totem master." "Cult-clan" refers to the general absence of self-esteem, conscientious, or postconventional needs, with consequent herd mentality. "Totem master" refers to the permanent authority figure that usually rides herd. "Totem" emphasizes the magical-mythical connotations given to this father figure, and "master" emphasizes the extraordinary power of legitimation rested in this individual (for psychodynamic reasons). Thus, Jim Jones was the totem master or temporal father of his entire community. He was not representative of the "eternal self" of each individual, as is an authentic guru. Rather, he was viewed as the *temporal* and even biological father of the group—a belief apparently supported by bizarre sexual-fertility (magical) rituals. Not "our Father who art in Heaven," but "our father who art next door." But regardless of actual sexual practices (they seem rather rare), the totem master is viewed as somehow being the temporal father of the entire group, literally or figuratively. He is *totemically* "in" the group and the group is "in" him, magically or mythically so. It is no accident that Jones, Moon, and Manson were often referred to as "father" (*not* meaning priest), and that more than one totem master has found *Führer* and *Vater* synonymous.

Such seems to be the general pattern of especially problematic groups: engaged in prerational realms, headed by a permanent and not phase-specific authority, and based on isolated, separative, or clannish legitimacy: the cult-clan and totem master. However much the specifics vary—and they vary immensely—I believe that is the single, simplest generalization that can adequately summarize the especially problematic "new religious" sects.

A CORROBORATIVE SCHEME

In this section I would like to mention very briefly the work of Dick Anthony and Tom Robbins, because they have categorized the new religions according to three (nondevelopmental) dimensions, and these dimensions tangentially support my own criteria. Those dimensions are (1) charismatic/technical, (2) one-level/two-level, and (3) monistic/dualistic.[55]

The monistic/dualistic dimension refers to whether a group believes that all individuals are ultimately one with Godhead (regardless of particular belief), or whether only a select "in-group" can achieve exalted status. One-level religion tends to look at the manifest or *presently* available level (usually material) as the arena of salvation, whereas two-level religion tends to see liberation as occurring in a transtemporal realm. Charismatic religion tends to center on the personality of the group leader, whereas technical religion tends to center on certain impersonal techniques and practices (or traditions).

Those three dimensions are not judgmental—they simply categorize, in terms perfectly acceptable to the various groups, the *types* of cognitive maps or belief systems embraced by each group itself. It is a simple classificatory scheme (see Fig. 8). Beyond that scheme, however, Robbins and Anthony have attempted to pinpoint those cells that seem to be problematic. This is what they found on the average (there are exceptions):

MONISTIC

	TECHNICAL	CHARISMATIC
One-Level	est Scientology Circle of Gold	Charles Manson Family Messiah's World Crusade Om Cult
Two-Level	Vedanta Hinduism Integral Yoga Zen Buddhism	Meher Baba Muktananda Bubba (Da) Free John

DUALISTIC

	TECHNICAL	CHARISMATIC
One-Level	Positive Thinking Robert Schuller Church of Hakeem	Unification Church (Moonies) People's Church (Jonestown) Synanon
Two-Level	Catholic Charismatic Renewal Groups Neo-Pentacostal Groups	Jesus Movement Christ Commune Christian Liberation Front

(Adapted by permission from D. Anthony)

FIGURE 8

Negative or problematic groups tend to be one-level, while positive groups tend to be two-level. Charismatic groups tend to be more problematic than technical groups. And dualistic groups tend to be more problematic than monistic groups.

Now what I am suggesting is that the developmental-structural criteria we have outlined form the substructure of the conclusions reached by Anthony and Robbins. Thus, dualistic groups tend to be more problematic than monistic groups because they foster the pseudostructural notion that only *some* people are qualified for (or can evolve to) the highest estate. This leads to an extreme emphasis on the in-group versus the out-group, which itself invites prerational regression to exclusively or overblown conformist or cultic involvement with separate and separative legitimation. Monistic religions, on the other hand, acknowledge temporary differences in development but emphasize potential equality or unity in only God.

One-level religions tend to be more problematic than two-level religions simply because they disregard vertical growth and development, and thus are always open to reinterpreting their own (however mediocre) level of structural adaptation as *the* highest level (as long as one merely adopts fully its present *legitimacy* criteria—a technique perfected by est). Genuine authenticity is ditched in favor of sturdy legitimacy, and the present level of development, however intermediate, is made the arena of final salvation. Two-level religion, on the other hand, *is* two-level because it refuses to equate the present level with the ultimate level (except in a paradoxical sense), and thereby holds open the possibility, indeed the necessity, of higher growth and development.

Charismatic religion is more problematic than technical (or traditional) religion because it necessarily relies on the authority of a sole person. Should the person prove to be less than genuine, then charismatic religions can degenerate into sole authority and isolated legitimacy—with all the problems therein. Technical religion, on the other hand, takes as ballast either an impersonal technique or a historical tradition, thereby counterbalancing the possibly idiosyncratic whims of any potentially totem master.

If we take the more problematic pole of each of these three dimensions and put them together, we arrive at the worst possible combination for a "new religion": one-level/charismatic/dualistic; second worst is one-level/charismatic/monistic. One-level, we saw, tends toward cultic separatism, and charismatic can tend toward permanent and sole authority. In short, the worst possible combinations follow exactly the general pattern of the "cult-clan and totem master." And if you look at those two cells in Fig. 8, you will indeed find *the* disastrous cults, Manson to Jonestown to Synanon to Moonies.

Conversely, at the other extreme, completely opposite in all three dimensions, are the monistic/two-level/technical religions—integral yoga (Aurobindo), Buddhist meditation, Vedanta, and so on—precisely the "new religions" that are at the forefront of the new and transcendental paradigm.

The Nonproblematic Group

According to Anthony and Robbins, the nonproblematic group will likely be monistic, two-level, and technical. Or, more realistically, we could recommend two out of that three: if the movement is charismatic, hope it is monistic and two-level; if dualistic, hope it is technical and two-level, and so forth.

In terms of developmental-structural criteria, we can suggest the following. A positive, authentic group will likely:

1. *Be transrational, not prerational.* Specifically, it will utilize teachings and disciplines that engage higher, subtle, and/or causal levels of structural adaptation, *not* prerational or irrational engagements. These disciplines generally involve sustained practice, concentration, and will; they explicitly rest on a moral foundation, which usually includes appropriate dietary and sexual relations; and they are at least as difficult to master and complete as is, say, a doctorate.

Most orthodox sociologists, unfortunately, seem intent upon seeing *all* "new religions" as nothing but a search for a new legitimacy prompted by the breakdown of traditional, orthodox, or civil religions, and fail to even consider that some of the new religions—the expressly transrational ones—are also in search of a higher *authenticity,* an authenticity *never* offered by the old religions. Say what you will, exoteric Protestantism never offered widespread, authentic, mystical, transcendental, superconscient experience. It offered, at best, a sturdy legitimacy at the *mythic* level. Some of the new religions are explicitly and structurally in search of that authentic, not merely legitimate, dimension (e.g., Zen, Vedanta, Raja Yoga, Vajrayana, etc.).

On the other hand, these authentic disciplines ought not be confused with the plethora of "pop mystical" and "quasitherapeutic" movements. The laid-back, blissed-out, Marin County high is exactly what these authentic disciplines are not; the beat Zen, *dharma* bum, go with the here/now—that, too, is exactly what these disciplines are not. In fact, virtually all of such "beat Zen" approaches are based on the pre/trans fallacy. As *Serial* so whimsically put it, "Everybody knew, in these days of heightened consciousness, that the rational mind was a screw-up; the really authentic thing to do was to act on your impulses." That, of course, is exactly the prerational mood that has so distorted mystical and Eastern teachings, and, alas, that prerational approach is behind perhaps 50 percent of humanistic, transpersonal, and "human potential" movements—not to mention the "new religions" so dubiously allied with them. Even worse, this pop mysticism, all-is-one, beat Zen has been used by more than one religious cult to rationalize their monstrosities. ("Since all is one," said Charles Manson, "nothing is wrong.")

2. *Anchor legitimacy in a tradition.* Legitimacy offered by a tradition—say, Christianity, Sufism, Buddhism—tends to be less problematic than legitimacy offered by a single person (leader), simply because it is less open to permanent, isolated, single-authority-figure domination and distortion. If, for example, you are a Buddhist meditation master, it is infinitely more difficult to proclaim yourself permanent authority and sole arbiter of legitimacy, because there lies behind you, as ballast, 2,500 years of corrective teaching. *Lineage,* in other words, is one of the greatest safeguards against fraudulent legitimacy.

3. *Have a phase-specific authority.* It is common knowledge that virtually all authentic Eastern or mystical traditions maintain that the guru is representative of one's own highest nature, and once that nature is realized, the guru's formal authority and function is ended. The guru is guide, teacher, or physician, not king, president, or totem master.

Buyer beware, then, of any religious movement headed by a permanent authority. Or—it comes to the same thing—any authority that cannot, at least in principle, be replaced. Even Dalai Lamas and Popes can be replaced by their successors; but there was, and could be, no replacement for Jim Jones or Charles Manson; when they die, their movements generally end or fizzle. Either religious teachers are there to bring you up to their level of understanding—in which case their authority is phase-temporary—or they exist to keep you in your place, which by definition is somewhere below or under them. The list of disastrous cult leaders is a list of permanent, not replacement and not phase-specific, "authorities."

As for the relation between the "good" gurus' authority and their disciples, I have been a participant-observer in almost a dozen non-problematic new religious movements, Buddhist, Hindu, Taoist. In none of those groups was I ever subjected to any harsh degree of authoritarian pressure (discipline, yes, pressure, no). In fact, the authoritarian pressure in these groups never even equaled that which I experienced in graduate school in biochemistry. The masters in these groups were looked upon as great teachers, not big daddies, and their authority was always that of a concerned physician, not totem boss.

There is another way to state what a nonproblematic authority looks like. That is, a positive group:

4. *Is NOT headed by a Perfect Master.* Perfection exists only in transcendental essence, not in manifest existence, and yet many devotees consider their master "perfect" in all ways, the ultimate guru. This is almost always a problematic sign, because the devotee, in confusing essence with existence, is invited to *project* his or her own archaic, narcissistic, omnipotent fantasies onto the "perfect" guru. All sorts of archaic and magical primary process cognitions are thus reactivated; the guru can do anything; how great the guru is; in fact, how great I must be to be among the chosen. It is an extremely narcissistic position.

But, of course, the guru eventually displays his or her human side (thank God), but the devotee is devastated, disillusioned, crushed. The devotee then either leaves, because the guru can no longer support the devotee's narcissistic glamour, or tries to rationalize the guru's actions. "Drunk? The master got drunk? Well, you know, like he was just emphasizing the evils of intoxicants by example." The notorious case involving Trungpa—he had a student stripped and verbally abused—was given all sorts of high explanations by his followers, none of whom got the correct one: Trungpa made an outrageous, inexcusable, and completely stupid mistake, period.

Good masters might indeed be divine, but they are also human. Even Christ was said to be one person (Jesus) with two natures (human and divine). Further, the fact that a guru has been thoroughly educated in soul and spirit does not mean he or she has been thoroughly educated in body and mind. I have yet to see a guru run a four-minute mile with his "perfect body" or explain Einstein's special theory of relativity with his "perfect mind." The Perfect Master cannot appear until the humanity in which he or she is grounded—until, indeed, all manifestation—has evolved to its own highest and perfect estate. Until that time, Perfection lies only in transcendence, not in manifestation, so beware the "perfect master."

There is a corollary to this; a positive group:

5. *Is NOT out to save the world.* It has often been pointed out that a very high percentage of those in problematic groups initially entered with apparently very altruistic and idealistic impulses, a desire to help people and better the world. But that "idealism" actually has a structure very similar to that of the "perfect master"—archaic and narcissistic. The underlying impulse is "me and the group are going to change the world," emphasis on me. Further, its narcissistic core is evidenced in the arrogance of the stance itself: we have the only (or the best) way, and we will change the world, that is, we will impose our ideas on the poor ignorant folks out there. Now they may not *state* it that way (I put it rather harshly); but they must in fact feel that way, more or less—how can you possibly presume to help someone, especially without being asked, unless you assume they are in need of help (i.e., inferior) and you are capable of providing it?

This narcissistic "altruism" usually shows up in a missionary zeal and proselytizing fury that no amount of high-sounding "idealism" can disguise. Such obsessive drivenness is always open to problematic occasions, not the least of which is the fact that if you have *the* way, then that end will justify virtually any means, up to and including holy war. And holy war, of course, isn't a sin, it isn't murder, because the people you are killing in order to save aren't really people—they're infidels.

On a smaller scale, in problematic new religious groups, the psychological dynamic is the same, if toned down. But any group "out to save the world" is potentially problematic, because it rests on an archaically narcissistic base that *looks* "altruistic" or "idealistic" but in fact is very egocentric, very primitive, and very capable of coming to primitive ends by primitive means.

9

Structure, Stage, and Self

Part of the search for a comprehensive or transcendental paradigm has included the attempt to compare and contrast different maps or models of consciousness, Eastern and Western, orthodox and transpersonal, humanistic and mystical. But what virtually all of these models and assessments have tended to overlook—and what, up to this point, our own mandalic maps (e.g., chapter 3) have not explicitly mentioned—is that there is a profound difference between levels or structures of consciousness and stages or phases of consciousness. The former are essentially permanent, enduring, basic components of consciousness; the latter are essentially temporary, transition, or replacement phases of consciousness. Just what that means, and why that distinction seems so important, is the topic of this chapter.

INTRODUCTION

One of the simplest facts of human ontogeny seems to be this: as various structures, processes, and functions emerge in the course of development, some of them *remain* in existence, some of them *pass*. For example, the need for food—the oral/anal alimentary structure—develops in the very earliest stages of development; so does

264

the oral stage of psychosexual development. The need for food remains; the oral stage passes (barring fixation/repression). One never outgrows the need for food; one ideally outgrows the oral stage.

That is by no means an isolated example; in fact, as a crude approximation, it appears that about half of development remains in existence (even if modified), and about half is lost or passes. In cognitive development, for instance, once a capacity emerges and matures—whether an image, a symbol, a concept, or a rule—it is by and large retained; the higher cognitive structures generally subsume and incorporate the lower ones. In moral development, however, the higher stages do not so much include the lower as *replace* the lower. The lower structures seem essentially to be dissolved or negated. The former might be called *basic structures;* the latter, *transition* or *replacement stages.*

Thus, for example, Piaget has demonstrated that cognitive development proceeds through four major stage-structures: sensorimotor, preoperational thinking ("preop"), concrete operational thinking ("conop"), and formal operational thinking ("formop"). Significantly, each of these cognitive structures is necessary for, and actively contributes to, its successor's operations. Thus, sensorimotor cognition provides the raw data for preop and conop thinking, which in turn provides the operand of formop logic. The point is that, even though sensorimotor intelligence emerges and is tentatively perfected by age two, it does not then cease to be active or important but rather continues to exist and function. Besides its own appropriate activities, it also contributes to and is incorporated in higher structural consciousness. That is a good example of what all basic structures have in common: once they emerge, they "remain."

Kohlberg's studies, on the other hand, are largely examples of transition-replacement stages. Kohlberg has demonstrated that an individual's sense of morality develops through (at least) six major stages. Most importantly, once a person has reached a particular stage—say #5—he or she virtually *ceases all responses characteristic of the lower stages*—in this case, stages #1 through #4 (only 25 percent stage #4 responses, virtually 0 percent stage #1, #2, or #3 responses). While each junior stage is necessary for the development of its senior, the junior stages are not incorporated by the senior stages but rather are almost totally replaced by them (a point clearly suggested by Flavell).[41] That is a good example of transition-replacement stages—the lower is a precursor of the higher but is not an ingredient of the higher; it emerges only to be replaced, not incorporated.

In a sense, then, the basic structures are stages of development that are never outgrown; the transition structures are stages that *are* outgrown; the former are stages that *remain as structures,* the latter, structures that serve *basically as stages. Both* of them display structure *and* stage attributes, but with different emphasis. For this reason I will usually refer to the former as basic *structures* (although they also emerge in stages) and the latter as translation *stages* (although they are also temporary structures).

As a simple analogy of how both basic structures and transition stages might operate in development, take the growth of the United States by the annexation of new territories. Hawaii, for example, used to be a sovereign and autonomous nation itself. It possessed its own sense of "selfhood"—or nationality—and its own basic geographical structures (land, rivers, mountains, etc.). When the United States annexed Hawaii and eventually made it into a state, two fundamental things happened: the basic geography of Hawaii remained unchanged, and was simply incorporated as part of the United States. The nationality of Hawaii, however—its existence as an *exclusive* nation—was simply and completely dissolved. It was *replaced* by U.S. nationality. From that point on, Hawaii could no longer (legally) declare war on other countries, make treaties, print currency, engage in international relations, and so on.

In that analogy there are three fundamental phenomena: the basic geographical *structures,* the *function* of nationality, and the replacement *stages* of actual national identities. I am suggesting that similar phenomena occur in human growth and development. The *basic structures* of human ontogeny are like the basic geographical features—even as growth includes more and more territories, the old ones are not abandoned but included. The *self-system* in human ontogeny is like nationality—it seems to include such basic functions as defense mechanisms ("war"), sense of identity, interpersonal relations, and so on. And the actual *stages of self-moral development* are like the stages in the growth of nationality—as a new one emerges, it negates, dissolves, or replaces the old one (barring fixation/repression).

Accordingly, this presentation is divided into three sections. The first deals with the basic structures of consciousness and their development—body, mind, subtle, causal, and so on. The third deals with the major replacement stages of consciousness—moral stages, self-sense stages, Maslow's needs hierarchy, and so on. The second section, "The Self System," discusses what I proposed as the theoretical link between them.

THE BASIC STRUCTURES OF CONSCIOUSNESS

Fig. 9 is a schematic presentation of some of the basic structures of consciousness. This schema, up to and including vision-logic, is based explicitly on the works of Piaget, Werner, Arieti, and Baldwin. The higher levels—which I have here condensed from five or six levels into two general realms, the subtle and the causal—are based largely on Hindu and Buddhist psychological systems and especially their modern interpreters, for example, Aurobindo, Guénon, Smith, Free John (see Wilber[137]).

This schema suggests that there are vertical developments *between* levels as well as horizontal developments *within* each level (the former we have called transformation; the latter, translation). Further, each level or basic structure seems to have a fairly circumscribed date of emergence, or chronological *starting* point, but no necessarily circumscribed *end* point of development. Thus, for example, formop thinking (the reflexive-formal mind) generally emerges around age twelve, but it can be further developed and exercised throughout one's entire life. The important point is not so much when it can be said to be "perfected," but rather that it rarely appears in any form prior to early adolescence. It is the emergent point, not the end point, that most helps us to locate a process on the hierarchy of structural organization (although that is by no means the only criterion; see Wilber[140]). In the schema of Fig. 9, I have therefore listed, at their branch or differentiation points, some generally accepted dates of the first emergence of the various structures.

(The dates of the three most senior levels are set in parentheses

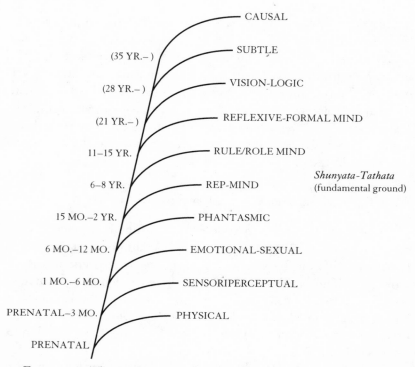

FIGURE 9. The Hierarchy of Basic Structures of Consciousness

because they do not yet seem to be collectively determined. Piaget had demonstrated that, barring abnormality, most individuals will reach a capacity for formop consciousness. But individuals today do not automatically develop beyond that point into the transpersonal regions of subtle, causal, or ultimate transcendence. My tentative hypothesis to account for this is that humanity on the whole has, up to this point in history, *collectively* evolved to the level of formop thinking, and therefore each individual born today is more or less assured of developing to that level. Beyond that level, however, "you're on your own." Conceivably, as more individuals strive for and reach the higher levels, as our ancestors fought for the capacity to reason, then these higher levels will be collectively bequeathed to subsequent progeny. In the meantime, my rather arbitrary earliest-point emergent dates are suggested in parentheses.)

One of the advantages of this type of branching-tree schema (first suggested by Werner) is that it clearly allows for the chronological development *of* and hierarchical ordering *between* the basic structures, without in any way denying ongoing and often parallel development *within* them. For example, the reflexive mind is of a higher order of structural organization than, say, the phantasmic or simple image mind, *and* the reflexive mind always emerges *after* the phantasmic mind—*but* the phantasmic level itself can still display significant development even as and while the reflexive mind is emerging and maturing. This occurs because once a basic structure emerges, then, as was suggested earlier, it *remains* in existence *simultaneously* with the subsequent higher structures; since it does remain it can be continuously and simultaneously developed and exercised. Significantly, this is *not* the case with transition or replacement stages. Persons at level-5 moral development do not simultaneously develop their capacity to be level-1 scoundrels. These stages, being replacements, are mutually exclusive.

It remains to give a brief description of the basic structures themselves, especially in the intermediate levels, which we heretofore have either lumped together (as "mind") or failed to define precisely.

1. *Physical.* The simple physical substratum of the organism (e.g., the first Buddhist *skandha*).

2. *Sensoriperceptual.* Here I am treating sensation, the second *skandha,* and perception, the third, as one general realm; typical sensorimotor cognition.

3. *Emotional-sexual.* The sheath of bioenergy, libido, élan vital, or *prana* (*pranamayakosha* in Vedanta, the fourth *skandha* in Buddhism, etc.).

4. *Phantasmic.* Arieti's term for the lower or image mind; the simplest form of mental "picturing" using only images.

5. *Rep-mind.* It is short for "representational mind," or Piaget's preoperational thinking. The rep or preop mind can form symbols and concepts, and thus *represent* not only things but classes, but it cannot yet *operate* on or coordinate those representations. Thus, to give a simple example, the rep-mind can count objects, but it cannot easily multiply or divide them—it lacks such *rule* coordination. Another striking feature of representational or preoperational thinking is that it *cannot easily take the role of other.* In other words, it is still very egocentric or narcissistic. In a classic series of experiments, Piaget precisely exposed the heart of preop consciousness: in a typical

experiment (I am greatly simplifying), Piaget would place an object, colored green on one side and red on the other, between the experimenter and the child. The child is allowed to examine the object, and then, with the red side facing the experimenter and the green side facing the child, the child is asked what color the experimenter (the other) is now looking at. The child answers "green." The object is turned so that green is now facing the experimenter and red is facing the child, and the question is again asked: what color is the experimenter now looking at? Answer: "red." In other words, in every instance the child imagines that others are seeing exactly what the child is seeing; the child has no real capacity to take the view of other, to cognitively change roles, to assume different perspectives. Because the rep-mind is still "close to the body," it is still bound to naive sensory data. What it *sees* is largely what it *thinks;* hence the incapacity for perspective; hence the egocentrism.

6. *Rule/role mind.* This is Piaget's concrete operational thinking. Conop thinking, unlike its rep-mind predecessor, can begin to take the *role* of others, and it can also clearly perform *rule* operations, such as multiplication, division, class inclusion, and so on. It is called "concrete operational" because it is still heavily bound to the immediate, gross, physical-sensory world. It can operate on the concrete world, but cannot yet operate on thought itself. One of the results of this is that conop, like its predecessors, is not a very imaginative or truly creative structure; still bound largely to the concrete and obvious world, it cannot imagine *possible* or *hypothetical* relationships. Again, in a series of extremely telling experiments, Piaget demonstrated that this structure lacks an understanding of "what if" and "as if" statements. That is, conop thinking simply cannot grasp statements such as "*If* this is the case, *then* this is the case"—it cannot grasp higher and nonobvious relationships.

7. *Formal-reflexive mind.* This is Piaget's formal operational consciousness. It is the first structure that can not only think about the world but think about thinking; hence, it is the first structure that is clearly self-reflexive and introspective (although this begins in rudimentary form with the rule/role mind). As such, formop can operate not just on concrete things but on subjective thoughts, and thus it is the first structure capable of imagining nonobvious *possibilities*. Among other things, this means it is capable of hypothetico-deduc-

tive or propositional reasoning ("if *a,* then *b*"), which allows it to apprehend higher or noetic *relationships*. Thus, far from being an "aridly abstract" structure, with little or no creativity, it is in fact the first truly creative or imaginative structure of cognition, as Piaget's studies clearly demonstrated. In fact—and Piaget is very explicit about this—this is the first stage that a person can become, in the true and best sense of the word, a "dreamer"—one capable of imagining possibilities not given to mere sensory evidence or sensory-concrete operations. And this leads directly to the next structure:

8. *Vision-logic.* Where the formal-mind establishes higher and creative relationships, vision-logic establishes *networks* of those relationships. The point is to place each proposition alongside numerous others, so as to be able to see, or "to vision," how the truth or falsity of any one proposition would affect the truth or falsity of the others. Such panoramic or vision-logic apprehends a mass network of ideas, how they influence each other, what their relationships are. It is thus the beginning of truly higher-order synthesizing capacity, of making connections, relating truths, coordinating ideas, integrating concepts. It culminates in what Aurobindo called "the higher mind," which "can freely express itself in single ideas, but its most characteristic movement is a mass ideation, a system or totality of truth-seeing at a single view; the relations of idea with idea, of truth with truth . . . self-seen in the integral whole."[2] This, obviously, is a highly *integrative* structure; indeed, in my opinion it is the highest integrative structure in the *personal* realm; beyond it lie more transpersonal developments.

9. *Subtle.* The general region of archetypal patterns or transindividual forms. We have already given a detailed breakdown of this realm in chapter 3; the reader is referred to that chapter for specifics.

10. *Causal.* The unmanifest source or transcendental ground of all the lesser structures. Again, a detailed breakdown is given in chapter 3.

11. *Ultimate.* Passing fully through the state of cessation or unmanifest absorption, consciousness is said finally to reawaken to its absolutely prior and eternal abode as spirit, radiant and all-pervading, one and many, only and all. This is Aurobindo's supermind, transcendental and unqualifiable consciousness as such. I am using

the paper on which Fig. 9 is drawn to represent this fundamental ground of empty suchness *(sunyata-tathata)*.

Those are some of the basic structures of consciousness. In the course of development, once they fundamentally emerge they remain in existence, not only fulfilling their own functions and carrying out their own tasks but also contributing to or even acting as ingredients of their senior structures. Although they can continue to grow, they are never outgrown.

SOME TRANSITIONAL ASPECTS ASSOCIATED WITH THE BASIC STRUCTURES

We said that the basic structures of consciousness, although defined as being essentially enduring structures, nevertheless emerge in *stages,* and therefore we would expect each basic structure to have certain temporary or phase-specific phenomena associated with it. And this indeed seems to be the case..

Since the basic structures are essentially *cognitive* structures, the temporary or phase-limited aspects of the basic structures simply concern the shifts in *cognitive maps* or *world views* that occur as successively new and higher structures emerge. I'll give several examples, which I'm sure will start to sound familiar:

The world view of the lowest levels—matter, sensation, and perception (treated together)—we have called "archaic," "pleromatic," "uroboric," and so on. This world view (so primitive as to hardly merit the name) is largely undifferentiated, global, fused, and confused—it's the way the world looks when you *only* have physical and sensoriperceptual structures. When the higher structures emerge, the archaic world view is lost or abandoned, but the capacity for sensation and perception is not. The latter are basic and enduring structures, the former is merely the transitional or phase-temporary cognitive map associated with them.

The world view of the emotional-sexual level we called "typhonic." It is more differentiated than the archaic and more body-stable, but it is still a largely premental world view, bound and confined to the felt present, capable of seeking only immediate release and discharge. When higher structures emerge, the *exclusively* felt-world will disappear; feelings will not.

The world view of the phantasmic and beginning preop we called "magic." Magic is simply the way the world looks when you *only* have images and symbols, not concepts, not rules, not formal operations, not vision. As in the world of the dream, the phantasmic images display magical condensation and displacement, wish-fulfillment, and release. As higher structures emerge, the magical world view per se is abandoned, but images and symbols themselves remain as important basic structures.

The world view of late preop and beginning conop we called "mythic." Myth is the way the world looks when you have concepts and rules, but no formal-operations or rational capacity. When the higher levels emerge, the mythic world view per se will die down and be replaced, but conop and rule/role will remain as important basic structures. Likewise, as development proceeds into the transrational realms, the exclusively rational world view—the way the world looks when you only have formop—is replaced with psychic and subtle world views, but the capacity to reason remains, and so on.

Thus, the archaic-typhonic world view (the way the world looks when you only have sensorimotor) is replaced by magic (the way the world looks when you only have preop), which in turn is replaced by mythic (the way the world looks when you only have conop), which itself is replaced by rational (the way the world looks to formop), and so on. The exclusive world views—archaic, typhonic, magic, mythic, and so on—are successively abandoned and replaced, but the basic structures themselves—preop, conop, formop, and so on—remain in existence, in awareness, functional and necessary. This is not to say that the old world views cannot in some cases be reactivated; when we dream, for instance, formop and conop are suspended, and thus we are reemersed in the phantasmic, preoperational, magical world view. But when the higher structures emerge or reemerge, the magical disappears, the preop remains.

THE SELF-SYSTEM

Perhaps the most striking feature of the basic structures of consciousness, at least as I have presented them, is that every one of them is *devoid of self*. That is, to no branch of the structural tree in

Fig. 9 can you point and say, *there* is the ego, or there is the self-sense, there is the feeling of personal "me-ness." The reason, I am suggesting, is that each of those basic structures is inherently without self-sense, *but,* in the course of development, a self-system emerges and takes as its successive substrates the basic structures of consciousness. In a sense, the basic structures form rungs in a ladder upon which the self-system then climbs, matter to body to mind to subtle to causal to spirit (generating certain self-transition stages in the process, as we will see).

But our point for now is that no single rung of the ladder, nor any combination of them, can be said to constitute an inherent self. This is very similar to the Buddhist notion of the five *skandhas*—roughly, the physical body, sensation-perception, emotion-impulse, lower cognition, and higher cognition. Each of these is said to be *anatta,* or without self, yet each (temporarily and unavoidably) serves as a substrate of the self-sense. When the self-sense passes through and beyond the *skandha*-structures, and thus ceases to exist in itself, the result is nirvana or selfless radiance, in which the *skandhas* can still continue to function but without the distortions of personalization. Essentially the same idea is found in the psychology of the yoga *chakras,* the Vedanta *sheaths,* and the Mahayana *vijnanas*—each system maintains that there are several basic structures, *sheaths,* or *chakras,* that are fundamentally without separate self-sense, evidenced by the fact that, for example, the enlightened sage has *access* to *all* the basic structures—for example, physical, emotional, mental, subtle—but she or he is not exclusively identified with or bound to them—there are structures *of* consciousness but no separate self *in* consciousness.

But this suggests that the self-system, although *ultimately* illusory, nonetheless serves an absolutely necessary if *intermediate* function. Namely, it is the vehicle of development, growth, and transcendence—or, to return to our simplistic metaphor, the self is the climber of the rungs in the ladder of structural organization, a climb destined to release the self from itself, "lest the last judgement come and find me unannihilate," said Blake, "and I be seiz'd and giv'n into the hands of my own selfhood."

The self-system, then, even if ultimately illusory is intermediately necessary, appropriate, and functional, and this brings us to the whole topic known generally as self psychology (a phrase first widely used by Maslow to describe his endeavors). It is actually only in the past few decades that self psychology—the study of what the self is, what its functions and constituents are, what developments it undergoes—has begun to receive serious attention. ("Only in the last twenty years has there been a shift in psychology back to the subject's consciousness of self.")[20] Spearheaded by such theorists as Hartmann, Sullivan, G. H. Mead, Erikson, Rogers, Fairbairn, Kohut, Loevinger, Maslow, and Branden, the study of the nature and function of the self-system has recently become of paramount importance. Indeed, the significance of self psychology might be indicated by the fact that the claim has already been made that "Kohut and Chicago are modern equivalents of Freud and Vienna"[20]— Kohut being the author of the landmark book, *The Restoration of the Self.*

All I wish to do in this section is suggest, on the basis of the above-mentioned theorists, what seem to be some of the major characteristics of the self-system. We might begin by noting that even such antiself psychologist-philosophers as Hume and James felt that the self-sense was connected to memory, or the capacity to connect and organize *this* moment around the *preceding* moment; that is, to *appropriate* the preceding moment by the succeeding one. For James, the innermost self—"the Self of selves"—consisted of "successive acts of appropriation, sustained for as long as one can sustain them."[66]

This definition—the self as locus of appropriation—can of course be used in a perverse fashion—to explain the self by explaining it away (as both Hume and James ended up doing). The idea is that, since the self is "merely" the act of this moment's appropriation of the preceding moment, there *is* no self, only a "stream of consciousness," evidenced by the fact that the self never sees itself as subject but always and only as a stream of objects.

The problem with this theory, however, is that the act of appropriation itself does not entirely enter the stream—and thus neither does the self. Put simply, the fact that the self cannot see itself doesn't necessarily mean there is no self, just as the fact that the eye does not see itself doesn't mean there is no eye. The self as intermediate seer of the stream is not necessarily part of the stream, at least not as entirely as Hume supposed. As appropriator of the stream, the self is constituted by functions *other than* the stream, and those functions are a legitimate field of study and research. Thus, as Brandt points out, it was only after this gap (or dead end) in the Hume-James approach became evident that the study of self psychology could proceed in earnest.[20]

One of the characteristics of the self, then, might be the capacity to appropriate and organize the stream of psychological events in meaningful and coherent ways. This is not very different from the modern psychoanalytic viewpoint which defines the self as "the process of organizing." Beginning with Freud's *The Ego and the Id,* and passing on to Heinz Hartmann, Edith Jacobson, Fairbairn, Spitz, Mahler, Kohut, Blanck and Blanck, the idea of the self as an *active organizer of psychological reality* was increasingly given credence. As Brandt summarizes this general view: "The self [is not merely] a synthesis of the underlying psychic parts or substructures [i.e., not merely a sum of the streams] but an *independent organizing* principle, a 'frame of reference' against which to measure the activities or states of these substructures."[20] Thus, in line with all the above, our first characteristic might be that the self is the executor of psychological organization, integration, and coordination.

In the same way and for the same reasons, the self might be viewed as the *locus of identification*. This is perhaps the most cogent definition or characteristic of the self-system, for the self, in appropriating and organizing the stream of structural events, creates for itself a *selective identity* in the midst of those occasions. This seems perfectly normal and necessary—we need only think of the disastrous results of the incapacity to form a stable self-identity (e.g., Erikson's "identity crisis") or the breakdown of self-identity in the borderline psychoses and neuroses (cf. Kernberg). As a simple generalization, then, I will speak of the self as the locus of identification as well as the center of the sense of identity—the intuitive apprehension of proximate "I-ness" which correlates with the act of appropriation.

Finally, the self might be thought of as the navigator of development, for at any point on the ladder of basic structures (except the two end limits), the self is faced with several different "directional pulls." On the one hand, it can (without limits) choose to remain on its present level of structural organization, or it can choose to release its present level in favor of another. If it releases its present level, it can move up the hierarchy, or it can move down. *On* a given level, then, the self is faced with preservation versus negation, holding on versus letting go, living that level versus dying to that level, identifying with it versus dis-identifying from it. *Between* levels the self is faced with ascent versus descent, moving up the hierarchy to levels of increasing structural organization and integration or moving down to less organized and integrative structures. We have already discussed these factors in Chapter 7. For convenience, I'll simply reproduce the figure:

<pre>
                    ASCEND
                       1

PRESERVE 3 ←————————|————————→ 4 RELEASE

                       2
                    DESCEND
</pre>

The self is located, so to speak, at the crossroads of the display. It must balance the two dilemmas—preserve/release and ascend/descend—and navigate its developmental course of those four compass points. The self does not merely float down the stream of consciousness—for better or worse, it pushes and pulls, holds on and lets go, ascends and descends, preserves and releases. How the self as "navigator" handles the resultant tensions and functional dilemmas appears to be a large part of the story of self-development and self-pathology.

Now, *if* the self is indeed the locus of organization, identification, and navigation, then we might expect the course of self-development to include the following: As each of the basic structures begin chronologically to emerge and develop, the self would *appropriate* those structures or *identify* with them (the self as the locus of identification). Once identified with a structure, the self, or the self's preservation drive (#3), would seek to consolidate and integrate the resultant overall self-complex (self plus appropriated basic structure; incidentally, note that the self's world view would be that of the appropriated basic structure—archaic or magic or mythic, etc.). This initial identification, consolidation, and preservation is normal, necessary, appropriate.

If, however, the self *as* self is to *ascend* the hierarchy of structural organization—to grow—then eventually it must *release* or negate its *exclusive* identification with the lower level (or levels) in order to allow a higher identification with more senior levels of structural organization. It must accept the "death," negation, or release (#4) of the lower level—*it must dis-identify with or detach from* an exclusive involvement with that level—in order to ascend (#1) to the greater life, unity, and integration of the next higher level (or levels) of structural organization. Once on the *new* level, the self then seeks to consolidate, fortify, and preserve the self-complex of *that* level (via factor #3), until it is once again strong enough to accept the death of that level, release or negate it, and so ascend to the next developmental level.

Thus, both preservation and negation, or life and death, apparently have important *phase-specific* tasks to accomplish. It is by the preservation-drive that a given level is appropriated, developed, consolidated, and integrated—only by making a level "its own" can the self intimately organize it. Once that task is accomplished, however, it is only by negation that the self can die to its exclusive identification with that level and thus ascend to the next higher integration. Pathology seems to develop if either (or both) of these phase-specific tasks are misnavigated. For example, *fixation* might be thought of as *morbid preservation*—a failure to release, negate, or die to a given level; the individual thus remains obsessed with gratifications he or she ought otherwise to have "outgrown." On the other hand, *repression* might be viewed as a type of *morbid negation*—a premature death; it is dis-identifying with a component before it is properly integrated, appropriated, and consolidated; the component is thus merely split off from the personality. The necessary dis-identification process becomes merely perverse dissociation.

In normal development, the phase-specific task of dis-identification from a given level seems to serve an extremely important function—namely, to denude that level of self (since self is the locus of identification). This phase-specific dis-identification does not destroy the level or the basic structure itself, but merely releases it from being the intermediately necessary substrate of the separate self-sense and returns it to its prior state of *anatta,* or selfless function and service. To return to our ladder metaphor: at each stage of growth, as the self steps from lower rung to a higher, the rungs of the ladder are not destroyed, deformed, or discarded. What *is* destroyed is the self's exclusive attachment to that rung.

We are now in a position to examine those self structures that are negated or released—they are, we have said, examples of transition-replacement structures. In particular, what we will be examining are the various *self-stages* constructed by a series of *exclusive identifications* with the hierarchic levels of structural organization or basic structures. As we will see, these "exclusivity structures" last as long as the self-attachment to the particular basic structure lasts. Once that identification is released, that exclusivity structure is destroyed.

THE SELF-STAGES OF CONSCIOUSNESS

The overall suggestion of this section is that if one takes the hierarchy of basic structures (as presented in Fig. 9) and then subjects each level to the influence of a self-system (whose characteristics I summarized above), one will generate the basic features of the stages of development presented and described by researchers such as Maslow, Loevinger, and Kohlberg. It is almost a process of simple mathematical mapping—for example, if the self is the seat of identification, what would the self look like if it identified with the emotional-sexual level? with the rule/role mind? with the formal mind? with the subtle? As I will try to demonstrate, by asking that question of each of the basic structures, we can generate—in precisely the same order and with quite similar descriptions—the stages of Kohlberg's moral development, Loevinger's ego development, and Maslow's needs hierarchy (to cite only the three examples I have chosen for this presentation).

I am suggesting (1) that the hierarchical stages presented by Loevinger, Kohlberg, and Maslow (also Erikson, Peck, Bull, Selman, Broughton, etc.) are referring to various aspects of *essentially similar* replacement-transition structures, and (2) that these particular types of replacement-transition structures are generated primarily by the enzyme of self-system acting on the substrate of basic structure. Since they are generated when the self's locus of identification centers more or less exclusively on successive basic structures, they can also be called "exclusivity structures."

Claim #1 is put in its strong form by Loevinger: "There is but one major source for all the conceptions of moral and ego [self] development, one thread of reality to which all of the conceptions give varying access."[78] But, to my mind, there is much room for latitude here, and I would (at this stage of our knowledge) prefer to make my own point with the weaker claim of similarity. Kohlberg, for example, feels that self-development is somewhat prior to moral development, and Selman feels that self-interpersonal development is a deep structure against which moralization occurs as surface structure (views I am inclined to agree with).

In addition to those (minor) differences, there are also variations in the comprehensiveness of the various theories of self-stages we are correlating. Thus, for each one of the Maslow's stages Loevinger has two (as does Kohlberg, up to a point). It might be that Loevinger is presenting substages; it might be that Maslow was inadvertently lumping different stages together—but that is not our concern for the moment. In all of these cases—the relation of self and moral sense, the number and types of stages and substages, and so on—future research alone will decide the issues. We need only the already acknowledged fundamental similarities between these theories to make our general point; as these systems are refined, we can likewise refine our scheme.

The correlations between the basic structures of consciousness and the hierarchic stages of Maslow, Loevinger, and Kohlberg are presented in Fig. 10. The correlations between Maslow, Loevinger, and Kohlberg are basically those given by Loevinger herself; further, the correlations between the Piagetian basic (cognitive) structures and the stages of Kohlberg and Loevinger are those suggested by Breger and by Habermas—in any case, these correlations are not merely my own readings of the data. Until research techniques are refined, however, these authorities generally acknowledge that such correlations are open to errors of ± one stage (e.g., some theorists place moral stage 2 under conop, and stage 4 under formop, etc.; these are very important distinctions, but again, quite incidental to our overall conclusions).

Because both the lower and the upper levels are more controver-

Basic Structures	Maslow (Needs)	Loevinger (Self-Sense)	Kohlberg (Moral Sense)	
Physical Sensoriperceptual	(Physiological)	Autistic Symbiotic	—	
Emotive Phantasmic		Beginning impulsive	—	
Rep-mind	Safety	Impulsive Self-protective	I. Preconventional	1. Punishment/ obedience 2. Naive hedonism
Rule/role mind	Belongingness	Conformist Conscientious-conformist	II. Conventional	3. Approval of others 4. Law and order
Reflexive mind	Self-esteem	Conscientious Individualistic	III. Postconventional	5. Individual rights 6. Individual principles of conscience
Vision-logic	Self-actualization	Autonomous Integrated	—	
Subtle	Self-transcendence	—	—	
Causal	"	—	—	
Ultimate	"	—	—	

FIGURE 10. Correlations between Basic Structures and Various Aspects of Self-Stages (Maslow, Loevinger, and Kohlberg)

sial (more difficult to research and interpret), I will start my discussion of the correlations in the middle—with the representational mind.

The rep-mind, which emerges around age two and predominates consciousness until around age seven, is capable of being *aware* of others but incapable of taking the *role* of others. A self identified with the rep-mind would thus be able to react *to* others but not act in conscious conformity *with* others; to that extent, it would be a rather self-centered or narcissistic structure, aware of its own tenuous and vulnerable existence but unable to fully comprehend the others who may threaten it, with a consequent concern, above all, for its own self-protection. This is, in my opinion, Maslow's safety needs and Loevinger's self-protective stage.

Further, since the rep-mind is also still "close to the body" (Piaget's summary of preop thinking)—or still partially identified and involved with emotional-sexual impulses—this general structure, especially in its beginning development, would display Loevinger's stage of "impulsiveness." The impulsive and self-protective stages correspond to Kohlberg's first two stages of moral development—punishment and obedience (stage 1) and naive hedonism (stage 2). The point is that, since the rep-mind is still close to the body, the self identified with that mind is likewise close to the body and thus largely motivated *by* the body—by concerns over bodily pain and punishment (stage 1) or bodily hedonistic pleasure (stage 2). With little or no actual comprehension of *others,* this overall stage is indeed rightly referred to as self-protective (Loevinger), narcissistic (Freud), egocentric (Piaget), preconventional (Kohlberg), and safety-bound (Maslow).

With the emergence of the rule/role mind, the capacity to take the role or perspective of others emerges. The self identified with the role-mind would thus be keenly attuned to the opinions and roles of others and to its own role in the midst of others. Further, since the role-mind is not yet capable of formal operational thinking, the self would have no inner capacity to easily judge the true roles from the false (or fraudulent) ones—it would thus tend merely to *conform* to the role assigned it, especially by authority figures. This, in my opinion, is Maslow's belongingness needs, Loevinger's conformist (and conscientious-conformist) stages, and Kohlberg's overall stage of *conventional* (conformist) morality.

The self identified with the role-mind escapes to some degree its narcissistic imprisonment in its own being and begins to enter the community of other viewpoints. Initially, however, it is "captured" by those viewpoints—hence, conformity. And the self would indeed actively *seek* this conformity because that is now its locus of identification, preservation, and life—to lose conformity is to "die." To lose face, to be an outsider, to not belong—there is the terror of the self identified with the role-mind.

By the time of adolescence, the formal-reflexive mind begins to emerge. This level is, as we saw, the first structure clearly capable of sustained self-reflection and introspection. The self identified with the reflexive mind would thus be involved in conscientious and self-inquiring modes of awareness and behavior. It would have the capacity to question conventional mores (something the role-mind could not easily do) and would thus be involved in postconventional moral decisions. No longer bound to conformity needs, the self would have to rely more on its own conscience, or its inner capacity to formally reflect and establish rationally what might be the good, the true, and the beautiful. Above all, it would have to see itself succeeding in—or at least attempting—this task, since it is now *identified* with the processes of self-reflection. Its "life" is now a process of self-reflection in the midst of other self-reflecting persons, and how it succeeds in this venture of self-reflection largely determines its own inner feelings of worth.

In my opinion, this is exactly Maslow's stage of self-esteem, Loevinger's conscientious and individualistic stages(s), and Kohlberg's postconventional morality. According to Kohlberg, the postconventional level consists of the stage of "morality by individual rights" (stage 5) and morality of "individual principles of conscience" (stage 6), which are almost exactly Loevinger's conscientious and individualistic stages, respectively.

We turn now to some of the highest levels of development, and here of course our data begin rapidly to thin out, but enough remain to conclude our general points. If the development of basic structures continues beyond the formal-reflexive mind, then—I have hypothesized—the next major basic structure is that of vision-logic, which was postulated as being the *highest personal-integrative level of consciousness.* The self identified with this level would thus be expected to attempt to fulfill the highest personal potentials it may possess, as well as to firmly integrate those it has already developed (we called the self-sense at this stage "centauric"). In my opinion, this is Maslow's stage of self-actualization, and Loevinger's integrated/autonomous stages(s). (For reasons that Kohlberg's studies "run out" at this point, see Loevinger,[78] Breger;[21] it's not that moral sensibility runs out at this stage, but that careful research into moralization has not yet been carried out beyond this stage, a situation I believe will soon be remedied.)

Beyond vision-logic lie the various levels of transpersonal structural organization—which, taken as a whole, obviously refers to Maslow's self-transcendence (a region usually ignored or denied by orthodox psychologists). The problem with even Maslow's presentation at this point, however, is that it fades out much too quickly. Although of pioneering importance in its day, Maslow's single category ("self-transcendence") slurs over the increasingly obvious fact that there are probably as many discrete stages of development beyond self-esteem as there are stages leading up to it. The transpersonal realm is far from being a single structure—it houses, in my opinion, at least five levels, perhaps as many as twelve or more (see Brown, Goleman). I simply include Maslow's highest need (self-transcendence) to finish our correlations. As research is expanded and refined, I think the existence of these higher dozen or so transpersonal levels—their characteristics, their development, and their moral correlates (such as the *bodhisattva* vow)—will become more obvious.

As for the very lowest levels, I do not think it necessary—or yet possible—to put the case as forcefully as I have for the middle realms. The reason is obvious: the lowest levels (up to and including the phantasmic) are preverbal; thus research is extremely difficult to conduct and even more difficult to interpret, and I in no way wish to hang my case on wild speculations about the first one or two years of infancy. I will simply say that, in my opinion, the studies of Piaget, Mahler, Spitz, Jacobson, and Fairbairn are definitely amenable to the theory I am here presenting. As for Loevinger's lowest levels (autistic, symbiotic, and beginning impulsive), I have simply listed them next to what I believe are the crucial correlations with the basic structures of consciousness. (Kohlberg has no correlations here because he was working solely and deliberately with verbal reports, and these early stages are entirely preverbal.) In any event, the lowest stages, as with the highest, are especially awaiting further research.

DISCUSSION

Perhaps we can now better appreciate why the self-moral stages can also be called "exclusivity stages," and how and why they differ fundamentally from the basic structures on which they rest. Take as an example the conformity stage(s)—my suggestion is that the actual *need to conform* (e.g., Maslow/Loevinger) is generated in large part by the *attachment to* the rule/role mind. Once that attachment is broken (via phase-specific negation or dis-identification), so is the conformity drive. But the rule/role mind—as a basic structure—is *not* broken; it can and does continue to function, at least as Arieti describes it, both in gathering its own information/rule-processing data and in serving as an ingredient-operand of the formal mind. And notice: A person at the rule/role mind has (barring pathology) *perfect access to and use of all the preceding and lower basic structures*— simultaneous access to the physical body, sensations, perceptions, feelings, images, and representational symbols (words). *However,* a person at the correlative level of self stage—in this example, a person at the conformity stage(s)—does *not* have access to, or does not use and simultaneously exercise, the lower self-stages (because, basically, they no longer exist). A person striving to be a conformist does not simultaneously and equally strive to be an impulsive maverick. As both Loevinger and Kohlberg demonstrated, a person at a given stage of self-moral development rarely gives responses of the lower stages (and the lower or more removed the stage, the less likely the response).

To suggest, however, that the basic structures are root supports of various self transition-stages does not imply that the latter aren't subjected to intermediate operations. This certainly seems the view of Habermas, Selman, and Kohlberg, all of whom tend to see cognitive base structures separated from moralization by interpersonal-self operations. Habermas, for instance, suggests that a single cognitive base structure, when subjected to different degrees of "interactive competence," supports two subclasses of self-moral response (Habermas's correlations of Piaget's base cognitive structures with Kohlberg's moral responses are exactly as given in Fig. 10). Further, this degree of "interactive competence" is related directly to "the core of identity formation" (our self-system identification-locus). I myself have already argued (above) that between the basic structures, on the one hand, and the self-moral stages, on the other, lies the self-system and its transcribing operations. Whether this transcription process takes place in one or two stages—indeed, three or four—is an extremely important point, but one that is incidental to our general thesis. At this time, I regard Habermas's discussion, and his correlations, as the most cogent, and therefore they are the ones I have here followed.

Finally, a note on Maslow's needs hierarchy. In my opinion, Maslow's hierarchy is almost entirely one of self-stages, *not* basic structures, of consciousness. I say this because (1) it fits almost perfectly the other schemes of self-stage development, as we have already seen (and as Loevinger emphasized); and (2) it fits very poorly with the traditional maps of basic structures (or levels of consciousness).

Take, for example, the Vedanta *koshas* or sheaths of consciousness—in order of ascending structuralization, they are: the *annamayakosha,* or physical (food) level; the *pranamayakosha,* or emotional-sexual level; the *manomayakosha,* or level of mind; the *vijnanamayakosha,* or level of intuition; and the *anandamayakosha,* or level of transcendental *enstasis* (beyond which lies the selfless being of ultimate spirit, or *sahaj* Brahman). *None* of those levels directly represents a self-sense—they are first and foremost levels of consciousness, not modes of self or self-needs. The Vedanta *koshas* are, in my opinion, perfect examples of *basic structures* (not self-stages). They correlate precisely, although in condensed fashion, with the scheme presented in Fig. 8, *not* Fig. 10. The same seems to be true, I would like to emphasize, of the yogic *chakras* (Hindu and Buddhist), the Mahayana *vijnanas,* Aurobindo's levels, the Christian mystic hierarchies, and others.

The perennial traditions are certainly aware of various stage, transition, or phase-temporary phenomena, including both transi-

This is a narrative of the appendix to the Atman Project.

tional world views *and* self-stages. Meditation, especially, is generally viewed as the unfolding of higher levels or basic structures of consciousness, but an unfolding that is accompanied by all sorts of phase-temporary events and stages (including also the fact that higher stages often include spiraling returns to and recapitulations of lower levels, in all sorts of complex patterns and combinations— see, for example, Brown and Engler's excellent account,[24] and also our own chapter 4). My point is rather that, in attempting to integrate and synthesize Eastern and Western approaches (as well as various Western approaches themselves), the differences between basic structures and transitional-stages ought to be kept in mind, lest we end up comparing apples and oranges. I have, for instance, seen probably a half-dozen attempts to equate Maslow's hierarchy with the yoga *chakras,* and they simply aren't the same phenomena, no matter how closely correlated they certainly are.

I have suggested that Maslow's hierarchy is basically one of transitional self-stages. The one exception is Maslow's physiological needs, his lowest level, which I have put in parentheses in Fig. 10. One never outgrows the physiological need for food, air, and so on. In other words, the physiological needs are not self-stages or transition-stages per se; nor are they prepotent (giving way to subtler needs: the need for air is never replaced, for example, by the need for belongingness). Thus, in my opinion, Maslow's physiological needs are the only basic structures in his hierarchy; they therefore ought to be replaced (à la Loevinger) with something like the symbiotic or impulsive needs (with the physiological needs moved back to the hierarchy of basic structures). Maslow's list would then be consistently a hierarchy of self-stages—self-impulsive, self-safety, self-belongingness, self-esteem, self-actualization, self-transcendence—and not physical, emotional, mental, subtle, and causal structures.

One last reason that it is important to distinguish basic structures from self-stages is that the two do not necessarily—not even usually—follow the same developmental timetable. They emerge in the same order, but not necessarily at the same time. To return one last time to our ladder analogy, the emergence of the basic structures can run far ahead of the self's willingness to "climb up" them. This, of course, raises many intriguing questions, but they are questions already faced by orthodox developmental psychologists, for it has long been acknowledged that cognitive structures are necessary but not sufficient for moral and self-development. For example, an individual can be at the basic structure of the conop mind but display a moral self-sense anywhere at or below it (but never above it). For just that reason, the actual times of emergence of the basic structures (up to and including formop) are largely *age-dependent* and relatively fixed (as evidenced, for example, by Piaget's cognitive structures and as indicated on Fig. 9), but the emergence of the self-stages are relatively *age-independent* (as Loevinger and Kohlberg have explained for their stage-structures). The hypothesis that the basic structures serve as substrates for the self-stages is compatible with that data.

In short, these distinctions have important implications for orthodox developmental psychology, because, even though rather elemental, they have been largely overlooked, as Flavell lamented. But they are also important for the scientists, philosophers, and psychologists who are in search of a new and higher transcendental paradigm, lest mere stages be confused with ontological structures (or vice versa). The dynamic, the timetable, the characteristics—these are all different in the development of the basic structures and the development of the self-sense through those structures. And while the former is the substrate for the latter, the two otherwise constitute different development strands.

10

The Ultimate State of Consciousness

T HROUGHOUT THIS VOLUME we have pointed out that the Absolute is both the highest state of being and the ground of all being; it is both the goal of evolution and the ground of evolution; the highest stage of development and the reality or suchness of *all* stages of development; the highest of all conditions and the Condition of all conditions; the highest rung in the ladder *and* the wood out of which the entire ladder is made. Anything less than that *paradox* generates either pantheistic reductionism, on the one hand, or wild and radical transcendentalism, on the other. Failure to grasp this paradox of instruction has led more than one modern theorist—in search of the new paradigm—to collapse and equate Spirit with any merely "holistic" findings in physics, biology, or psychology—a confusion of the sum total of the shadows in the cave with the Light beyond the cave. Accordingly, as a counterbalance to this modern and widespread pantheistic reductionism, I have throughout this book largely emphasized the developmental, transcendental, "highest rung" aspect of Spirit.

But, indeed, the other side of the paradox ought not be overlooked in the process. If Spirit is completely transcendent, it is also completely immanent. I am firmly convinced that if a new and comprehensive paradigm is ever to emerge, that paradox will be its heart. Since I have heretofore been emphasizing the transcendental or "highest rung" aspect, I can think of no better way to conclude this volume than with a sustained emphasis on the immanent or omnipresent aspect.

One without a Second

In the *Chandogya Upanishad,* Brahman—the absolute reality, the ultimate state of consciousness—is described in glaringly simple and straightforward terms: the Absolute is "One without a second."[62] That inspired Upanishadic text does not describe the ultimate as the creator, controller, ruler, or lord of a second; neither does it speak of One opposed to a second, nor One outside a second, nor over, above, or beyond a second—but One without a second. The Absolute, in other words, is that which has nothing outside It, nothing apart from It, nothing other to It, a fact expressed in Isaiah as "I am the Lord, and there is none else." All of which means that there is really nothing outside Brahman, nothing outside the Absolute. In the words of an old Zen Master:

> All the Buddhas and all sentient beings are nothing but the One Mind, beside which nothing exists. Above, below, and around you, all is spontaneously existing, for there is nowhere which is outside the Buddha-Mind.[15]

Of course, if there were anything outside the Absolute, that would immediately impose a limitation on It, for the Absolute would then be one outside a second instead of One without a second. And so it is in this sense that Brahman, the Buddha-Mind, the Godhead is called absolutely all-encompassing, all-inclusive, and all-pervading. When the Upanishads say "All the world is Brahman," and "This, too, is Brahman"; when the *Lankavatara Sutra* proclaims that "The world is nothing but Mind," and "All is Mind"; when the *Awakening of Faith* states that "All things are only of the One Mind"; when the Taoist texts insist that "There is nothing outside the Tao; you cannot deviate from It"—well, they mean just that. To quote the apocryphal Acts of Peter:

> Thou are perceived of the spirit only, thou art unto me father, thou my mother, thou my brother, thou my friend, thou my bondsman,

thou my steward: thou art All and All is in thee: and thou ART, and there is nought else that IS save thee only.[65]

This being true because, as Christ said in the Gospel of St. Thomas:

I am the Light that is above them all, I am the All, the All came forth from Me and the All attained to Me. Cleave a piece of wood, I am there; Lift up the stone and you will find Me there.[57]

Now the statement that all the world is really Brahman usually fires up in overly imaginative minds such fancies as uniform, all-pervading, featureless but divine goo; the instantaneous and total evaporation of all diversity and multiplicity, leaving behind an immaculate but amorphous All-knowing, All-merciful, celestial Vacuum. We flounder in such mental frenzies only because we expect the statement "All is Brahman" to be a logical proposition, containing some type of mental information about the universe, and taken thus, we can only picture its meaning to be the reduction of all multiplicity to uniform, homogenous, and unchanging mush.

But "All is Brahman" should not be mistaken as a philosophical conclusion, a logical theory, or a merely verbal explanation of reality. For the sages of every time and place have unanimously maintained that the Absolute is actually ineffable, unspeakable, utterly beyond words, symbols, and logic. And not because it is too mysterious or too sublime or too complex for words, but rather because it is too simple, too obvious, too close to be caught in the net of symbols and signs. Because there is nothing outside It, there is no way to define or classify It. As Johannes Scotus (Erigena) remarked, "God does not know Himself, what He is, because He is not a *what;* in a certain respect He is incomprehensible to Himself and to every intellect." Or, as Shankara, the Master of Vedanta Hinduism, explains:

Now there is no class to which Brahman belongs, no common genus. It cannot therefore be denoted by words which signify a category of things. Nor can it be denoted by quality, for it is without qualities; nor yet by activity because it is without activity—"at rest, without parts or activity," according to the Scriptures. Neither can it be denoted by relationship, for it is "without a second" and is not the object of anything but its own self. Therefore it cannot be defined by word or idea; as the Scripture says, it is the One "before whom words recoil."[120]

This, indeed, is also the point of Wittgenstein's philosophy; namely, we cannot make any valid statements about Reality as a whole because there is no place outside it where we can take up a stance so as to describe it. In other words, "we could only say things about the world as a whole if we could get outside the world, if, that is to say, it ceased to be for us the whole world. . . . (But) for us, it cannot have a boundary, since it has nothing outside it."[142] And having no boundary, no limits—being one without a second—it cannot be defined or classified. You can define and classify, for example, a "fish" because there are things that are not fish, such as rocks, trees, and alligators; and drawing a mental line between what is fish and what is not fish, you are able to define and classify it. But you cannot define or say "what" Brahman is, for there is nothing It is not—being one without a second, there is nothing outside It and so nowhere to draw the classifying line.

Hence, the Absolute, the real world as it is, is also called pure Emptiness, since all definitions and propositions and statements about reality are void and meaningless. Even such statements as "Reality is the Limitless" won't quite do, for the "limitless" excludes that which is "limited." Rather, the Absolute is finally Void of all conceptual elaborations, and so even the word "void," if taken to be a logical idea, is to be denied validity. In the words of Nagarjuna:

> It cannot be called void or not void,
> Or both or neither;
> But in order to point it out,
> It is called "the Void."[124]

Since all propositions about reality are void and invalid, the same of course holds true for the statement "All is Brahman," if this statement is taken as a logical proposition. If, for instance, Brahman were taken as a concrete and categorical fact *among other facts*, then "All is Brahman" would be sheerest nonsense: as any logician will tell us, to predicate something of everything is to predicate it of nothing. But Brahman is not so much a fact among other facts, but the Fact of all facts. "All is Brahman" is not a merely logical proposition; it is more of an experiential or contemplative revelation, and while the logic of the statement is admittedly quite flawed, the experience itself is not. And the experience All-is-Brahman makes it quite clear that there is not one thing outside the Absolute, even though when translated into words, we are left with nonsense. But, as Wittgenstein would say, although It cannot be *said,* It can be *shown.*

Now the insight that there is nothing outside of Brahman implies also that there is nothing *opposed* to It; that is to say, the Absolute is that which has no opposite. Thus It is also called the Nondual, the Not-two, the No-opposite. To quote the third Patriarch of Zen:

> All forms of dualism
> Are ignorantly contrived by the mind itself.
> They are like visions and flowers in the air:
> Why bother to take hold of them?
> When dualism does no more obtain,
> Even Oneness itself remains not as such.
> The True Mind is not divided—
> When a direct identification is asked for,
> We can only say, "Not-Two!"[116]

But, as Seng-t'san points out, "Not-two" does not mean just One. For pure Oneness is most dualistic, excluding as it does its opposite of Manyness. The single One opposes the plural Many, while the Nondual embraces them both. "One without a second" means "One without an opposite," not One opposed to Many. Thus, as we have already hinted, we mustn't picture the Absolute as excluding diversity, as being an undifferentiated monistic mush, for Brahman embraces both unity and multiplicity.

Now the import of what has been said thus far is that since there is really nothing outside the Nondual, there is no point in either space or time where the Absolute is not. And it isn't that a *part* of the Absolute is present in every thing—as in pantheism—for that is to introduce a boundary within the infinite, assigning to each thing a different piece of the infinite pie. Rather, the *entire* Absolute is completely and wholly present at every point of space and time, for the simple reason that you can't have a different infinite at each point. The Absolute, as St. Bonaventure put it, is "A sphere, whose center is everywhere and whose circumference nowhere," so that, in the words of Plotinus, "while it is nowhere, nowhere is it not."

Yet notice that the Absolute can be entirely present at every point of space only if It is itself spaceless. Just as, to use Eckhart's example, your eyes can see things which are colored red only because your eyes themselves are without red color or "red-less," so also the Absolute can embrace all space because It is itself without space or "space-less."

Thus, the infinite is not a point, or a space—even a very Big Space—or a dimension among other points, spaces, and dimensions; but is rather point-less, spaceless, dimensionless—not one among many but one without a second. In just this fashion, the *whole* of the infinite can be present at all points of space, for being itself spaceless, it does not contend with space and so is free to utterly embrace it, just as water, being shape-less and form-less, can fill containers of all shapes and forms. And since the infinite is present in its entirety at every point of space, *all* of the infinite is fully present right HERE. In fact, to the eye of the infinite, no such place as *there* exists (since, put crudely, if you go to some other place over *there,* you will still only find the very same infinite as *here,* for there isn't a different one at each place).

And so also with time. The Absolute can be present in its entirety at every point of time only if It is itself timeless. And that which is timeless is eternal, for, as Wittgenstein rightly pointed out, Eternity is "not infinite temporal duration but timelessness." That is to say, Eternity is not everlasting time but a moment without time. Hence, being timeless, *all* of Eternity is wholly and completely present at every point of time—and thus, all of Eternity is already present right NOW. To the eye of Eternity, there is no *then,* either past or future.

Point without dimension or extension, Moment without date or duration—such is the Absolute. And while It is nowhere, nowhere is It not. That, simply, is the meaning of omnipresence—the Absolute is simultaneously present everywhere and everywhen in its entirety. "Who sees not God everywhere sees him truly nowhere."

With all of the foregoing, it won't be hard to understand that all metaphysical traditions have universally claimed that the Absolute is literally Unattainable. For if it were possible for a person to *attain* the Absolute, this would imply moving from a point where the Absolute is not to a point where It is—yet there is no point where It is not. In other words, it's impossible to attain It because it's impossible to escape It in the first place. And so it is important to realize that since the Absolute is already one with everything everywhere, we can in no way manufacture or attain to our union with It. No matter what we do or don't do, try to do or try not to do, we can never attain It. In the words of Shankara:

> As Brahman constitutes a person's Self, it is not something to be attained by that person. And even if Brahman were altogether different from a person's Self, still it would not be something to be attained; for as it is omnipresent it is part of its nature that it is ever present to everyone.[120]

Or read carefully the following from the great Zen Master Huang Po:

> That there is nothing which can be attained is not idle talk; it is the truth. You have always been one with the Buddha, so do not pretend you can attain to this oneness by various practices. If, at this very moment, you could convince yourselves of its unattainability, being certain indeed that nothing at all can ever be attained, you would already be Bodhi-minded. Hard is the meaning of this saying! It is to teach you to refrain from seeking Buddhahood, since any search is doomed to failure.[15]

Or, just to push the point home, consider the words of Sri Ramana Maharshi:

> There is no reaching the Self. If Self were to be reached, it would mean that the Self is not here and now but that it has yet to be obtained. What is got afresh will also be lost. So it will be impermanent. What is not permanent is not worth striving for. So I say the Self is not reached. You *are* the Self; you are already That.[95]

Thus the Absolute, the Buddha-Mind, the real Self cannot be attained. For to attain union with the Absolute implies bringing together two things, and yet in all reality there is only One without a second. The attempt to bring the soul and God together merely perpetuates the illusion that the two are separate. As the above quotes make clear, the Self is already present, and we're already It.

Now it is sometimes said that whereas we are indeed already one with the Absolute, most of us nevertheless do not realize that this is so; that whereas union with God cannot be attained, *knowledge of that union can be attained;* that whereas we cannot manufacture the Supreme Identity, we can realize it. And that realization, that attainment of the knowledge of our Supreme Identity, is everywhere said to be the very Ultimate State of Consciousness, enlightenment, satori, *moksha, wu,* release, liberation.

Now there is certainly some degree of truth in the statement that we are all Buddhas but don't know it, and that we must therefore attain this knowledge for complete liberation. But on closer inspection this is not entirely satisfactory. For by the truth of nonduality, to know God is to be God: the two are not at all separate. So there is not one thing called God and another thing called knowledge of God. Rather, it is that knowledge is but one of the names of God. And if we cannot attain God, neither can we attain knowledge of God—since the two are actually one and the same. Put it another way: since the Ultimate State of Consciousness *is* Brahman, and since Brahman cannot be attained, neither can the Ultimate State of Consciousness.

If this conclusion seems odd, then go ahead and suppose, on the contrary, that the Ultimate State of Consciousness could be attained, or reached, or entered. What would that imply? Only that that state of consciousness which you *entered* would necessarily have a beginning in time; that that state of consciousness is therefore not timeless and eternal; and that, in short, that state of consciousness is precisely not the Ultimate State of Consciousness. The Ultimate State of Consciousness cannot be entered because it is timeless, without beginning or end, and conversely, any state of consciousness you can enter is not the Ultimate State of Consciousness.

Hsuan-tse heard of a meditation master named Chih-huang, and when he went to visit him, Chih-huang was meditating.

"What are you doing there?" inquired Hsuan-tse.

"I am entering into a *samadhi*, a highest state of consciousness."

"You speak of *entering*, but how do you enter into a *samadhi*— with a thoughtful mind or with a thoughtless mind? If you say with a thoughtless mind, all nonsentient beings such as plants or bricks could attain *samadhi*. If you say with a thoughtful mind, all sentient beings could attain it."

"Well," replied Chih-huang, "I am not conscious of either being thoughtful or being thoughtless."

Hsuan-tse's verdict was swift-coming. "If you are conscious of neither, you are actually in *samadhi* all the time; why do you even talk at all of entering into or coming out of it? If, however, there is any *entering* or *coming out*, it is not the Great *Samadhi*."[116]

So what does it mean that you can't enter the Ultimate State of Consciousness? What does it mean that never, under any circumstances, at any time, through any effort, can you enter the Ultimate State of Consciousness? Only that the Ultimate State of Consciousness is already fully and completely present. And that means the Ultimate State of Consciousness is in no way different from your ordinary state of consciousness or from any other state of consciousness you might have at this or any moment. "Your ordinary mind, just that is the Tao," says Nansen. Whatever state you have now, regardless of what you think of it and regardless of its nature, is absolutely It. You therefore cannot enter It because you have always been in It from the very beginning.

Of course, this should have been obvious all along. Since the Ultimate State of Consciousness is Brahman, and since Brahman is absolutely all-inclusive, the Ultimate State of Consciousness is equally all-inclusive. That is to say, the Ultimate State of Consciousness is not a state among other states but a state inclusive of all states. This means most emphatically that the Ultimate State of Consciousness is not an altered state of consciousness, for—being one without a second—there is no alternative to It. The Ultimate State of Consciousness is perfectly compatible with every state of consciousness and altered state of consciousness, and there is no state of consciousness apart from or outside of It. As René Guénon explains it, "The state of *Yogi* is not then analogous with any particular state whatsoever, but embraces all possible states as the principle embraces all its consequences."[56]

All of this points inescapably to the fact that you not only are already one with the Absolute, you already know you are. As Huang Po said, "The Buddha-Nature and your perception of it are one." And since, as we have seen, the Buddha Nature is always present, then so is your perception of It. If you maintain that you are Buddha but don't know it, you necessarily introduce a very subtle dualism between the Buddha Nature and your perception of It, imagining that the one is while the other is yet to come, and such is not possible. Truly, as we cannot manufacture the Absolute, we cannot manufacture knowledge of the Absolute. Both are already present.

> Rekison Roshi was asked by a monk, "What is this 'apprehending of a sound and being delivered'?" Rekison took up some fire-tongs, struck the firewood, and asked, "You hear it?" "I hear it," replied the monk. "Who is not delivered?" asked Rekison.[116]

That the Ultimate State of Consciousness is not a state apart or in any way different from the Present State of Consciousness is the point so many people seem to miss. Hence, they misguidedly seek to engineer for themselves a "higher" state of consciousness, radically different from their present state of awareness, wherein it is imagined that the Supreme Identity can be realized. Some imagine that this particular and exclusive "higher" state of consciousness is connected with specific brain-wave patterns, such as predominant amounts of high amplitude alpha waves. Others maintain that an individual's neurological system must undergo several changes, evolving as it were to a point where this "higher" state of consciousness can finally emerge. Some even believe that physiological stress has to be removed through meditative techniques and *then* the "higher" state of consciousness will result. But all this chatter totally overlooks the inescapable fact that *any* state of consciousness that can be entered, or that emerges after various practices, must have a beginning in time, and thus is not and could never be the timeless and eternal Ultimate State of Consciousness.

Moreover, to imagine that certain steps can be taken in order to realize the Ultimate State of Consciousness and attain liberation is actually to make the Ultimate State an *effect*. That is to say, to believe certain stages or various steps or particular practices can lead to liberation is inescapably to make liberation the *result* of these steps, the *consequence* of these stages, the *effect* of these causes. Yet long ago Shankara saw the utter absurdity of such a notion:

> If Brahman were represented as supplementary to certain actions, and release were assumed to be the effect of those actions, it would be temporal, and would have to be considered merely as something holding a preeminent position among the described temporal fruits of actions with their various degrees.
>
> But as Release is shown to be of the nature of the eternally free Self, it cannot be charged with the imperfection of temporality. Those, on the other hand, who consider Release to be the effect of something maintain that it depends on the action of mind, speech, or body. So, likewise, those who consider it to be a mere modification. Noneternality of Release is the certain consequence of these two opinions; for we observe in common life that things which are modifications, such as sour milk and the like, and things which are effects, such as jars, etc., are noneternal.[120]

And what of the opinion that we all have Buddha Nature but as yet just don't know it? And that through some sort of action, such as meditation, we can attain to this knowledge? Shankara is decisive:

> It might be said that Release might be a quality of the Self which is merely hidden and becomes manifest on the Self being purified by some action; just as the quality of clearness becomes manifest in a mirror when the mirror is cleaned by means of the action of rubbing. This objection is invalid, we reply, because the Self cannot be the abode of any action. For an action cannot exist without modifying that in which it abides. But if the Self were modified by an action its noneternality would result therefrom; an altogether unacceptable result.[120]

In short, since the Ultimate State of Consciousness is your Present State of Consciousness, there is obviously no way to cause, produce, effect, or manufacture that which is already the case—and even if you could, the result would be noneternal. But when we imagine that the Ultimate State of Consciousness is different from the state of consciousness we have now, we then foolheartedly seek ways to usher in this supposedly different and miraculous state of "higher" consciousness, totally ignorant of the fact that even if we get this "higher" state of consciousness it is not the Ultimate State because it is the result of certain steps and therefore has a beginning in time. And yet, think we, some knowledge of the Absolute awaits us in this particular higher state of consciousness. But as Eckhart so forcefully explained, if we imagine God can be found in a *particular* state of consciousness, then when that state slips from us, that god slips with it.

"Contrary to widespread belief," writes Alan Watts, "the knowledge and contemplation of the infinite is not a state of trance, for because of the truth that there is no opposition between the infinite and the finite, knowledge of the infinite may be compatible with all possible states of mind, feeling, and sensation. [This] knowledge is an inclusive, not an exclusive, state of consciousness."[125]

In fact, it's only because we keep insisting that the Ultimate State of Consciousness be different from the Present State of Consciousness that makes it so hard to admit to ourselves that we already know our Buddha Nature. We imagine, for instance, that nirvana is different from samsara, that enlightenment is different from ignorance, that Brahman is different from maya (illusion). Yet Nagarjuna clearly states: "There is no difference whatsoever between nirvana and samsara; there is no difference whatsoever between samsara and nirvana. There is not the slightest bit of difference between these two." And Hsuan-chueh begins his celebrated *Song of Realizing the Tao:*

> See you not that easygoing Man of Tao, who has abandoned
>   learning and does not strive?
> He neither avoids false thoughts nor seeks the true,
> For ignorance is in reality the Buddha nature,
> And this illusory, changeful body is the body of Truth.[116]

And pure Vedanta has never understood maya or illusion to be different from Brahman, but rather as something Brahman is doing.

And yet we seek to escape samsara as if it weren't nirvana; we try to overcome ignorance as if it weren't enlightenment; we strive to wipe out maya as if it weren't Brahman. Fénelon, Archbishop of Cambrai, has the only acceptable comment on this state of affairs: "There is no more dangerous illusion than the fancies by which people try to avoid illusion."

Hence, all seeking, spiritual or otherwise, is ultimately irrelevant; and viewing the Ultimate State of Consciousness as a particular altered state of consciousness is absolutely unacceptable. I am not at all denying that some very miraculous altered states of consciousness can certainly be attained—they can be attained for the simple reason that they are partial and exclusive and hence can be developed and perfected. But what has that to do with the all-inclusive Ultimate State of Consciousness? You can surely train yourself to enter alpha states; you can develop your ability with a mantra; you can learn to halt all thoughts from rising—but only because these are exclusive and partial states of consciousness apart from other states, and for that very reason can selectively be given more attention and effort than the others. But you cannot train yourself to enter that state of consciousness which you have never left and which includes all possible states of consciousness. There is just no place outside the Ultimate State of Consciousness where you can take up a position to train yourself in It. Listen to Huang Po once again:

> Bodhi (knowledge of the Buddha-Nature) is no state. The Buddha did not attain to it. Sentient beings do not lack it. It cannot be reached with the body nor sought with the mind. All sentient beings are already of one form with Bodhi.
>
> If you know positively that all sentient beings are already one with Bodhi, you will cease thinking of Bodhi as something to be attained. You may recently have heard others talking about this "attaining of the Bodhi-Mind," but this may be called an intellectual way of driving the Buddha away. By following this method, you only APPEAR to achieve Buddhahood; if you were to spend aeon upon aeon in that way, you would only achieve the Sambhogakaya (blissful states) and Nirmanakaya (transformed states). What connection would all that have with your original and real Buddha-Nature?[15]

Upon hearing this, many of us nevertheless feel that "Yes, I do understand that somehow I must already be one with the Absolute, but I still just don't know it!" But that is manifestly not true. The very fact that you are now seeking Buddha shows that you already know you are Buddha. "Console thyself," wrote Pascal, "'thou wouldest not seek Me if thou hadst not found Me." And St. Bernard expressed the very same sentiment, "No one is able to seek Thee, save because he has first found." Or, as Blyth put it, "In order to be enlightened, we must first be enlightened."

Of course, individuals might indeed feel that they don't really know It, despite all the best assurances of the Masters. And the reason It might not seem evident to them is the somewhat peculiar nature of this ever-present Bodhi-knowledge; namely, it is nondual. A person doesn't seem to know It only because he is so used to seeing things dualistically, where he as subject holds out and looks at an object, either mental or physical, and feels that, yes, he sees that object very clearly, with "he" and "that object" being two different things altogether. He, as subject, then naturally assumes that he can also see Brahman in the same way, as an object out there to look at and grasp. It thus seems that he, the grasper, should be able to get Brahman, the grasped. But Brahman won't split into getter and got. In all of reality there is only One without a second, and yet out of habit the person tries to make It two, to split It so as to finally grab It and exclaim, "Aha! I've got It!" He tries to make it an experience to be grasped among other experiences. But Brahman is not a particular experience, being one without a second, and so he is left grasping at ghosts and clutching at smoke.

And so it is that we all inevitably end up feeling that we just can't see It, no matter how hard we try. *But the fact that we always can't see It is perfect proof that we always know It.* In the words of the *Kena Upanishad:*

> If you think that you know Brahman well, what you know of Its nature is in reality but little; for this reason Brahman should still be more attentively considered by you. . . . Whoever among us understands the following words: "I do not know It, and yet I know It," verily that man knows it. He who thinks that Brahman is not comprehended, by him Brahman is comprehended; but he

who thinks that Brahman is comprehended knows It not. Brahman
is unknown to those who know It and is known to those who do
not know It at all.[62]

That is, the very state of not-knowing Brahman is the Ultimate
State of Consciousness, *and that is exactly how you feel right now.* Says
a Zen poem:

> When you seek to know It, you cannot see It.
> You cannot take hold of It,
> But neither can you lose It.
> In not being able to get It, you get It.
> When you are silent, It speaks.
> When you speak, It is silent.
> The great gate is wide open to bestow alms,
> And no crowd is blocking the way.[124]

Since you are Brahman, you obviously can't *see* Brahman, just as,
for instance, an eye cannot see itself and an ear cannot hear itself.
The *Brihadaranyaka Upanishad* says, "Thou couldst not see the seer
of sight, thou couldst not hear the hearer of hearing, nor perceive
the perceiver of perception, nor know the knower of knowledge."
And the *Zenrin* puts it simply, "Like a sword that cuts, but cannot
cut itself; Like an eye that sees, but cannot see itself." In fact, if your
eye tries to see itself, it sees absolutely nothing. Likewise, the Void
is what you right now don't see when you try to look for Brahman.
That Void is exactly what you have always been looking for and
have always never found nor seen. And *that* very not-seeing is It.
And since you always don't see It, you always know It. Because any
individual, explains St. Dionysius, "by the very fact of not seeing
and not knowing God, truly understands him who is beyond sight
and knowledge; knowing this, too, that he is in all things that are
felt and known."

As you rest in your present awareness, you might perceive some
sensation in the body, or you might be aware of thoughts passing by
in front of the mind's eye, or you might be seeing the clouds float
by. But there is one thing you cannot see: you cannot see the Seer.
You see thoughts, things, clouds, mountains, but never the Seer,

never the Self, never the pure Witness. Precisely because it sees thoughts, it is not itself a thought; precisely because it sees things, it is not itself a thing—it is radically free of all such objects, all such sights, all such ripples in the stream.

So what is this Witness in you that is aware of you? Who is aware of your thoughts, your feelings, your self, right now? What is that pure awareness? Of course, you cannot see this Seer! Anything you see is just more objects: you see thoughts float by, clouds float by, sensations float by. But the Seer itself is not an object, and thus can never be seen.

And so, for just a moment, simply be the Seer. Simply rest as the Seer, rest as the Witness, rest as that which sees but cannot be seen. As you rest in that emptiness, that absence, that clearing, that opening, you will begin to sense a vast freedom, a vast release from things seen, a vast release from the pain of being an object. You will rest as Emptiness, as the ancient Unseen, as the primordial Unborn, floating in the great Liberation.

When you rest as Emptiness, you are seeing your Original Face, the face you had prior to the Big Bang. This great Emptiness is the primordial background that has always already been your True Self, a Self never lost and therefore never found. This Emptiness is the great background in which the entire universe arises moment to moment. And this great background is—by any other name—God.

That which is aware of you right now, is God. That which is your own innermost awareness, right now, is God. That which sees but is never seen, is God. That Witness in you right now, ever present as pure Presence, is God. That vast Freedom, that great Emptiness, that primordial Purity, your own present state of awareness, right now, is God. And thus, most fundamentally and forever, it is God who speaks with your tongue, and listens with your ears, and sees with your eyes, this God who is closer to you than you are to yourself, this God who has never abandoned you and never could, this God who is every breath you take, the very beat of your tender heart, who beholds the entire majesty before your eyes, yet is never, never seen.

Still don't see It? How right you already are. For each and every one of us, "by the very fact of not seeing and not knowing God, truly understands him who is beyond sight and knowledge; knowing this, too, that he is in all things that are felt and known."

Epilogue

THE POSSIBILITY of a genuinely comprehensive paradigm is an alluring notion. This book, of course, has presented no more than a few fragments of what such a paradigm might look like. In other books I have tried to suggest what form the paradigm might take in the fields of anthropology and history, developmental psychology, sociology, and psychotherapies (see *A Brief History of Everything* for a summary). The real point of this book, however, was not so much to present a final paradigm—we are decades away from such—as to point out some of the major obstacles now blocking its emergence. And we saw a half dozen or so: category error, the pre/trans fallacy, the confusion of legitimacy and authenticity, the confusion of structure and stage, the failure to grasp the paradox of spirit as goal and ground. For there are now a tremendous number of gifted scholars working on or toward a comprehensive-transcendental paradigm, and yet most of them, in my opinion, fall into one or more of those fallacies. The most common seems to be to take the results from a monological science (physics, physiology, systems theory) and attempt to stretch them, as it were, to cover what in fact can only be covered with dialogical and translogical sciences. This is, of course, a profound category error. The next most common seems to be the pre/trans fallacy—especially in psychology and sociology; and next, structure-stage confusion.

But in any event, I have simply offered what seem to me to be several such fallacies or errors, with the hope that the quest for the new paradigm may more easily move forward. I have suggested and outlined what I think aspects of the new paradigm might look like. But what I most wanted to leave with the reader was not a final view, but hints on how better to reach that view; not a final knowledge, but a balance in the quest itself; not a way to stop, but a way to carry on. And, indeed, we might eventually discover that the new paradigm is nothing but the quest itself; that the only constant is the search; that Being, as Hegel said, is simply the process of its own becoming. When a famous Zen Master was asked the meaning and nature of absolute reality, he replied only: "Walk on."

References

1. Arieti, S. *The Intrapsychic Self.* New York: Basic Books, 1967.
2. Aurobindo. *The Life Divine/The Synthesis of Yoga.* Pondicherry: Centenary Library, XVIII-XXI, n.d.
3. Ayer, A. *Language, Truth and Logic.* New York: Dover, 1952.
4. Baldwin, J. *Genetic Theory of Reality.* New York: Putnam, 1915.
5. ———. *Thought and Things.* New York: Arno Press, 1975.
6. Barrett, W. (ed.). *Zen Buddhism: Selected Writings of D. T. Suzuki.* New York: Anchor, 1956.
7. Battista, J. "The Holographic Model, Holistic Paradigm, Information Theory and Consciousness." *ReVision,* vol. 1, no. 3/4, 1978.
8. Becker, E. *The Denial of Death.* New York: Free Press, 1973.
9. Berdyaev, N. *The Destiny of Man.* New York: Harper & Row, 1960.
10. Bernstein, J. "A Cosmic Flow." *American Scholar,* Winter-Spring 1979.
11. Beynam, L. "The Emergent Paradigm in Science." *ReVision,* vol. 1, no. 2, 1978.
12. Blake, W. *The Portable Blake.* A. Kazin (ed.). New York: Viking, 1968.
13. Blanck, G., and Blanck, R. *Ego Psychology: Theory and Practice.* New York: Columbia Univ. Press, 1974.
14. Blanco, M. *The Unconscious as Infinite Sets.* London: Duckworth, 1975.
15. Blofeld, J. *The Zen Teachings of Huang Po.* New York: Grove, 1958.
16. ———. *The Tantric Mysticism of Tibet.* New York: Dutton, 1970.
17. Bohm, D. "A Conversation with David Bohm." Conducted by Renée Weber. *ReVision,* vol. 1, no. 3/4, 1978.
18. Bohm, D., and Hiley, B. "Some Remarks on Sarfatti's Proposed Connec-

tion between Quantum Phenomena and the Volitional Activity of the Observer-Participator." Pre-print, Dept. of Physics, Birkbeck College, Univ. of London, 1975.

19. Branden, N. *The Psychology of Self-esteem.* New York: Bantam, 1971.
20. Brandt, A. "Self-confrontations." *Psychology Today,* October 1980.
21. Breger, L. *From Instinct to Identity.* Englewood Cliffs: Prentice-Hall, 1974.
22. Broughton, J. *The Development of Natural Epistemology in Adolescence and Early Adulthood.* Doctoral dissertation, Harvard, 1975.
23. Brown, D. "A Model for the Levels of Concentrative Meditation." *Internat. J. Clinical Exper. Hypnosis,* 25, 1977.
24. Brown, D., and Engler, J. "A Rorschach Study of the Stages of Mindfulness Meditation." *Journal of Transpersonal Psychology,* vol. 12, no. 2, 1980.
25. Brown, G. *Laws of Form.* New York: Julian, 1972.
26. Brown, N. O. *Life Against Death.* Middletown: Wesleyan Univ. Press, 1959.
27. Bubba (Da) Free John. *The Paradox of Instruction.* San Francisco: Dawn Horse, 1977.
28. Bull, N. *Moral Judgment from Childhood to Adolescence.* Beverly Hills: Sage, 1969.
29. Campbell, J. *The Masks of God,* 4 vols. New York: Viking, 1959–68.
30. Capra, F. *The Tao of Physics.* New York: Bantam, 1977.
31. Copleston, F. *A History of Philosophy.* New York: Image, 1959.
32. Crittenden, J. "A Review of Person/Planet." *ReVision,* vol. 2, no. 1, 1979.
33. Dean, S. (ed.). *Psychiatry and Mysticism.* Chicago: Nelson-Hall, 1975.
34. Deikman, A. "Deautomatization and the Mystic Experience." *Psychiatry,* vol. 29, 1966.
35. Descartes, R. *Rules for the Direction of the Mind.* Quoted in Copleston (reference #31, above).
36. Deutshe, E. *Advaita Vedanta.* Honolulu: East-West Center, 1969.
37. Erikson, E. *Childhood and Society.* New York: Norton, 1963.
38. Fairbairn, W. *An Object Relations Theory of the Personality.* New York: Basic Books, 1954.
39. Fenichel, O. *The Psychoanalytic Theory of Neurosis.* New York: Norton, 1945.
40. Feuerstein, G. *Textbook of Yoga.* London: Rider, 1975.
41. Flavell, J. "Concept Development." In P. Mussen (ed.), *Carmichael's Manual of Child Psychology,* vol. 1. New York: Wiley, 1970.
42. Flavell, J., and Wohlwill, J. "Formal and Functional Aspects of Cognitive Development." In D. Elkind and J. Flavell (eds.), *Studies in Cognitive Development: Essays in Honor of Jean Piaget.* New York: Oxford Univ. Press, 1969.

43. Freud, S. *Beyond the Pleasure Principle.* S.E. vol. 18. London: Hogarth, 1960.
44. ———. *The Ego and the Id.* S.E. vol. 19. London: Hogarth, 1961.
45. ———. *New Introductory Lectures.* S.E. vol. 22. London: Hogarth, 1962.
46. ———. *An Outline of Psychoanalysis.* New York: Norton, 1969.
47. ———. *A General Introduction to Psychoanalysis.* New York: Pocket, 1971.
48. Frey-Rohn, L. *From Freud to Jung.* New York: Dell, 1974.
49. Fromm, E. *Escape from Freedom.* New York: Farrar, Straus, & Giroux, 1941.
50. Gard, R. *Buddhism.* New York: Brazillier, 1962.
51. Gardner, M. "Quantum Theory and Quack Theory." *NYRB,* May 17, 1979.
52. Garfield, C. "Ego Functioning, Fear of Death, and Altered States of Consciousness." In C. Garfield (ed.), *Rediscovery of the Body.* New York: Dell, 1977.
53. Gilson, E. *The Unity of Philosophical Experience.* London: Sheed & Ward, 1938.
54. Goleman, D. *The Varieties of Meditative Experience.* New York: Dutton, 1977.
55. GTU research seminars, 1980–81. Jacob Needleman and Dick Anthony, coordinators.
56. Guénon, R. *Man and His Becoming According to Vedanta.* London: Luzac, 1945.
57. Guillaumont, P. (trans.). *The Gospel According to Thomas.* New York: Harper & Row, 1959.
58. Hall, C. *A Primer of Jungian Psychology.* New York: Mentor, 1973.
59. Hartmann, H. *Ego Psychology and the Problem of Adaptation.* New York: International Universities Press, 1958.
60. Hegel, G. *The Phenomenology of Mind.* J. Baillie (trans.). New York, 1949.
61. Hixon, L. *Coming Home.* New York: Anchor, 1978.
62. Hume, R. *The Thirteen Principal Upanishads.* London: Oxford Univ. Press, 1974.
63. Jacobson, E. *The Self and the Object World.* New York: International Universities Press, 1964.
64. Jakobson, R. "Child Language Aphasia and Phonological Universals." Quoted in H. Gardner, *The Quest for Mind.* New York: Vintage, 1974.
65. James, M. *The Apocryphal New Testament.* London: Oxford, 1924.
66. James, W. *Principles of Psychology,* 2 vols. New York: Dover, 1950.
67. ———. *The Writings of William James.* J. McDermott (ed.). New York: Random House, 1968.
68. Jung, C. "The Psychological Foundations of Belief in Spirits." *Collected Works,* vol. 8. Princeton: Princeton Univ. Press.

69. Kaplan, P. *Toward a Theology of Consciousness.* Doctoral dissertation, Harvard, 1976.

70. Kernberg, O. "Borderline Personality Organization." *Journal of the American Psychoanalytic Association*, vol. 15, 1967.

71. ———. "Prognostic Considerations Regarding Borderline Personality Organization." *Journal of the American Psychoanalytic Association*, vol. 19, 1971.

72. Klein, M. *Psychoanalysis of Children.* New York, 1966.

73. ———. *Narrative of a Child Analysis.* London: Hogarth, 1961.

74. Kohlberg, L. *The Philosophy of Moral Development.* San Francisco: Harper & Row, 1981.

75. Kohut, H. *The Restoration of the Self.* New York: International Universities Press, 1977.

76. Lacan, J. *The Language of the Self.* Baltimore: Johns Hopkins, 1968.

77. Lasch, C. *The Culture of Narcissism.* New York: Norton, 1979.

78. Loevinger, J. *Ego Development.* San Francisco: Jossey-Bass, 1976.

79. Mahler, M., et al. *The Psychological Birth of the Human Infant.* New York: Basic Books, 1975.

80. Marin, P. "The New Narcissism." *Harper's*, October 1975.

81. Maslow, A. *Motivation and Personality.* New York: Harper & Row, 1954.

82. ———. *Toward a Psychology of Being.* New York: Van Nostrand Reinhold, 1968.

83. ———. *The Farther Reaches of Human Nature.* New York: Viking, 1971.

84. McCarthy, T. *The Critical Theory of Jürgen Habermas.* Cambridge: M.I.T. Press, 1978.

85. McPherson, T. "Religion as the Inexpressible." In Flew and MacIntyre (eds.), *New Essays in Philosophy of Religion.* New York: Macmillan, 1964.

86. Mead, G. *Mind, Self, and Society.* Chicago: Univ. of Chicago Press, 1934.

87. Ogilvy, J. *Many Dimensional Man.* New York: Oxford Univ. Press, 1977.

88. Ornstein, R. *The Psychology of Consciousness.* San Francisco: Freeman, 1972.

89. Ouspensky, R. *A New Model of the Universe.* New York: Vintage, 1971.

90. Peck, R., and Havighurst, R. *The Psychology of Character Development.* New York: Wiley, 1960.

91. Piaget, J. *The Child's Conception of the World.* New York: Humanities Press, 1951.

92. ———. *The Construction of Reality in the Child.* New York: Basic Books, 1954.

93. ———. *The Essential Piaget.* Gruber and Voneche (eds.). New York: Basic Books, 1977.

94. Prince, R., and Savage, C. "Mystical States and the Concept of Regression." *Psychedelic Review,* vol. 8, 1966.

95. Ramana Maharshi. *The Collected Works of Ramana Maharshi.* A. Osborne (ed.). London: Rider, 1959.
96. Randall, J., and Buchler, J. *Philosophy: An Introduction.* New York: Harper & Row, 1971.
97. Reich, W. *Selected Writings.* New York: Farrar, Straus, & Giroux, 1973.
98. *ReVision,* vol. 1, no. 3/4, 1978.
99. Riesman, D. *The Lonely Crowd.* New York: Doubleday, 1954.
100. Rogers, C. *On Becoming a Person.* Boston: Houghton Mifflin, 1961.
101. Rogers, C., and Holdstock, T. "Person-centered Theory." In R. Corsini (ed.), *Current Personality Theories.* Itasca: Peacock, 1977.
102. Roszak, T. *Person/Planet.* New York: Anchor, 1978.
103. Russell, B. *A History of Western Philosophy.* New York: Simon & Schuster, 1945.
104. Sarfatti, J. "Implications of Meta-physics for Psychoenergetic Systems." *Psychoenergetic Systems,* vol. 1, 1974.
105. Schumacher, E. *A Guide for the Perplexed.* New York: Harper & Row, 1977.
106. Schuon, F. *Logic and Transcendence.* New York: Harper & Row, 1975.
107. ————. *The Transcendent Unity of Religions.* New York: Harper & Row, 1976.
108. Selman, R., and Byrne, D. "A Structural Analysis of Levels of Role-taking in Middle Childhood." *Child Development,* vol. 45, 1974.
109. Shepherd, A. *A Scientist of the Invisible.* Quoted in J. White and S. Krippner (eds.), *Future Science.* New York: Anchor, 1977.
110. Smith, H. *Forgotten Truth.* New York: Harper & Row, 1976.
111. Smuts, J. *Holism and Evolution.* New York: Macmillan, 1926.
112. Smith, H. *Forgotten Truth.* New York: Harper & Row, 1976.
113. Sullivan, C., Grant, M., and Grant, J. "The Development of Interpersonal Maturity: Applications to Delinquency." *Psychiatry,* vol. 20, 1957.
114. Sullivan, H. *The Interpersonal Theory of Psychiatry.* New York: Norton, 1953.
115. Suzuki, D. T. *Studies in the Lankavatara Sutra.* London: Routledge & Kegan Paul, 1968.
116. ————. *Essays in Zen Buddhism.* London: Rider, 1970.
117. Taimni, I. *The Science of Yoga.* Wheaton: Quest, 1975.
118. Tart, C. *States of Consciousness.* New York: Dutton, 1975.
119. ———— (ed.). *Transpersonal Psychologies.* New York: Harper & Row, 1975.
120. Thibaut, G. (trans.). *The Vedanta Sutras of Badaryana.* New York: Dover, 1962.
121. Van der Leeuw, J. *The Conquest of Illusion.* Wheaton: Quest, 1968.
122. Wachsmuth, G. "The Etheric Formative Forces." In J. White and S. Krippner (eds.), *Future Science.* New York: Anchor, 1977.

123. Washburn, M. "Observations Relevant to a Unified Theory of Meditation." *Journal of Transpersonal Psychology,* vol. 10, no. 1, 1978.
124. Watts, A. *The Way of Zen.* New York: Vintage, 1957.
125. ————. *The Supreme Identity.* New York: Vintage, 1972.
126. Welwood, J. "Self-knowledge as the Basis for an Integrative Psychology."
Journal of Transpersonal Psychology, vol. 11, no. 1, 1979.
127. Werner, H. "The Concept of Development from a Comparative and Organismic Point of View." In Harris (ed.), *The Concept of Development.*
Minneapolis: Univ. of Minnesota Press, 1957.
128. ————. *Comparative Psychology of Mental Development.* New York: International Universities Press, 1964.
129. Wescott, R. *The Divine Animal.* New York: Funk & Wagnalls, 1969.
130. Whitehead, A. N. *Science and the Modern World.* New York: Macmillan,
1967.
131. Whyte, L. *The Next Development in Man.* New York: Mentor, 1950.
132. Wilber, K. "The Ultimate State of Consciousness." *JASC,* vol. 2, no. 1,
1975–76 (revised as chapter 10 of this volume).
133. ————. *The Spectrum of Consciousness.* Wheaton: Quest, 1977.
134. ————. "A Developmental View of Consciousness." *Journal of Transpersonal Psychology,* vol. 11, no. 1, 1979 (expanded and revised as chapters 3
and 4 of this volume).
135. ————. "Eye to Eye." *ReVision,* vol. 2, no. 1, 1979 (revised as chapter 1
of this volume).
136. ————. *No Boundary.* Los Angeles: Center Press, 1979 (new edition:
Shambhala, 1981).
137. ————. *The Atman Project.* Wheaton: Quest, 1980.
138. ————. "The Pre/Trans Fallacy." *ReVision,* vol. 3, no. 2, 1980 (chapter 7
of this volume).
139. ————. *Up from Eden.* New York: Doubleday/Anchor, 1981.
140. ————. "Odyssey." *Journal of Humanistic Psychology,* vol. 22, no. 1, 1982.
141. ————. *A Sociable God.* New York: McGraw-Hill, 1982.
142. Wittgenstein, L. *Tractatus logico philosophicus.* London: Routledge &
Kegan Paul, 1969.
143. Zimmer, H. *Philosophies of India.* London: Routledge & Kegan Paul, 1969.

Afterword

FOR MANY YEARS I have told students of transpersonal psychology that they must read Ken Wilber if they want to know how transpersonal theory integrates psychology and spiritual teachings from the world's religions. No one is expected to agree with everything he says, but they need to understand why his perspective is important.

The depth and scope of Ken Wilber's vision is not easy for most of us to encompass. Many of his critics take issue with the details of one small segment or another, but never address his philosophical position as a whole. It seems that there are few people who can challenge the overarching view that integrates so many disciplines and perspectives.

My own acquaintance with Wilber's work dates back to 1975, when I was an associate editor of the *Journal of Transpersonal Psychology* and we had the privilege of being the first to publish his paper "The Spectrum of Consciousness." When his book by the same title was published soon afterward, I realized what a great service he was doing for us all. His ability to articulate in a clear and coherent manner the integral vision that many of us had been attempting to formulate, with limited success, expanded the field of psychological and spiritual inquiry to encompass a truly global view of the spiritual quest.

Wilber is undoubtedly one of the greatest thinkers of our time. His cross-disciplinary syntheses encompass the psychology, philosophy, and religion of East and West, as well as sociology, anthropology, and postmodern thought. In the last two decades he has been widely recognized as an outstanding philosopher. Some people have compared him to Hegel, but to my mind he is much easier to read! He has been hailed as the Einstein of consciousness studies, and his work offers a healthy antidote to the dogmatic reductive thinking in many disciplines. His contribution to psychology has been compared to that of Sigmund Freud, Carl Jung, and William James. His brilliant and fundamental reformulation of theories of human development and the evolution of consciousness have earned him an international reputation and the respect of scholars in a wide range of fields. I believe he offers a worldview that will, in time, affect all of our academic, social, medical, religious, and scientific institutions.

In his work Wilber demonstrates an indomitable warrior spirit that matches any adversary with fearless integrity. His dedication to service is evident in his uncompromising commitment to doing the work that he feels called to do, despite the arduous discipline that it demands. Through it all he remains open to feedback and keeps a cheerful sense of humor about his own human foibles in personal relationships. He has also demonstrated his willingness to revise his ideas in response to new information, as evidenced by the evolution of his own thinking, whose phases he calls Wilber I, II, and III.

When he responds to critics, Wilber often reflects the tone of their own remarks, and this leads some observers to feel that he can be unduly sharp. However, it seems to me that he has demonstrated both wisdom and compassion in his willingness to reply to critics who are familiar with only a small portion of his work. His compassion may seem ruthless at times, but I know his heart is open, and he writes from experience as well as a prodigious amount of reading. I have been a student of psychology, religion, and philosophy for nearly forty years and, with the possible exception of the Dalai Lama, I have yet to meet or read anyone who can match the laser-like quality of his intellect.

Wilber's rare intellectual genius is matched by an emotional intensity that we can feel by reading the account of his passionate love relationship with his late wife, Treya Kilham Wilber, as portrayed in his book about her life and death, entitled *Grace and Grit*. I know many people whose lives have been deeply affected by reading this book, and many who have been helped to deal with their own illness or loss of a loved one.

I have had the privilege of knowing Ken very well for the better part of two decades. He has been a spiritual friend, a teacher, and a shining star of inspiration. What I value most about his work is the fact that I see it always pointing to liberation and enlightenment. His exquisite mastery of language always points beyond itself to the ineffable mystery. For those inclined to jnana yoga, a thorough study of Wilber's work can be deeply rewarding. For those who feel confused on the spiritual path, his clarity is unmatched. For those who are familiar with the farther reaches of spiritual practice, his pointing-out instructions are a delight. In each of the dozen books he has written to date, his penetrating vision-logic brings a kaleidoscope of ideas into a meaningful pattern that offers us a window on the wisdom of the ages.

Index